BUILDING
THE GREEN
MOVEMENT

also by Rudolf Bahro:

The Alternative in Eastern Europe (Verso/NLB, 1979)
Socialism and Survival (Heretic Books/GMP, 1982)
From Red to Green (Verso/NLB, 1984)

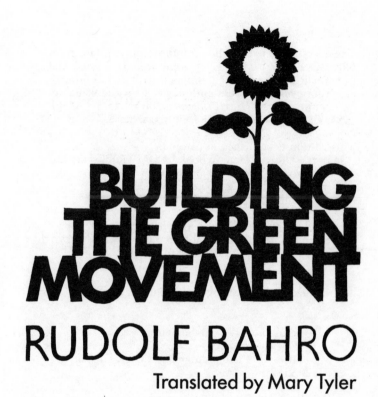

BUILDING THE GREEN MOVEMENT

RUDOLF BAHRO

Translated by Mary Tyler

new society publishers

The texts collected in this volume range in date from
November 1982 to June 1985. Some were first published
in periodicals, as indicated, others distributed in mimeo-
graph form. Several were anthologized in Rudolf Bahro,
Pfeiler am anderen Ufer (Bridgehead on the Other Bank),
1984, a special issue of the Berlin magazine *Befreiung*.

This edition is published in parallel:
  – in the UK as a Heretic book by GMP Publishers Ltd,
    P O Box 247, London N15 6RW
  – in the USA by New Society Publishers,
    4722 Baltimore Avenue, Philadelphia, PA 19143

British Library Cataloguing in Publication Data

Bahro, Rudolf
  Building the Green Movement
  1. Political science
  I. Title   II. Pfeiler am anderen Ufer. *English*
  320.9182'1   JA66

  ISBN 0-946097-17-8 (UK paperback)
  ISBN 0-86571-078-3 (US hardcover)
  ISBN 0-86571-079-1 (US paperback)

Cover art by Louis Mackay
Photosetting by M C Typeset, 34 New Road, Chatham, Kent
Printed and bound by Billing & Sons Ltd, Worcester

Contents

Introduction

When Rudolf Bahro arrived in West Germany after his release from an East German prison in October 1979, a new political grouping was in the process of being born there. The Greens, in various guises and under various names, had already begun gaining seats in local councils in 1977, and in June 1979 they attracted some 900,000 votes in the elections to the European Parliament – too few, however, to cross the 5 per cent threshold required by West German electoral law before a party's votes can be translated into seats. Just over a week before Bahro's arrival, that threshold was crossed for the first time at the level of provincial elections by Greens in the *Land* of Bremen. Meanwhile, a programme commission was working away at a common platform for the country's various Green groups, and its efforts finally bore fruit in January 1980 when delegates to the founding conference in Karlsruhe brought into being the Green party at the Federal level. This was the party that in the Federal elections of 6 March 1983 was to gain 5.6 per cent of the vote, and hence occupy 28 seats in the Bundestag: the first new party to join the established trio of conservatives (CDU/CSU), liberals (FDP), and social-democrats (SPD) in the West German parliament since the early 1960s.

Bahro lost no time in getting involved with the Greens. Indeed, some criticized the haste with which he threw himself into West German politics; others, though, had already noted signs in his book *The Alternative* that he was, as he puts it, "a suspect ecologist when I was still locked up in East Germany". A founder member of the new party, he was elected to its Federal executive, and was from the outset a prominent participant in the very public internal debates that have been a distinguishing characteristic of Green politics in West Germany.

The outside world, intrigued by their electoral success, has tended to perceive Die Grünen simply as an "ecology party", and has hardly registered the complexity of inputs, arguments, and activities that this label conceals. The Greens have their roots in a number of political traditions, including in particular the student movement of the late 1960s and the campaigns against atomic energy of the 1970s, whilst their organizational beginnings lie in the "citizens' initiatives" that sprang up around predominantly environmental concerns throughout the Federal Republic in the mid-1970s. These essentially extra-parliamentary and non-party origins have bequeathed to the Greens a philosophy that resists accommodation to pressures – both from within and even more from outside their own ranks – to adopt a formal structure, to join in the party game, to stand in elections, win seats, and fight other parties in the parliamentary arena.

Their establishment as a party has thus been accompanied by serious misgivings that are epitomized in the image of the "anti-party party" and their deliberate avoidance of the name by which they are usually known in the foreign media – the Green Party. They have confronted these misgivings by building into their structures devices such as the two-yearly "rotation" of members of parliament, limits on the proportion of their salary that MPs may retain for personal use, the direct accountability of the elected to the electors, and a prohibition on the holding of party offices by those who sit in parliament. The aim of these measures, which reflect the fiercely democratic convictions of the Greens, is to avoid the creation within their ranks of those professional politicians that typify the hierarchies of the established parties. But above all, the Greens insist that representation in parliament and other legislative chambers is not the be all and end all of political activity: it is only one of the two legs on which they stand, the other being firmly planted in the wider movement with its demonstrations, campaigning, and grassroots activities.

Debates within the Greens have tended to crystallize around attitudes to the role and significance of parliamentary activity, and hence have focused in particular on such matters as their relationship with other parties – the question of coalitions or less formal "toleration" arrangements to enable minority administrations to function. For most Greens, if there *is* a potential coalition partner, then it is the social-democratic SPD; but so far coalitions have only been entered into in town and district councils. There have been phases of Green toleration of SPD governments at *Land* level, whilst in the Bundestag the question of Green coalitions remains a purely theoretical matter for possible future elections.

But the question of parliamentary involvement, of coalitions and toleration remains the most visible part of one end of a complex spectrum of attitudes that runs the whole breadth of the very broad Green movement. At the other end of that spectrum stands Rudolf Bahro, the epitome of Green fundamentalism, resolutely critical of the compromises with the system that such "realists" as his favourite bogey-man Joschka Fischer are prepared to enter into. The Green *Realos* are the butt of Bahro's most scathing critique: they are the dupes of a system that simply wants them to help with repairs, when in fact the disintegration of the industrial world "is the best thing about it and . . . we must say 'yes' to it and assist it as far as possible". Reformism for Bahro simply means postponing the ecological catastrophe – "euthanasia as Green politics" – and is symbolized in the anti-pollution filters of the "eco-industrialists" and their "catalytic converters for the next boom in the car industry". "It is the time," he asserts, "not of reformists, but of a reformation, which has now commenced."

The religious analogy is not accidental: Bahro's essays and speeches abound with millenarian sentiments and calls for a new spiritual awakening. He talks of "the politics of salvation", of the need to "correct the last ten thousand years of evolution", of "a change so deep that one must speak of a break with basic European patterns of behaviour", and "the building of a new psychology". He is fascinated by the fall of the Roman Empire – "the only event which can be compared in dimension with the present-day crisis of civilization" – and intrigued by the communal monastic orders, the Benedictines in particular, that emerged out of its collapse: they, he proposes, may provide a model for *our* way forward.

But the way forward is also a way out: a way out of the doomed system of industrial capitalism (and Bahro subsumes the Soviet Union and the countries of Eastern Europe under this heading too). It is an exit that will be prepared by acts of liberation, by the creation of "zones liberated from the industrial system", by the liberation of "surplus consciousness" and the "surplus energies" that we have not yet surrendered. For Bahro the hope for the Greens lies not in accumulating a greater share of votes, but in steadily accumulating a greater share of people's consciousness, irrespective of their formal political allegiance.

Bahro has never been a comfortable colleague for the Greens. His constant recall to fundamentals has been a permanent irritant to their consciences, and for many within the party his comparison, at the December 1984 party conference in Hamburg, of the political rise of the Greens with that of the Nazis in the 1920s was the last straw – the pretext to dismiss him to the margins as an eccentric and troublesome one-man band. Bahro returned to the next party conference in Hagen in June 1985 – and resigned. The last straw for *him* was ostensibly the issue of animal rights: the Greens had turned down a motion banning all animal experiments, and adopted instead a compromise resolution. But animal rights for Bahro are not simply a matter of sentiment: "Animal experiments," he says, "are one of the most political questions we have ever had to deal with"; such experiments are "one of those foundation stones whose removal could cause the whole house to collapse". Moreover, "the question of animal experiments is so central to testing whether we are really ready for conversion that there is no better litmus paper by which we can find out what we really want and what we no longer want." The Greens had failed Bahro's litmus test. He wrote an explanation of his departure from the party: it was not just a matter of the Greens' sell-out to the system; he had grasped that the attempt to work as a *party* was itself inherently mistaken. Bahro will now continue his campaigning and writing outside that structure.

Rudolf Bahro's writings are heady stuff. They are informed by an excitement that is apocalyptic, visionary, and urgent. They will also strike many English-speaking readers as very German. Their references – historical, literary, philosophical – are often German, and so of course are their immediate political concerns. Bahro also makes it clear that West Germany, "this richest, most powerful European province", is the country in which he places his greatest hope for an exemplary exit from the industrial society, and fulfilment of his vision of "a gentle, non-violent, green republic". Certainly there is evidence enough of a spread of "post-materialist values" among the young in West Germany – a spread that is reflected in the disproportionately high support that young people in West Germany give to the Greens (well over a quarter of first-time voters have supported the Greens in recent elections). But those values, and the attitudes and behaviour that accompany them, are certainly not unique to the Federal Republic. Nor, of course – as he makes abundantly clear – are the problems with which Bahro concerns himself unique to the wealthy First World. That these thoughts of West Germany's most articulate Green fundamentalist are now available in English will make them more widely accessible to that world whose fate he seeks to address.

John Sandford

Basic Positions of The Greens
For an Ecological Answer to the Economic Crisis

I. The Greens and the Economy

In the richest, industrially over-developed countries of the West a
fundamental opposition is growing – above all in the diverse form
of the new social movements. It is reacting to the now clearly and
markedly self-destructive, outwardly murderous and inwardly
suicidal character of our industrial civilization, and to its
institutional system which is geared to continuing in the same
old way. What makes this opposition fundamental is above all the
fact that it throws into question both the material foundation and
its counterpart in our basic attitudes which are oriented towards
possessions and having. It gives expression to the ever more
obvious truth that we shall only survive if we equip ourselves to
live differently than we have up till now. The Greens see
themselves as the parliamentary political arm of this fundamental opposition movement.

The development that has proceeded from Europe in the past
two hundred years and more has been decisively characterized by
the simultaneously most expansive (aggressive) and most effective (productive) economic system in world history, the capitalist
mode of production. The merciless struggle to remove competi-
tors – first between private individuals, then between firms, and
finally between multinational and state corporations – has proved
to be the mightiest economic impetus of all times. The East and
the South are only emulating it; they are doing so under different
political systems and socio-economic conditions, resulting from a
weaker and more or less dependent position, and often with even
worse direct consequences for the people affected.

Whilst the independent, alienated Megamachine is preparing to
collide against the bounds of the Earth, pressing us – its original
creators – up against the wall and crushing us, it is already
destroying untold millions of human lives in the Third World
each year, where we have for a while diverted war, unemployment, hunger and misery of all kinds. To stop the industrial
system – and first of all the military machine it has created – in
its tracks, here in the metropolises where it started, is just as
much the first command of solidarity with the most wretched of

this Earth as it is the requirement of a reasonable self-interest. For we shall not be able to bear the backlash of either the social crises or the ecological catastrophes which our way of work and life leads to on a world scale.

The global industrialization process not only devours and destroys its own preconditions, the resources which it soaks up in ever greater quantities, but also the natural foundations of human life, of the very biosphere which sustains us. The completion of this process on a world scale would be the ultimate natural catastrophe. It cannot be continued for a further 200 years and it must be braked and stopped much earlier. The work which made us into human beings, the specific ability of our species comprehensively to change nature, has developed in such a way that it can become the cause of our downfall. Our planet can be transformed by the nuclear bomb and other direct means of annihilation into a desert largely devoid of human beings. Seen as a whole, industrialized labour of the kind which has dominated up till now – notwithstanding its numerous individual blessings – has proved to be fatal. Production for war is only the tip of the iceberg.

This industrial system must not be further extended. On the contrary, we must begin to dismantle the Tower of Babel before it collapses on top of us. We want to gain the assent of the majority so that a restructuring of our civilization, which is necessary for survival, can be decided, planned and executed step by step. For this we need a Great Moratorium on any kind of expansionist investments of the old type and a critique of all products and conditions of labour. Even so-called "investments in the future" must be examined to determine whether they too do not only serve to facilitate the breakthrough to a new thrust of industrialization and to build a new storey onto the industrial system – for example, in the form of expanded large-scale production for environmental protection. Too many "alternative" investment ideas reinforce the existing structures, as for example the installation of district heating networks reinforces the concentration of the population in industrial conurbations.

II. The Greens and Unemployment

When those interested in an investment breakthrough reproach us that environmental protection costs jobs, the Greens don't immediately respond with a zealous attempt to prove – correct though it often is – that on the contrary our policies would create jobs, but rather with an unambiguous explanation that we want to combat the approaching total ecological catastrophe even at the cost of the loss of jobs. Industries in which products are produced on a mass scale to compete for profits on the world market, and with a material- and energy-intensive division of labour, must shrink in size.

We still regard the ecological crisis as the overriding and broader challenge. The economic crisis and the capitalist response of mass unemployment and dismantling of the welfare state may well change the conditions for the ecology and peace movement. But it would simply be a further victory for the existing order if we let ourselves be pushed into giving priority to the fight against unemployment and social decline in the wake of the old trade-union and left socialist defence strategies. We are not here to defend or create jobs in the industrial system.

In our view the present crisis, which we see not least as a crisis of industrial society, a society of labour and achievement, must be used to detach the question of an income, a secure basis of life for everybody, from the compulsion to wage-labour for the world market. It is not our aim to give everybody back "wages and bread". It is rather a case of reducing the expenditure of labour – wage-labour for the anonymous market – far beyond the extent of the present restructuring which is taking place in the interest of profit. There is not too little work but still too much.

The creation of new jobs is not our actual goal even where the restructuring of the economy will in fact lead to that. For us the main point is to withdraw investments and the deployment of human energies from all large-scale projects whatsoever. If we decentralize the work process and make the units smaller, what will come about in the first place are not new jobs but new conditions of life. Though decentralization as a rule creates jobs and working conditions more worthy of human beings than those in large-scale production.

With regard to our policy on working hours, we will support everything which:

a) minimizes the amount of work as a whole, i.e. cuts down relatively on work;

b) above all relaxes time structures in every respect so as to increase the freedom of individuals to do what they want with their own time.

Minimization of working hours presupposes first of all a critique of production and of needs. It is actually aimed at the total structure of conditions of reproduction of life, because only thus can certain needs – as for example the need for private cars – become superfluous.

III. Where Are The Greens Going?

We consider the complexity of industrial society based on the worldwide division of labour as the cause of multiplied consumption and the tendency to anonymous bureaucratic rule or administration to death. There is no salvation without dismantling this complexity, which in itself means an intolerable susceptibility to sudden breakdown and is thus one of the most important sources of anxiety.

A fundamental reorientation of the economy such as we are striving for can only succeed hand in hand with the spread of a new ("post-modern, post-industrial") way of life. Only a different society will found a different technology and organization out of the arsenal of sciences and skills that have been handed down.

In this respect lasting new solutions presuppose the existence of a network of interlinked base communities. The social weight and political influence of this new social formation must be sufficient to increasingly subordinate the remaining industrial sector and the other institutions and organizations necessary for overall social functions to the requirements of the base community network. The present social and economic crisis goes so deep that it favours steps towards this by making them urgently necessary, while the old remedies no longer help. Now is the very time to take our fundamental ecological attitude onto the offensive in the attempts at a solution.

As yet the numerous beginnings of alternative ways of life do not represent a complete context. In most cases they do not have their own economic cycle but exist on the margins, more or less dependent on the general market, relying on the one hand on the welfare state, and on the other on gaps in supply. The real alternative, which at the same time would begin to reconcile us with the peoples of the Third World, can only be the building of base communities (of – it is suggested – a maximum of 3,000 people), which agree on a mode of simple, non-expanded reproduction of their material basis.

These would produce their basic needs in the way of food, clothing, housing, education and health care to a large extent by their own labour, decide on some specialized production mainly for exchange in the immediate locality, and contribute to the upkeep of general communications (transport and exchange of information) and conditions of production either by the manufacture of parts designed for this or by contributing labour-power.

Instead of the communities being unilaterally dependent on the more or less centralized functions, these functions will on the contrary be dependent on the needs of a society which realizes its basic functions in a decentralized fashion. Above all, this will not be an economic society in the sense of a society geared towards economic success and economic development. Material production and reproduction are only undertaken as the basis, which has to be kept relatively constant, for a learning process geared to people's psychological capabilities and for personal communication.

Having regard to the scarcity of resources, we must develop an expenditure norm for basic supplies which tends to minimal consumption of materials and energy. Ending material expansion will prove not only necessary for survival but also desirable and useful for the higher development of human beings in relation to their "non-material" needs (though these needs are still bound to material realities, endogenous and social). The new culture will once more have a spiritual dimension, if only because it will otherwise be impossible to break through the vicious circle of material expansion. Without a system of values which from the start is set above the purely economic, this ecological cyclical economy we are striving for cannot come about.

And here too is the real place for intermediate steps leading towards the radical, ecological and pacifist alternative. It is not a case of making something palatable to people, of seducing them to a certain degree to the new perspective, but of providing them with an opportunity for active experience in dealing with the concrete contradictions of their everyday existence. Above all, it is a question of opening up for them a minimum of space that affords them security, into which they can step when they want to risk withdrawal from the industrial system.

This involves on the one hand material possibilities for a new beginning beyond the "formal" structures, and on the other hand a social cohesion for the project, which is perhaps even more important. Since the new structures have first to be founded, small groups or individual personalities must seize the initiative in order to create an active nucleus for the project in question and in order to be able to face the rest of society, or the state, as initiators.

Within the remaining industrial sector (which at first will by no means function in dependence on the society of base communities which is anticipated as the ideal) we will support everything which favours the power of disposal, the free space, the creative activity of those active in it. (In this we are to some extent following the concept of the dissident trade-union group at Daimler-Benz; what interests us above all in the experience of Lucas Aerospace are the ideas about a technology subordinated once more to human beings and at the disposal of their creativity.)[1] In principle, the criteria for technology and organization must not be primarily cost efficiency and competitiveness, but providing the conditions for the workers to develop.

The Greens do not deny that in the long term our overall policy runs counter to the predominant trade-union efforts to secure jobs in the industrial system. And the contradiction between environmental protection and jobs is not merely an apparent one. At least in the short term, a rigorous implementation of ecological priorities would raise the cost of production in the Federal Republic and thus worsen our chances of selling on the world market. We are faced with the question as to whether we are prepared consciously to run this risk in the country of Western Europe with the greatest economic reserves. It would be a shabby kind of politics if the Greens were to try to conceal from the public and our potential voters the consequences that our political influence can have. The sincerity of our position is our greatest capital. As on the question of unilateral disarmament, we must not hide the risks, but rather try to motivate people so that they obtain the psychological bonus for the courage of their decision. The point we must really use to enlist support is the long-term advantage of a timely change. Precisely in this sense fundamental opposition is constructive.

Above all, in this the richest industrial country of Europe we must not just try to carry out repairs and shift our problems elsewhere. Those involved must unite their strength in order to force a restructuring different from that which is likely to result from the new international division of labour and the shift towards a new phase of super-industrialization. Then it can even become a gain to abandon the old advantages of the strong economic position by making use of them to start along a completely new course. In any case the Federal Republic is of all European countries the one where the impoverishment of the population in the old industrial locations is least likely. More is needed than just a conventional slogan of "protection against danger levels". The workforce must demand power of disposal over production plants which no longer have any market, they must win the right to use the capacities and resources for any purposes they consider worthwhile – including dismantling them in favour of completely new, decentralized enterprises.

As experience shows, the German trade unions as currently constituted are only to a very limited extent an institution for such struggles, so that new structures must be created at the grassroots. The Greens will support every step towards concrete appropriation by the workforce, at the same time asserting our particular standpoint that the means available should be used by those sections of the workforce involved and by the unemployed for a new social beginning beyond large-scale industrial production.

IV. Ecological Economic Policy – Baselines

1. Industrial disarmament and adaptation.

The Greens start from the realistic assumption that the new social forces which we rest on and our influence in the realm of politics are still nowhere near sufficient to achieve such a fundamental reorientation of the economy. Therefore we see our first and most important task as being to continue and to extend into the political realm precisely that practice which has defined the conduct of the new social movements: to put up resistance against continuing in the same old way.

It is not only the economy, which wants to make its profits in the customary way, but also the entire institutional system – the state, the legal system, the political parties, the trade unions and the other traditional interest groups – which taken as a whole is committed by its history and constitution to continuing along the same path and can aim at nothing more than at best adjusting externally to the new demands. We shall oppose this force of inertia, which rests upon a multitude of habits in the general consciousness, is preserved and strengthened by the media, and also has a share in our own personal interests.

Our parliamentary practice, following the example of the extra-parliamentary practice (the peace movement, the citizens' initiatives, the alternative movement, the women's movement and so on), must concentrate on preventing any steps which continue in the same dangerous direction. This means in particular all investments in the expansion of the Big Machine, i.e. any military installations, any installations of the nuclear industry, any projects to extend the heavy transport infrastructure (airports, motorways, trunk roads, canals, river straightening, ports), all large industrial projects, as well as all large projects in the school and university system, in the health service, and in public administration, the police, computerized control of society, etc.

Investments in the formal sector are only permissible at all if they do not require a single square metre of land not previously built on. If however there has to be new building, then at least the equivalent area must be balanced against it for recultivation. The Greens will pursue locally a consistent policy of environmental and nature protection, aimed at the restoration of varied landscapes and the elimination of buildings that ruin the natural habitat. Everywhere that we have influence we will oppose expansion, prevent industrial subsidies, combat construction with all conceivable counter-measures, stimulate and support the extra-parliamentary resistance.

Even where, as it is now fashionable, projects claim to be "investments in the future", the Greens will examine whether these are not in fact steps which simply create for the industrial system an outlet into new directions, which presuppose the continuation of the existing structure and indirectly help it to continue. We are – for example – not in favour of a new industry to manufacture filters for the chimneys of power stations; we want to save the forests from acid rain by replacing large power stations with small, locally controllable and responsible units of energy production. We are in general against the concentration of plant and capital, against mergers, in favour of breaking up and decentralization, right down to technology.

Taken as a whole, this first point primarily involves a strategy of prevention, an anti-investment and a deconcentration strategy, an emergency brake against any further "progress" in the fateful direction which the accumulation of capital, driven by the world market, is taking. According to all previous experience capital needs expanded reproduction and concentration in ever greater conglomerations. Our practice is aimed at the encirclement and restriction of capital in terms of investment opportunities, material and energy supplies and marketing. We shall attack both the products and the technology, the motivation to work and the motivation to buy, and do everything to encourage inside the market-orientated enterprises the growth of scepticism as to whether one should research, develop, produce, advertize and sell at all in the present context.

People will then ask us how our economy is to maintain its position against international competition, where it is after all dependent to the highest degree on imports and exports. Our reply is that we want to withdraw from the world market and believe that as a result our standard of living will not quantitatively deteriorate but will be qualitatively changed. We have in mind an economic order of the greatest possible self-sufficiency at a local, regional, provincial and national level. We envisage markets for the exchange of activities between base communities and cooperation at levels above this, complementing each other to form a market-free economy for basic needs and built from the bottom up.

The international division of labour – as it affects the flow of materials and energy across state frontiers and oceans, as opposed to the flow of information – we conceive as strictly limited. Our question, which we shall examine more thoroughly, is: how can the population – in a situation where the supplies for our gluttonous Big Machine will in any case fail to materialize and the war-mongering struggle for resources will increase – reproduce its life on the given territory with the resources still available?

In contrast to the merely reformist strategy of the Social-Democrats and the old left, this is also the truly anti-capitalist and anti-colonialist answer to the challenges of our time.

2. *Defend and extend the space for the development of the new social movements.*

The Greens believe we will represent in parliament not only heads (the number of our voters) but also growing parts of the consciousness of those people who still vote for the traditional parties. What we regard as decisive is that the scope for each individual to make new decisions should increase, right down to a new fundamental decision about his or her life. That includes the extension of the political space, where citizens must not be limited to voting and the expression of individual opinions but must have the opportunity of expressing themselves in demonstrative actions right through to non-violent civil disobedience.

The basic tendency of established politics (already visible at the end of the SPD-FDP coalition) is to allow the polarization of society between a tied, pacified core and a growing number of fringe existences, if not actually promoting this in order to keep those excluded as socially and politically weak and atomized as possible. The CDU's cuts in the welfare state have as their main objective to weaken the social base of the ecology and peace movement, which is rightly regarded by Franz-Josef Strauss as a danger to the stability of government insofar as it is dissolving the previous consensus.

In the most fundamental interest of our constituency we oppose any deterioration in social services. We absolutely refuse to be deflected back to discussions about financeability within the framework of the usual budget procedures, and instead challenge the monstrous sums spent on all the deadly and harmful investments which we want to prevent.

Every mark that is withdrawn from investment in large-scale industry or from expenditure on the expansion of the state machine, and flows instead to the alternative movement, is already in itself a contribution to the protection of life, quite

independent of whether we use it for subsistence purposes or for
the construction of "lifeboats" (which is what it primarily comes
down to). Since the alternative movement in the metropolises is
near enough to the centre of power to disturb significant parts of
the established forces and their social following, it has a chance of
keeping the issue open.

If the decisive point here is not to sever the link between the
wage-earners in the factories and offices and those who have
opted out, this question must not be settled in such a way that
the new forces subordinate themselves to the traditional patterns
of trade-union politics. On the contrary, the release of the
potential in the factories and offices depends upon the union
bureaucrats losing their ideological influence and organizational
control. In any case the new social movements will not stop at
the gates of the factories and institutions, precisely because they
are not proceeding via the old structures. The question of
organizing working conditions in accordance with human rights
and the wholesomeness of the products can today only be
effectively posed from the ecological perspective.

The Greens will support organized alternatives to the German
Trade-Union Federation and its constituent unions, wherever
these appear on the scene. It is in this way and not through
adjustment and subordination to the traditional rules of the game
that the new forces can have the strongest influence on the
debates inside the trade unions. Here too it will be a case of how
consistently we can articulate the new contexts and link actions
to them. Only in conflict will the unsuitability of the old
structures and their role as a constant hindrance become apparent
in the general experience. Our arguments must consciously
appeal to needs which go far beyond the wage-earning interest as
monopolized by the trade unions, and play for maximum stakes.

3. *Begin withdrawal from the industrial system.*

The specific response of the Greens to the challenge of mass
unemployment is the use of our political influence to facilitate
departure from the industrial system into a positive new way of
life. Only if there is a genuine provision of start-up assistance will
we be able seriously to test, not only how many of the
unemployed, but also how many people who are still employed
and perhaps even relatively successful functionaries, are already
prepared or inclined to change their general perspective.

The Greens set themselves the goal of diverting one thousand
million marks into the alternative sector, to make possible there
a kind of primary accumulation for the new social formation. On

this foundation a comprehensive network of autonomous base communities can emerge, which will subsequently support and reproduce themselves. This objective also includes support for all those alternative undertakings of the most diverse type and level which are only (or as yet) halfway between the old and new ways of production and life. We consider it our main task to provide political cover for this long-term transitional process and to help secure the material foundation for it.

For this end, we basically want to bring into existence, against the present *de facto* Grand Coalition of the established parties and at right angles to the traditional political and social division, a Grand Coalition of our own (which should not be envisaged in the form of a new party system). To build this up, we shall pick up on the uncertainties and the new attitudes which the ecological crisis has already aroused in almost everybody in our society. There will soon be two souls dwelling in almost every breast, and the process is leading slowly but surely to the general upheaval which will enable us to start out on a new overall course. Psychologically the exodus from the capitalist industrial system has already begun, and the same process is already beginning to reach across to our Eastern counterpart.

4. Corrections and repairs within the present system – learning processes.

This basically involves critical and selective cooperation in all projects which make up the catalogue of ecological reformism (and which have in common above all that they appeal to the existing state, the existing institutional system, and taken in themselves do not point beyond it). In this the focal point is not a compromise with the old parties, which are pursuing a different basic direction, but an appropriate appeal beyond them to their supporters, designed in each case to expose their half-measures and demagogic subterfuges and to promote a change in thinking.

In all factory initiatives for alternative production plans, the Greens support those tendencies which press for the achievement of self-determination by those concerned against the power of disposal held by capital, the management hierarchy and the trade-union bureaucracy. Here more and more battles are being decided on the field of manufacturing technology and data processing. Our position is to spread the experience that large-scale industrial production for the world market has become altogether questionable, continuously comes up against the limits of toleration of both external nature and human nature, here and abroad, and inevitably frustrates hopes for self-management and humane working conditions.

Decisive in all developments inside the so-called "formal" sector are the social learning processes which transcend the horizon of the labour-divided and bureaucratic industrial society of both Western and Eastern types and in which the subjective preconditions of a new culture are maturing.

November 1982, for the Hagen Congress[2]

Human Beings Are Not Ants

KIKERIKI: How, in brief, would you assess the current historical situation?

BAHRO: We're in the process of industrializing the world to destruction and death. Civilization is becoming self-destructive. The ecology and peace movement is the answer. The Bomb is only the most direct expression of these self-destructive forces. Christa Wolf was surely right to say that the Bomb is not a chance or accident, its development was inevitable. In this perspective, the differences between classes which struggle against each other on the basis of industrial society are no longer particularly important. The struggles waged on social questions in the rich countries, struggles of the workforce, have proved to be instrumental for the central position of the industrial metropolises and for their colonial role. This means that social-democracy and trade unions are sub-functions of this industrial society here, team-mates of capital. We must break with the entire logic of this social formation. Even the institutions of the left are among the things that have to be overcome. That is: the SPD, the French Socialist Party, even the Italian Communist Party. After all, they all want to solve the old questions.

The main reason for criticizing them today is not that they are not revolutionary. Revolution was traditionally supposed to bring about a complete release of the material forces of production. Today the main criticism of reformism is that it wants to repair a system that we must leave behind us altogether.

KIKERIKI: What you are saying is that the entire perspective of social-democratic politics is wrong.

BAHRO: Yes, but of course it's not just social-democracy. For example, this ordinary apartment we're sitting in now requires an incredible amount of expenditure of materials and energy because of the way that the infrastructure is organized. If we wanted to have the same thing for the whole of humanity – for according to the principles of social justice everyone should have what we ourselves have – that would mean multiplying by twenty the madness we have here, which would mean total natural catastrophe. The interest of the wage-earners, as defined in the rich countries, is bound up with the self-destruction of civilization. We must reject any perspective which would result in workers wanting to remain workers and engineers engineers. On the contrary: if they want to survive as human beings and have a future for their children, they must question their existence as workers and engineers, instead of merely wanting to slave away in their old roles of extracting better conditions from capital.

KIKERIKI: How under this perspective do you think that production can continue? What alternative method of production do you see which will both satisfy physical needs and remove alienation?

BAHRO: Nowadays production is not geared to human needs but has become an end in itself. The result is that today we consume around ten times as much energy for a worker to be able to sit in front of the TV in the evenings with his bottle of beer as was needed in the eighteenth century for Schiller to create his life's work. Not because the worker wants to have so much but because the total structure has changed so greatly, for example the infrastructure which means that he needs a car to get to work. This entire mechanism of the market-oriented international division of labour means that the whole of consumption has become detached from what would in nature be necessary in order to reproduce physical existence. And in this sense production must be abolished. We must stop working in this sense. A society of gatherers and hunters didn't work as we understand it today. They did what was necessary for the total process of their lives. If they found favourable natural conditions they were active for four hours. Nowadays we would say that they worked for four hours. But at that time work and pleasure were not separated, it wasn't asceticism when they went hunting. When you talk of work in this society today you mean wage-labour for the world market. You must produce cars, but human beings don't need cars. On this point we must correct the last 10,000 years of evolution. Human beings defined themselves through work by creating for themselves a second nature, alias material culture. Human energies and the specifically human capabilities have gone principally into material expansion.

This process of expansion has now become independent. Human beings must learn to transfer the competition that seems to be part of their nature to non-material regions. I don't mean this in a moralistic or religious way, but it is essential that it should no longer be satisfied through things which cost materials and energy. People cannot compete over the construction of bridges. There must be an end to the situation where one engineer competes with another over technical objects, a complete end. The only way is for the energy expenditure of the individual to be completely shifted to matters of communication – with other humans and with themselves. Everything else, expanded reproduction in the material sense, must be halted.

The famous cyclical economy that many Greens conceive of can't be achieved by, so to speak, introducing a bit of ecological reason into this economic system. Recycling, etc. are all primarily reformist ideas. They are better than the strategy of achieving a breakthrough via new investment. But it is an illusion to think that we can turn back this tenfold multiplication since Schiller's time with a bit of reason. For that we need the founding of a new society which no longer makes itself dependent on the production machine.

KIKERIKI: There's a traditional left criticism of that, namely the accusation that you want to throw overboard the achievements of a highly developed technology.

BAHRO: There are no achievements that one can contemplate in isolation from the question of where the development is leading. People who talk about being able to do something different with technology are talking about apples growing on a tree, some of them maggoty and others sound. They start sorting them. But what actually needs to be done is to chop down the tree which bears rotten fruits. I simply don't believe that any one of the outcomes of the last 2,000 years *taken by itself* can be defined as an achievement. If our first point is to say "but we don't want to destroy this and that" then we're condemning ourselves to keep on playing the same old game.

KIKERIKI: How do you think this reasoning would gain acceptance as against the automatism which is after all inherent in capitalist production? For society develops inevitably, independent of the good or bad intentions of the owners of capital. They by no means determine the course of events as individuals, but are themselves governed. Now what chance has a movement which has realized the destructive character of the accumulation of capital of taking up a stand against this automatism? What real possibilities of change do you see? Do you see a parliamentary path, or a path of revolution with the ensuing dictatorship of the proletariat?

BAHRO: Well, capital, the accumulation of capital, contrary to the old socialist expectations, does not come to a halt by being burst asunder from the inside but rather by meeting external limits. Thus in principle the smaller the Earth, the more favourable for us in a certain respect. The accumulation of capital, by reducing or at least tending to reduce human beings to automata, has also generated the counterforces of industrial society, that is, forces opposed in principle to the consciousness objectified in the Big Machine, to dead spirit or dead labour as Marx called it.

After all, ten thousand years ago, when we had an agrarian revolution, the basic ability to work was the same as it is today. Human beings have not changed biologically, so it is also conceivable that we can return to this early point of evolution. For unlike the ants which by nature are bound to the anthill, we are not irreversibly committed to the social structure we have erected. And perhaps we have not got it sufficiently clear in our own minds that in the last instance capital, seen against the historical evolution of 10,000 years, is not the cause of this expansion, but the means.

KIKERIKI: So catastrophe, the apocalypse, is not ruled out . . .

BAHRO: No, it is quite possible, as I see it.

KIKERIKI: You seem almost to depair of civilization.

BAHRO: I think the apocalypse can only be averted if it is clear to us that it is quite probable.

KIKERIKI: So in your opinion the main problem lies in the specialization of human beings in externally directed labour, in "exosomatic" evolution. Consequently to correct this we should rather develop the so-to-speak inner capabilities of human beings?

BAHRO: They should indeed be awakened and mobilized. Human beings must now make a different use of their brains than previously. It is not for nothing that bourgeois society is the final victory of abstract reason focussed on the instrumental world. Mind you, humanity has not yet achieved self-awareness. Self-awareness in the sense of self-control, control of one's own forces. We do not control our own forces. What takes place collectively and socially in the process of material reproduction is not controlled, it still operates independently. In this situation everything that withdraws energy from this uncontrolled operation is good for a start. Dropping out in this most general sense is the start of any alternative.

We must only bear in mind that for the time being most people will remain inside the system, and that we must also work as facilitators. Therefore I believe that the main issue in the economic policy of the Greens (alongside the anti-investment strategy by which we will prevent continued industrial expansion), is for us to divert parts of what the system wants to invest into providing the means needed for people who want to start afresh outside the industrial system, i.e. outside the system of wage-labour. Among other things, the Greens should try to secure the means for unemployed people and their dependants to be able to build up a new way of life for themselves.

We don't want a restoration of full employment. Those for whom the industrial system has no more work should found a new society outside the industrial system. That is quite important in distinguishing us from the old left stuff.

KIKERIKI: . . . from all the proposals for repairs.

BAHRO: I mean this economic programme that was put forward to the Greens (the paper of the Federal Economic Action Group), with the demand for wage-labour for all. But our problem is that we don't want everyone to come back into the industrial system for "wages and bread"; what we want and must want is to finance a withdrawal from the industrial system.

KIKERIKI: You mean that the development actually has its roots in human nature . . .

BAHRO: . . . and that I don't see the main problem as being how we overcome capital as a specific form. I see the main problem much more as how living spirit can overcome dead spirit. You know there is actually no guarantee that it will succeed. The development of the species, like the development of other species, *can* come to an end. That is conceivable, it is not out of the question, on the contrary.

KIKERIKI: Does that mean that you envisage decentralization as the form of a utopian alternative?

BAHRO: I think that is necessary even from a material point of view alone. For with the current international division of labour, costly transports of materials and energy, infrastructure and so on are unavoidable.

So you can only come down from the tenfold multiplication of per capita material and energy consumption if you start from the premise that people's basic needs are produced on the spot and that even exchange takes place for the most part only within the surrounding area. Of course this can't actually be decreed, but the degree of division of labour that humanity can materially afford will be determined simply according to the criterion of minimal material and energy consumption. They will then make a new use of science for it.

KIKERIKI: And would that mean in practice that a new social form which would some day come to prevail would develop in the womb of society, of capitalist society?

BAHRO: I think so, and I think so because the possibilities for the expansion of capital, simply in the material dimension, are now really limited. As capital hits the limits of the Earth, accumulation is becoming visibly fatal. For example, in the Amazon basin an area the size of West Germany is being razed every two and a half years, that's how the Big Machine is working there.

Therefore in my opinion the main argument is between those who want to repair all this and those who want to drop out. In this respect I consider social-democracy to be our main ideological opponent.

KIKERIKI: Is that not analogous to the theory of social-fascism?

BAHRO: Not at all. What I mean is . . .

KIKERIKI: Not that one should struggle against the SPD more than the CDU?

BAHRO: No, the point is . . .

KIKERIKI: To create a line of separation . . .

BAHRO: Because we recognize that it is not the CDU which can ruin the new political approach which the Greens and Alternatives have. That is, ideologically and intellectually ruin and put a brake on it. Only the eco-reformists in the SPD can do that.

In this sense "Eppler[1] is worse than Schmidt". Please don't think I'm being fanatical. As far as his intentions are concerned Eppler is very close to us in spirit. But by kidding us that ecology and the present type of economy are in principle reconcilable and that SPD-type "realpolitik" could be the instrument of such a reconciliation, he is taking the movement for a ride.

To counter that we must formulate our absolute independence. Radicals against reformist ecologism!

KIKERIKI: What concrete possibilities do you envisage in the alternative counterculture? Alternative production runs into precisely the same danger of producing for a market.

BAHRO: There would have to be a certain number of people so that basic production such as food, clothing, housing, health, schooling, etc. is possible. But first of all of course a few particularly active and receptive individuals will face the rest of society as initiators and say: We are now gathering together a few people and we will take, let's say, 0.15 hectares per head. That would seem to be the area we will be able to feed ourselves from, not to supply products for the market, but to feed ourselves. And we need buildings . . .

KIKERIKI: Do you have a self-sufficiency model in mind?

BAHRO: Self-sufficiency for the most part in all the necessities of daily life. A certain surplus will be available for exchange, but in principle self-sufficiency, autarchy, seems to me to be what is necessary. I don't know whether you know Lao Tzu? His economic concept was that communities should not get too close to each other. The best thing would be never to visit the neighbouring place. That is naturally exaggerated, but it has a rational core.

KIKERIKI: Are you therefore saying that agrarian production is the ideal?

BAHRO: The point is to produce food oneself and not to buy it in the supermarket. So it's not that agrarian production is the ideal but that you produce things – from food and housing to schools and universities, everything that people need in order to become socialized and to reproduce themselves physically – to a large extent by your own labour. And to do that you must have the land. But not as just another productionist end in itself that everything else revolves around.

KIKERIKI: So, agriculture as a necessary condition.

BAHRO: It is indeed the fundamental condition, that's why we need the "acquisition of land". It is also good for further reasons. The land will then in any case be taken away from the EEC's common agricultural policy. To bring it down to the basic concept, we must build up areas liberated from the industrial system.

That means, liberated from nuclear weapons and from supermarkets. What we are talking about is a new social formation and a different civilization.

> *Conversation with* Kikeriki, *the paper of the*
> *Bremen Culture Workshop, on the opening day of*
> *the Hagen Congress, November 1982*

This Time The Greens – Why?
Draft for an Election Appeal

Not only have we reached the end of our economic system, but also we and our whole industrial civilization have reached a state of crisis which will prove terminal if we are not prepared to change our total course.

The foreground is now dominated by fears about unemployment and social decline because these evils have for many of us become immediate problems, or could suddenly become so.

But behind that there rises menacingly the danger of atomic extinction which is to be increased by the stationing of new means of mass annihilation – particularly Pershing II and Cruise missiles but also chemical and biological instruments of murder.

In the Third World hundreds of millions of people are living in destitution as a result of the unjust world economic order. Approximately 15 million children die annually of hunger alone – more than the number of deaths claimed by each year of World War II.

And at an ever-increasing pace the form of production and lifestyle which has spread out from Europe across the whole world is destroying the Earth which sustains us, above all the biosphere from which we come.

If the trees die, human beings will not live. Not only is the German forest dying – we're still losing it only hectare by hectare – but an area of tropical rain forest equivalent to the whole of the Federal Republic is being lost every two years, and of topsoil in just over one year.

In the end it won't need the Bomb to wipe us out. But if the monstrous squandering of resources on the arms race and the exploitation of the Third World don't cease there is no hope at all of really stopping the ecological crisis.

From this alone it's already obvious that we have to play for maximum stakes.

If in future we want to live lives at all fit for human beings, or even if we just want to survive, we must fundamentally change our way of life. We must design civilization anew. Everyone who has already reached these conclusions should vote for the Greens. Insofar as we really are talking about such a conversion, are we promising to achieve it from a minority position simply by taking up seats in parliament? Are we claiming to have got together the new overall plan and the detailed prescriptions consistently enough to succeed?

We can at least promise one thing: to raise so unreservedly for debate in parliament the challenges which now face us that the CDU/CSU and SPD (not to mention the FDP) can no longer go on talking and governing regardless, unperturbed by questions of life and survival.

What this general election is about above all is a signal that the new fundamental philosophy is spreading. It's about as unforgettable a warning as possible for all those who want to pursue the same politics as before or at most believe in a solution through reformist tinkering.

We do not dispute that they too would like "a little peace", an "undamaged environment" and "bread for the world", but on their conditions, which have to do with gaining power and/or the level of profits.

Therefore in practice they are neither capable of peace (which first of all means disarmament) nor will they protect the environment and leave the destitute people in the southern hemisphere of the Earth even the bare means of subsistence.

We will make no compromises with them on matters concerning life and survival. We know from experience that it can't be done with "a little ecological reason" and with "responsible peace policy" à la Franz-Josef Strauss, because there is no such thing as "a little cancer" and "a little death".

Anyone who votes for us is deciding in favour of the following positions, which we shall fight for in Bonn, in order to lend a new momentum to West German politics. Ours is a new total alternative to the offer of the previous party cartel which has worn itself out in an unimaginative continuation of the crisis situation, stagnation and corruption.

Foreign Policy as Peace Policy

1. Creating peace without weapons, swords to ploughshares in East and West. Beginning at home.

The first thing is to reverse our thinking on the "threat": we are threatened because we threaten others. The fact that our country is used as a military base against the second superpower, the Soviet Union, is the main reason for the deadly danger in which we are suspended. The planned new missiles will finally make Germany a firing range for the superpowers. They can reach the heart of the Soviet Union within a matter of minutes. Therefore they don't deter the blitz, they attract it.

Helmut Kohl wants expressly to interpret your vote as a "yes" to the stationing of missiles which he has pushed for, while Hans-Jochen Vogel is the candidate for the party of Helmut Schmidt who talked us into the missile decision and is not dissociating himself from it.

Anyone who no longer wants to base peace on nuclear deterrence or the so-called balance of terror (which moreover has been rejected by the arms strategists themselves) can vote for no other party but the Greens.

We also oppose the hypocritical policy of the German Communist Party in the peace movement, which represents the analogous deterrence doctrine of the Eastern military bloc and is worried that the Soviet Union might have to stop pointing missiles at our country, in which there are still as yet no medium-range missiles aimed at it.

For us, every missile which either side keeps at the ready is one too many. Anyone who like us considers the very possession of atomic weapons to be a crime, and their use – in the words of a North American bishop – to be the final crucifixion of Christ, should vote for us.

We are also unconditionally – that is, regardless of the outcome of the Geneva negotiations – opposed to the new missiles, because they do not in any way enhance our security but programme suicide and add fuel to an arms race which must sooner or later end in catastrophe.

Furthermore we are also opposed to every other step of arms build-up and militarism. As far as we have any say there will be no build-up of conventional weapons. There will be no production and no export of arms. No women will join the army. There will be no extension of military service and community service, no test of beliefs for conscientious objectors, no persecution of those who object to any kind of service. There will be a ban on producing and selling war toys and on brutalizing contributions by the media, particularly by television. We want education for peace and instruction in non-violent forms of resistance in schools.

But it is not enough to prevent the arms build-up. Nations must insist upon disarmament, each first of all in its own country. Since nuclear defence wipes out along with life every value which might be worth protecting, we demand first of all the removal of all nuclear warheads – 5,000 times Hiroshima! – from our country. We no longer want to be under the North American nuclear umbrella.

West Germany must become a nuclear weapon-free zone, and over and above that a nuclear-free zone altogether (free also from nuclear power stations which in the event of war would function as super-bombs), in which no chemical and biological weapons are stored either.

In remembrance of the terrors of the Second World War, which would be exceeded, we demand steps towards unilateral disarmament also in the conventional field: the removal from service of all kinds of weapon systems like tanks, aircraft, etc. which can be deployed offensively (i.e. to cross borders). Our minimum demand is to change to an exclusively defensive defence system.

Our ideal goes far beyond that. It is a society which no longer has to defend itself because its mode of existence no longer provokes any external threat. As long as a defence problem exists we want non-military, decentrally organized social defence supported by society as a whole, which above all means non-cooperation with the potential occupying power.

2. Germany in the peace movement: out of the military blocs.
Solo initiative by the Federal Republic for peace and
disarmament.

We Germans in the Federal Republic can and should contribute our own initiative to release the dynamic of disarmament, and in doing so count on a response from the population of the GDR.

In the face of the danger that we are now being plagued with in the third and fourth generation for the sins of our fathers, and against the background of our ecology and peace movement, we have the right and also the reason, with the necessary self-awareness, to demand full sovereignty for our country and to desire a government which also aspires to this.

In the face of the politics of preparation for war pursued by the Western alliance as represented by the governments of the USA under Reagan, Great Britain under Thatcher and France under Mitterrand, we need as soon as possible a government which is prepared for the Federal Republic to take a solo initiative for peace and disarmament.

The partners we shall count upon in this are not primarily other states, but rather the grassroots peace movements in the other European countries and in the United States, together with whom we want to achieve a nuclear weapon-free Europe from Poland to Portugal.

We will support everything which helps overcome the division of Europe into military blocs and the confrontation between the two halves which is caused by the dominance of the two superpowers.

Because the strategies of both blocs are built on nuclear deterrence, anybody who doesn't want to be "defended" to death by nuclear weapons must back military neutralization. Therefore we want to remove the Federal Republic from military integration in NATO. Our objective is first of all a largely demilitarized, neutral West Germany. The more distant perspective, which we see also in connection with the increasing weakness of the Soviet system in Eastern Europe, is demilitarization on both sides of the border between the military blocs which divides Europe and partitions Germany.

Taking up the political legacy of Gustav Heinemann[1] and his supporters from the time before rearmament and integration into the West, we want a neutral belt in Central Europe, so that the neutralization of the Federal Republic can facilitate and lead to neutralization of the GDR.

The key to solving the German question, which consists mainly of a situation where outsiders cause the two German states to be heavily armed against each other, is the withdrawal of all foreign troops from the Federal Republic; this can lead to the freeing of the GDR and in probable consequence the release of Eastern Europe into full sovereignty.

Since in the end it comes down to the fact that the foreign troops in both German states are still stationed on the basis of their rights as victors in the Second World War, Germany needs at last a long overdue peace treaty which should establish its neutrality in perpetuity on the Austrian model, initially as a commitment of both German states.

We aspire to a Germany newly unified out of the ecology and peace movement on both sides. The unqualified recognition of the GDR as presently constituted will open the way to a German confederation.

By this we do not mean the restoration of that centralized nation-state with which not only other peoples but also the Germans themselves had such terrible experience. There will be no new edition of the Bismarck Reich.

We have in mind rather a "Germany of regions" in which municipalities have precedence over districts, districts over the *Länder* (or the regions in the GDR) and finally the *Länder* (or regions) over the federal government. We conceive of the whole as a gentle, non-violent, green republic without armed forces for use either externally or internally.

Sovereignty will rest not with the federal government, but – as in the time before 1871 – with the *Länder* (or regions) which federate voluntarily to it.

Since our programme links military disarmament with industrial disarmament, that is with the renunciation of capitalist expansion on the world market, this policy can bring about reconciliation with the other peoples of Europe, especially with Eastern Europe and the Soviet Union.

3. *Solidarity with the peoples of the Third World.*

Military and industrial disarmament in the rich countries is also a decisive factor for solidarity with the peoples of the Third World. In particular we refuse to consider any measures to militarily "secure" the supply of energy and raw materials or access to markets. Likewise we Germans must not participate either directly or indirectly in "rapid deployment forces".

Apart from ecological demands in our own country, the interests of the exploited, poverty-stricken, hungry and starving in the Third World – and even more in the so-called Fourth World of the absolutely poor countries – demand our withdrawal from the prevailing international division of labour.

Only a reduction in economic relations with these countries, or rather with their "elites" in whose interest export production takes place, can leave room for the people there at least to satisfy their basic needs.

"Development aid", "partnership", "technology transfer", "new world economic order" and industrial capitalist "development" *per se* are only so many names for the conspiracy between the elites of North and South, who are simply struggling for a share of the cake and to socially secure their positions of power. Behind this are concealed the main causes of the continuing dependence and impoverishment of half of humanity.

We Greens consider it one of our most important international obligations to get rid of the disastrous model of the "good life" here at home, which lures the rest of humanity into a tunnel without exit. Unless we are prepared to dismantle and transform our industrial system all our sympathy remains nothing but empty gestures and phrases.

Material and financial aid from the rich countries will only be effective for the recipients as "help for self-help", if it serves to restore, support and develop those conditions under which the people there can obtain or retain food, clothing, housing, health and education in accordance with the local circumstances, on their own responsibility.

The question for us is what can we do here to help protect the local conditions of reproduction and life against the forces of the world market. It then becomes decisive to bring to a halt the expansion of national and multinational corporations and banks and to cut off their outlets, and reducing the demand for their products is a part of this. In the final analysis it means dissolving their material and financial structures and putting a stop to their activity. We Greens are considering anew how this task, which is important too for our own survival, and which the workers' movement was unable to accomplish, can be tackled in a different way.

Work Differently, Live in Solidarity

4. Finding an ecological answer to the economic crisis.

The existing world economic order impoverishes half of humanity, forces whole nations below the basic subsistence level, and everywhere smothers local cultures, makes hundreds of millions of people landless and unemployed, destroys the fertility of the land, extends the deserts, fells the rain forests, and drives one country after another into state bankruptcy and towards military dictatorship.

But now we in the metropolises from which this all emanates – North America, Western Europe, Japan – have ourselves been caught up by the crisis. The "free market economy", so highly praised, is here too devouring its own natural basis, materially impoverishing and above all psychologically depressing the people dependent upon it. The democratic facade is crumbling accordingly. And as in every place where contradictions intensify it is women who are usually affected first and most seriously.

We by no means see an alternative in the Soviet type of system, which has never been able to escape completely from the wake of the materially superior West, but rather adds its own indigenous weaknesses to it. In the end what we are faced with is a single world system of unrestrained power rivalry, social injustice and destruction of nature.

We are prepared to take up the social question which has been thrown up with new intensity and variety in our own country – mass unemployment, social decline, decay of political culture, restriction of civil liberties.

But we do not forget that the economic crisis in the rich countries is embedded in the more fundamental dangers of nuclear war, of mass extermination through wars, hunger, disease and privations of all kinds, and of the ecological crisis which encroaches on everything and is the quintessence of the worldwide industrialization process.

In this situation all purely traditional attempts at a solution –

which are in any case effective only in the short term – will only serve to advance us further towards the total catastrophe which threatens us. For this reason we are advocating an ecological answer to the economic crisis. Social justice must in future be established under the conditions of a contracting economy and in particular, of a commitment to minimize the burdens placed on nature.

Let us admit at last that the more it expands, the more our industrial system is devouring its own basis. There is in the Federal Republic not too little industrial production but too much: too much consumption of raw materials and energy, too much production of harmful substances, too many cars eating up materials and belching out exhaust fumes, too much plastic and concrete, not to speak of the armaments and nuclear industries. Instead of starting new export drives and thereby exporting some of our unemployment to other countries, we want needs-oriented work in economic and living zones which are as decentralized as possible.

For there is too little self-determined, satisfying work. There are numerous areas of deficiency to which too little work is devoted – for example, alternative ecologically harmless systems of energy, local public transport, dwellings fit for human habitation, processing and re-use of waste, non-toxic healthy food. And there is too little leisure time for the working population.

5. We Greens won't accept unemployment with its psychological and financial afflictions as a forced situation of life. But the demand for jobs at any price is not what we're about either. We want to know what is produced, how and where, and who determines this.

We differentiate between socially and ecologically meaningful and destructive work. We demand the dismantling of anti-life branches of the economy, primarily of the nuclear and armaments industries, and the extension of socially useful, future-oriented areas of work.

The policy of curing mass unemployment by boosting economic growth, as proclaimed by all the established parties, is illusory, misleading, and disastrous in its effect on living conditions and the environment.

Have not the investments of yesterday ensured the unemployment of today? Today's investments will drive tomorrow's unemployment figures sky high, since for the greater part they serve to replace human work by machines.

At the same time the working conditions of those still

employed are deteriorating as a result of rationalization: as the mad rush for work increases, so do monotony, the devaluation of skills and the strain on health. Meanwhile control over the actual work process decreases and creative ability is driven out.

We support all efforts aimed at self-determination for workers employed in factories, offices, shops or wherever; and we are in favour of generous support for all self-managed alternative projects outside this sector.

6. *For justice and against social decline.*

We desire the equal distribution of socially necessary work amongst all members of society. One precondition for this is a drastic reduction in working hours. As a first step we demand a 35-hour week with no loss of earnings for lower and middle income earners. A decrease in the number of hours worked for pay will at the same time create better conditions for people's own work in their personal sphere of life and for a different division between men and women of the necessary child-rearing and housework.

We are against a gender-specific division of labour which assigns to women mainly work in the home and family, as well as the badly paid and low-skilled activities in the sphere of employment.

We are strongly opposed to the dismantling of social services and public services in the very situation in which more and more people are becoming dependent on them.

At the same time we want to get away from centralized, bureaucratic social administration and build up self-administered social services on a community basis.

In the long term there can only be social security if the constant growth in the need for state-managed social support and services ceases. And our perspective is not to build more and more hospitals, addiction clinics and sanitaria, but to overcome the competitive growth society that makes people sick, this society that needs the so-called welfare state as a repair workshop for a multitude of ills.

Nevertheless some short-term measures have to be taken now in order to alleviate the most urgent problems of the people affected and to protect the social progress that has been achieved. The scope for far-reaching reorganization can depend significantly on calming people's most acute anxieties.

It is necessary to fix decent minimum levels for wages, unemployment benefit, social security, educational assistance and child allowance. In this context we will support further measures which ensure equal opportunities for women.

7. *There is a lot of work to be done for conversion to a humane ecological cyclical economy and repairing damage to the environment, the workplace and society.*

An ecological and social type of economy demands a completely different system of production: small units, locally integrated and self-administered, with soft technologies which save resources and spare the environment. The present big industrial establishments, including infrastructures for the flow of energy and materials, must be reduced step by step (not only on account of the market difficulties which will in any case arise), and in part also cease operation and be dismantled.

If we don't go beyond minor reforms and repairs, we can neither save water, forest, sea and soil for any length of time, nor protect ourselves as human beings from the physical and mental consequences. Nor are large organizations capable of self-administration, especially if they operate transnationally.

We want to achieve in the foreseeable future a majority consensus for determining, planning and beginning the rebuilding of our civilization, which is necessary for survival.

Apart from that we must here and now seize all opportunities to remove danger and prevent further damage. And we must use the crisis to change whatever can be changed in the existing industrial complexes and infrastructures, so that from the point of view of both product and work process, things are done in a more environmentally and socially tolerable way.

All these measures must aim towards decentralized and alternative solutions, and as we see it the most significant bottlenecks in the process will be caused by the necessary reorganization of energy and water supplies. We know that we are thereby raising the question of whether the industrial conurbations should not be rapidly broken up. All this should facilitate a bit more free development of the personality.

Yet whatever we undertake in order to reduce unemployment, it is improbable within the existing circumstances that there will ever be full employment. Should we then recommend, even to those who don't really want it any more, only the perspective of reintegration into capitalist wage-labour for the world market? Is it not true that many people who are still inside the system want to drop out too?

For both reasons there must be an adequately assured possibility of changing to new living conditions beyond the capitalist industrial system; and we mean more than those alternative projects which are still dependent on the niches of the general market.

We should like to divert some of the millions wrongly invested in armaments, in the nuclear state, in the various giant projects, into the hands of those who want to get involved in the positive adventure of exiting or changing to a post-industrial self-sufficient economy. Whether there is a need for this will be seen when we can politically guarantee the relevant opportunity.

We need money for our utopian alternative, because land and tools are distributed in our society in such a way that men and women cannot easily start work with their own hands.

8. The Green alternative can be financed!

We are devoting a small separate section to this because the cooks who have stirred the crisis broth they have found say, as a result of the material constraints in which their interests are tied up, that many of our proposals are quite good, but sadly just not feasible.

This is said by the same people who have committed the money for arming us to the teeth for nuclear holocaust, for industrializing the world to destruction and for the state and police apparatus which must provide cover for all this. We do not accept their "material constraints", and therefore don't accept either the small play areas in their fully booked budgets where they want to tire us out.

Financing of the ecological and social investment programme, including the minimum income, is possible if we can gain priority for it in the budget.

The main areas from which we want to redistribute are armaments, the nuclear programme and the other projects of insanity. Let us take the money away from death and give it to life!

Besides that we would like to cancel the various privileges for the upper income groups in the tax and national insurance system.

We are in favour of a supplementary tax and we support a broadening of the autonomous financial basis of local government.

The Federal Republic is the richest of the big industrial states of Europe. The means for the great conversion exist here and are obtainable. We must ask the voters: If you want conversion, give us enough influence! Not only through the ballot paper, but above all through extra-parliamentary action.

Domestic policy: Risk more grassroots democracy!

9. *For an alternative democratic culture which helps the civic will convincingly to prevail and renounces the use of violence.*

Green politics aims to strengthen the elements of decentralized and direct democracy.

Far from wanting to abolish the rule of law, we want to make full use of and broaden the legal scope for resistance by those affected.

We regard civil disobedience as legitimate where the policies pursued affect life itself and the future.

Without maintaining and extending civil rights and liberties the people cannot defend themselves with any effect against the daily threat to their environment, and protect their working and living conditions.

Ecological, social and democratic demands, even if at first they are expressed only by a minority, must find a way into decisions at all levels.

In order to improve the prospects for this, it is necessary:
– to create a form of self-government which is close to the citizens and controlled from below, and to counteract the increasing monopolization of economic power, the growing bureaucratization and centralization of government, and the expansion and brutalization of the police force.
– to ensure the right to unrestricted, timely and comprehensible information for the citizen about all government measures.
– to extend the right to public control through stronger involvement by the citizens and establishing the right for citizens' groups and associations to institute legal proceedings.
– to end the criminalization of legitimate political and social resistance and the erosion of the right to demonstrate.
– to open up the mass media widely for the social movements.
– to allow minorities and people with fundamentally critical opinions the right to present their views in the media and to prevent access by the big media companies to radio and TV.
– to prevent the broad-band cable network and computerized data gathering as instruments of increasing the isolation, control and intimidation of the citizen.

The prevailing politics must no longer encourage the isolation of our immigrant fellow-citizens and their deprivation of rights.

We Greens defend the right of asylum for victims of political persecution and condemn its restrictive use.

What We Want Responsibility For and What Not

10. How will we conduct ourselves in the Federal parliament?

We Greens are taking up seats in parliament to give a voice to the pacifist, ecological and social opposition in our country in parliament too, to obtain information for these movements and to further our objectives in this field.

At the same time we are striving for a new relationship between members of parliament and the party base, the social movements and the voters, including those of the other parties. To this end we shall counteract the possibility of our deputies becoming independent, for example by limiting their period in office.

Our elected representatives will divert a major part of their allowances to the support of alternative projects and initiatives. They may not hold seats in other elected assemblies and may not hold any additional offices in the party.

The basis of their work is to provide complete and comprehensible information which makes our political decision-making process clear and controllable for the public.

We shall also in future place our main emphasis on giving the extra-parliamentary and opposition movements and trends a party-political and parliamentary voice. We shall remain closely linked to those forces out of which we ourselves have grown:
– to the ever-growing peace movement;
– to the multi-layered ecology movement and the citizens' initiatives, to all those who are committed to the humanization of our everyday environment, the protection of cultural monuments, cityscapes and landscapes, and not least to nature conservation and animal protection;
– to the movement against nuclear power, which has been fighting for longer than we Greens have existed against this life-threatening and uneconomic energy policy;
– to the women's movement, which stands for the real equality of women and young girls, for their right to self-determination over their own bodies, and their self-defence against the violence which they continually encounter in our society;
– to those people in factories and offices who no longer subordinate to the tactics of the SPD and the trade unions their commitment to meaningful work, to their rights at the workplace, and against reductions in earnings, unemployment, and everyday repression;
– to the wide network of efforts directed at self-organization by the unemployed and opposed to achievement pressure and the

selection system in schools and universities; against the erosion of cultural life; against the shunting of old, sick and handicapped people away from the life of society; against sexual oppression, ostracism and commercialization; against discrimination of deviant minorities; against the dismantling of democratic and constitutional rights, and the *Berufsverbot*;[2] against fascist and neo-nazi activities; for extending freedom of the press and of expression; for the integration of our immigrant fellow-citizens on the basis of equal rights; for moral and material support of liberation struggles in the Third World . . .

We Greens are definitely prepared to take on political responsibility in order to carry through the above-mentioned objectives.

And we are definitely not prepared to take on joint responsibility for continuing the life-threatening policies currently practised by the parties represented in parliament.

We challenge these parties to public discussion in order to sound out whether it is possible to work with them on the basis of problem-oriented cooperation from case to case, in order to achieve objectives which are vital for survival.

We are at all times willing and able to cooperate on material issues, as our numerous representatives in the state and municipal assemblies prove.

But the Greens will not vote for any Chancellor nor support any government that wants to continue the armaments and nuclear programmes and to continue subordinating the protection of the natural foundations of human life to the needs of the profit economy. We reject all "progress" in the wrong direction.

We do not want to help repair industrial mass production and the bureaucratic institutions. We will not let ourselves be dictated to as to where to deploy our still meagre forces. We will not run with sandbags to where others tell us there is a breach.

This will not make the Federal Republic ungovernable – there is no such thing as a constitutional duty to form coalitions. But we will force the old parties, especially the SPD, to nail their colours to the mast and show whether they are prepared to take the new challenges into account, or whether they prefer majorities within the framework of the old common ground of growth and armaments. If the latter, let them show us their Grand Coalition! It is in any case the real truth of the present situation, far more than many people think.

If we are not deceiving ourselves completely:

Green is in '83 the only colour of hope.

We are the party of peace. For us, *dona nobis pacem* (grant us peace) is not only a plea for external peace. We seek a culture of peace inside the country too and we know that peace begins with non-violence in one's own conduct.

We want to overcome the highly dangerous division of Europe and Germany between the armed military blocs. West and East are no longer alternatives to each other. Against the status quo we pose our vision of a new third way which leads beyond confrontation.

We should like to win a majority in favour of changing our life here in such a way that our rich country ceases to oppress and exploit the nations of the Third World and keep them dependent.

We want to get at the deepest causes of the economic crisis by throwing into question the whole of modern capitalist factory and office society. As is only now becoming clear, the motto over its entrance is: "Abandon all hope, ye who enter here." The future lies only in the other direction.

We have recognized the growth economy driven by competition for the highest profit as the motor which we have to stop if we want to halt the total catastrophe which it is bringing upon human beings and their world.

In opposition to the material constraint towards death, human beings – men and women – must regain the freedom to set off wherever they will and to live their lives in the way for which they are actually disposed by their original nature.

We can't go on like this, above all we can't go on satisfactorily on the basis of *things* which can be *had*. Do we not above all need to return to ourselves, to find leisure for meaningful communication with others, and to find ourselves again in one community?

We are now the party for the general emancipation of human beings – men and women. At least we should like to be so, and would like people to help us by participating – perhaps with us, but above all in the social movements which sustain us.

Anyone who has had enough of the dissipation of forces and wants to join together with us for resistance and for the transition to a different and healing civilization:

This time vote for us, vote Green.

Sindelfingen, January 1983[3]

Overcoming the Gravitational Pull of the Industrial System

What will be completely decisive for our extraordinary national congress is whether we put forward an ideologically defensive concept on the lines of the programme against unemployment which we let ourselves be pressured into by the established forces, who themselves no longer have any solution to offer, or whether we self-confidently, positively and forcefully outline our Total Alternative.

If it is not disputed that the ecological crisis is the historic quintessence of the capitalist industrial system and therefore cannot be solved by repairing the symptoms but only by a break with its total logic, each individual measure which we support must be fitted into the perspective of this transition. In view of the pace at which the train is heading for the abyss, what we are talking about first of all is an emergency brake strategy. More precisely expressed: our action must be aimed primarily against the driving dynamic of industrial development, bearing in mind particularly that the accumulation of capital is a general international process, whose engine must however be switched off above all in the metropolises.

In our Hagen declaration on economic policy, the question whether we give priority to alternatives *within* the system or alternatives *to* the system was not clearly settled. It is not contested that we must put forward both, that we must provide links and connections with the current situation. But what matters is that we should set down at the beginning as a general criterion *where* we want to go in order to "count down" from there and thus examine whether our proposals lead towards the new social formation. Everything we offer must be aimed clearly against the industrialist bloc which wants to carry on as before. Measures that remain within the system must be recognizable as such, and from the context it must be clear that we want to go beyond that, that we want to achieve the "second cosmic velocity" needed to overcome the gravitational pull of the industrial system.

So far we have got out of the question of the relationship between perspectives within the system and those transcending the system by saying "both one and the other", for instance with the proposition: "We support all efforts aimed at the self-determination of workers in factories, offices and shops; and we support generous aid for all self-administered alternative projects outside this sector". Anyone who still has a trace of Marxist training in them as far as method is concerned, can never be satisfied with this eclecticism, that is with the mixing of positions instead of integration on one particular position. A consistent programme will only be possible if we build either on the old principle or the new.

A "programme against unemployment" is defined by its very name as bound to the system and preserving the system. It sends human beings back into wage-slavery for the world market and reminds them of the inescapable nature of this urban-industrial civilization pregnant with the embryo of death. It ties our forces to a job which we neither can nor in the final analysis want to solve, because it is contrary to our task.

Are we at least agreed that the ecological crisis is the quintessence of the industrial system as a historic whole? That industrial-urban civilization as such is becoming intolerable?

Concretely, for example: that even such a "triviality" as water supply demands the breaking up of conurbations like Hamburg (Lüneburg Heath!) or Frankfurt (Vogelsberg!)? The basis of our decision cannot be whether we can "explain it to the colleagues at work", i.e. whether we can convince them about it right away. The new movements we rest upon (including the Green-Alternative election movement) did *not* arise primarily in the workplace, but – in a historic sense – against the workplace as core component of the industrial capitalist social formation embracing capital and labour, which must be dismantled completely. But then we must not confirm the people there as workers or engineers, but must make every effort to bring them psychologically away from their fixation upon *this* as their position of interest and to motivate them in every way to drop out or to change tracks. This is not a question of "welcoming unemployment", of "giving notice today" or of "handing in one's union card", but of reorientation against the destructive work, fatal in its results, which they must inevitably continue if they remain inside the system.

Rainer Trampert[1] does not want to call on the people in the factories to drop out, because he can't tell them where to go. He just doesn't start from the assumption that the train is heading for the abyss. But I am not sure whether he would find dropping out desirable even if it were possible.

Would he *like* to know where he can send them? If so, my concept is not to send them into the void but to use our potential share of power to offer them a material support for the change, a proposal which he ought to agree to. I envisage a *different* redistribution. One beyond the industrial system, beyond the arena of the struggle for distribution between capital and labour in the workplace, which has proved to be historically devoid of perspective. A diversion of material (financial) resources away from capitalist investment, subsidy, support and insurance into the beginnings of a new social formation (which does *not* mean into an "informal sector" which complements and reinforces a "formal" one).

We must in principle deal with the crisis from the new perspective. At the threshold on which we now stand, to want to staple together for a "new majority" concepts that are contrary in their perspective is only evidence of mistrust in the new forces.

Deliberations as to whether a clear statement on this matter could cost us votes are absolutely short-sighted. Even in the medium term our success will not depend upon getting as close as possible to the SPD/trade-union point of view, but upon differentiating ourselves from it as much as possible. The more thoroughly we now define our position, the longer a run-up we take, the further we will jump. Let us leave to the others the frog-like perspective of emergency measures – which in any case will not solve the social problems, so that our participation in them can only discredit us – and not let ourselves be forced to join in the patch-up.

We cannot put greater pressure on the SPD to transform itself than by effectively confronting it with the choice between the ecological and peace movement on the one hand and a Grand Coalition on the other. The SPD is afraid of a Grand Coalition precisely because it would set the seal on our rise to being a 20 per cent party, while they themselves might break up because of it. And in this fear the SPD is the organ of the *whole* establishment, which is suffering from increasing wear and tear and lack of credibility.

The more determined we are and the more clearly we present our completely different perspective, the more we shall be promoting a long-term restratification in the electoral base of the SPD and also that of the CDU/CSU. It is a sceptical misreading of the situation to base ourselves only on short-term manoeuvres for trapping potential defectors from the other camp. The social process is moving towards a qualitative leap in the public consciousness. For that we must establish the opposite camp.

It is precisely our pressure from an Archimedean point outside the previous world of ideas that can effect a change in the political landscape. The more unavailable we are for the SPD, the stronger in its inner-party power play will be the wing that is turned towards us.

Tageszeitung, 5 January 1983

No Stand-in for Eppler

STERN: Rudolf Bahro, as an advocate of fundamental opposition you reject any approach by the Greens towards the Social-Democrats. Are you afraid of contact with the SPD?

BAHRO: Not in the slightest. I think I've proved that through my many public appearances with Social-Democrats. But I'm asked about it so often nowadays, as if there were a legal requirement to form a coalition and a duty to join the game. That's not the case.

STERN: For what reason do you refuse then?

BAHRO: Because even with the SPD it is not really possible to do what is indispensable if we want to avoid atomic annihilation and destroying the world through industrialization. What an illusion is the assumption that we only need to help the SPD back into government to be able to stop the new missiles! Anyone who believes that still doesn't understand how inescapably bound up in the arms logic this party is when it is in power.

STERN: Don't you think it's possible that the SPD might withdraw from the Brussels resolution?[1]

BAHRO: Social-democrats and socialists have always played pacifist when they were in opposition. In government they were always "responsible peace-lovers" in a similar manner to Franz-Josef Strauss. Can you see the slightest sign of the SPD wanting to revoke the foreign policy they share with the Christian-Democrats? They will do what the North Americans demand. Should we, for the sake of the illusion that they wouldn't do it, vote in favour of the budget, including the arms budget?

STERN: If you refuse to cooperate with the SPD, the conservatives are sure to continue in government. Is it really a matter of indifference to you whether Helmut Kohl or Hans-Jochen Vogel becomes Chancellor?

BAHRO: No, because I'd rather have a man like Gerhard Baum as minister of home affairs than someone like Friedrich Zimmermann. But in the decisive military and ecological spheres the difference doesn't show. In both cases the SPD persists in the logic of the arms race and world market competition. It is only for "moderation" in nuclear armaments, and where the CDU pushes private investments the SPD give preference to public ones. We want to get away from these disastrous compulsions to expand.

STERN: Why can't you imagine any possibility at all of doing that with the SPD?

BAHRO: First and foremost, the SPD takes people in their capacity as industrial workers, engineers, wage-earners, and wants them to remain like that. With the SPD you can't get beyond the industrial system. According to them people have to keep on producing although they get less and less pleasure out of it – and even if the world is destroyed because of it. I on the contrary would like as many people as possible to have a real option of dropping out and switching over to a different context of life, beyond wage-labour and the market.

STERN: But there is a reformist trend among the Greens as well.

BAHRO: If you look at what is happening where the forces described as willing to compromise are active, as for example in Hamburg, you will realize that the differences within the Greens are in practice not so great. And ideologically there is the need to be fundamentally ecological if only because the left wing of the SPD has already occupied eco-reformist positions. Surely we don't need to find a stand-in for Erhard Eppler outside the SPD.

STERN: Are you not running into the danger of sectarianism with your rigorous opposition?

BAHRO: Can it be sectarian to insist on the interests of life and survival? There is now a deeper conflict than ever between the long- and short-term interests of one and the same human being. What people have to do today to pay off the mortgage on their house can cost the lives of their own children tomorrow.

STERN: On the theme of disarmament the orthodox Communists of the DKP have also tagged along with the Greens. How do you propose keeping them at a distance?

BAHRO: Even without me the Greens are distanced from the DKP by their decision in favour of non-alignment. In Hagen I had the approval of a very great majority for my declaration that I was unconditionally opposed to the deployment of the new missiles, and equally unconditionally opposed to the politics of the DKP in the peace movement. So my election to the national executive is a signal that the door is well and truly closed.

An unpublished interview for Stern *magazine shortly before the March 1983 election*

To What End Are We Consolidating Our Forces?

Propositions in Preparation for the Open National Delegate Conference (Hanover)

The national committee decided on 27 March [1983] to call an open national delegate conference at the earliest possible opportunity. It will take place on 4/5 June in Hanover. Its sole purpose is for us, together with as many interested individuals as possible from the social movements to whom we owe our entry into parliament, politically to digest the election result of 6 March.

We want to reach the greatest possible degree of understanding of what is in store for us over the next few years and how we wish to meet these challenges with regard to the foreseeable long-term trends. If we think of the global situation in 2000 as threatened on a world scale by the forces of the arms race, the destruction of nature, exploitation and poverty – to what end are we now consolidating our forces?

We want this conference to aim for as broad as possible a consensus, reaching out beyond the Green party, on the evaluation of the situation, its dangers and possibilities, but also on our own presence as an alternative force; and to focus more closely on the substance and actual extent of the differences of opinion which emerge in the process.

We must discuss the main lines and emphases of our social and political actions, primarily outside, but also inside or rather through parliament, and the best possible way for them to be linked.

With the presence of the Greens in parliament, organizational and constitutional questions and also the pressure in favour of paid political activity have naturally once more become relevant. Nevertheless the national committee proposes to deal with this theme at a later national delegate conference, in order to keep the political debate which is urgently needed in the new situation after the conservative election victory free from the political backbiting which would otherwise assert itself. We want first to fix criteria of aims, which will facilitate an objective decision on these problems which despite all their importance have been subordinated.

The following propositions on the election result and on the focal points of discussion for the national delegate conference are intended to make it easier for the district and state associations, and everyone in the social movements interested in the further development of Green politics, to form their opinions before the conference.

1.   We Greens are in parliament. But on 6 March a solid majority decided to ask only which of the two big parties would be better at preventing the disintegration of the "German model" founded under Adenauer and Erhard and renovated under the Socialist-Liberal coalition. It was not only the lie about economic upturn, but also the remembrance that the CDU stands traditionally closer to the economic power base and that it founded the model, which was the deciding factor in favour of the Union parties.

The SPD was not an alternative to the conservatives before this election and is not an alternative now. It stands on the same ground, defends the same system and wants to continue the same overall course. The 94 per cent or more concerned with preserving the system had to decide whose hand would tremble less. Logically the CDU now has the general task of defending the status quo, above all the ability of the West German economy to function, and of continuing as before.

The majority of voters were so keen on charity beginning at home that in voting they once more suppressed in their minds all the dangers which the system as such holds in readiness for them. In view of this general socio-psychological state the 5½ per cent for the Greens is an even more meaningful signal.

More than two million people have given their vote to a new party which promises nothing in the short term. They voted for the priority of their long-term and basic life interests. They no longer wanted as the lesser evil the "constructive opposition" that the SPD candidate promised in the very hour of defeat, in order that in industry and the bureaucracy as well as in Washington and the other NATO capitals there should be no doubt as to the loyalty of this state-supporting force.

2.   The negative meaning of the election result would be over-estimated if we were to evaluate it as a decision in favour of *everything* the CDU objectively stands for. The crisis of economy, society and above all of civilization can only grow more intense in the next few years. The "yes" in favour of defence and preservation of the status quo can and will be reversed in many people when it becomes clear that the task is insoluble, even for the CDU.

We now say above all to those voters for the old parties who are already well aware of the deadly consequences of a prolongation of the present policies but still shunned the risk of at least giving a warning to those responsible: You will not be innocent if the house of cards should collapse on us in a way which would make the outcome of the Hitler war look like an idyll.

This time we are less sure than ever of having four years to reflect on it, even if the Bomb isn't dropped – ruin moves on apace, at home and throughout the world. Therefore be active with us in the new social movements. Only outside, not inside the badly elected parliament, can we still put a stop to some things and take the first steps in the right direction.

3.   Together with those who voted for us so that the new social movements would also have a parliamentary arm, we want to be clear in our minds without any illusion how little we can achieve with the Green election result. We have only gained a symbolic position and, regardless of the intention of our parliamentary representatives, there is a great danger that the parliamentary group will be lost to the party and the Green party lost to the social movements.

If we become dependent on the constraints of the system which work through the machinery of parliament, and allow ourselves to be occupied there mainly with what is "feasible" within this framework, we will divert energy from the movement to the mills of state, and this energy will then be lost to the resistance and the forces of social renewal. Didn't the delay between the change of government in October and the election on 6 March have something to do with the existence of the Greens, with false expectations nurtured of their possible effectiveness as a power factor and of a parliament altered by their presence?

The present unfavourable constellation in parliament has at the same time the advantage of disillusionment. It leaves no scope for the assumption that we might be able to directly advance or even to push through any of our substantial concerns. We will be faced – regardless of whatever other guises the SPD might assume – with a Grand Coalition. They will all be united even against our demand just to raise uncompromisingly in every issue the interests of life and survival, and at best will dismiss us as utopians.

Our task in parliament is clearly defined: we have to make fundamental opposition politically workable. There is no need for the usual parliamentary realpolitik, for Green reformism and pragmatism. There is nothing to negotiate with the SPD, although of course from issue to issue, with due regard to its inadequacy in principle and the inconsistency of its solutions, we can vote with it as well as with the other parties if at least the direction is right.

The main function which has fallen to the Greens in parliament is to be multiplier and amplifier for the alternative consciousness outside, and to supply the public promptly with information about all attacks on the common good, all omissions in protection from danger, which they must resist.

4.   Like the Green party as a whole, its parliamentary group regards itself as an instrument of support to the movement. For us as for our members of parliament politics must never be primarily what takes place in Bonn. In this sense we say to all our friends in the country: Count upon our will and our readiness to use the platform we have won and the other opportunities in Bonn as well as possible for our common concern − but don't rely on us!

We are not thereby calling upon you to mistrust us; on the contrary, your active trust will lead us further than any system of control. It's rather a case of making it clear from the outset that while parliamentary politics may perhaps restrain the state machine a little here and there, it does not give us a position of power in favour of the change of course that is so imperative.

If on some points we can prevent the state from behaving in a wrong way, that will only be the expression of the courageous resistance which is arising in the country against the life-threatening policies of the government and the other parties.

5.   The hopes entertained as to the possibility of a "red"-green coalition have for the time being been dispelled by the election outcome, insofar as there emerged an absolute majority for a CDU/CSU government (if you include the second votes of FDP supporters). But the essential lesson should be that there was not yesterday, is not today, and will not be even tomorrow either, any such thing as a "red"-green bloc of reform.

A concept of reform which lumps Social-Democratic and Green politics together under the same roof is deceptive. It's not like counting apples and pears together, but rather concrete and vegetables. Those parts of the SPD which now stand with Richard Löwenthal firmly in the industrial bloc were indeed once in favour of certain reforms. But they have proved to be technocratic and centrist in their orientation, and the new social movements, including the Greens, have grown up precisely in opposition to their conclusions.

It is simply not true that the barely 44 per cent "red" and green vote could be counted together and then with some political skill be led in 1987 to a workable left majority under an ecological and pacifist banner. The SPD can only strive for reforms that stabilize the system and therefore definitely does not belong to the forces of reform which we are talking about. Its left/green wing may subjectively sympathize with us, but since they never manage to determine party policy, they will only ever play the role of deceptive fig-leaf. Anyone in this camp who is serious about peace politics and ecology must leave their old home.

The remainder of the SPD, together with the voters who support it, belong at present to the conservative centre of society and in a historic sense to the same party as the Christian-Democrats (excluding the followers of Strauss). Whether or not we like that and whether or not we are afraid of losing the cover provided by the SPD, the 100-year-old "tanker", which has been on the road through both prosperity and ruin for the capitalist industrial system, is bound for the breaker's yard.

The immediate political reality we must gear ourselves to cope with is a three-quarters majority for the conservatives in the country, with half the voters being relatively indifferent between Schmidt and Kohl, while a quarter would like to let Strauss and Lamsdorff[1] sort things out. The other quarter of the voters are reformist in the broadest sense, the majority of them temporarily eco-reformist minded in the style of Erhard Eppler, and for the most part still prefer the SPD as being concerned with conservation of the system, rather than the adventure with the Greens.

There may be a radical ecological force of barely 5 per cent, if you include an appropriate share of non-voters. But this force, which is in favour of a total alternative to the capitalist as well as the (pseudo-) communist industrial system, will grow in the next few years. For the integrative power of the industrial-bureaucratic core is in decline.

More and more individuals are disappointed and directly or indirectly marginalized. In particular large parts of the younger generation can no longer be held to the old values.

6. In the debate for hearts and minds, the SPD is no less our opponent than the CDU. On the contrary, it occupies the front line from which the system defends itself against us. In comparison with this, the fact that we are together in opposition in Bonn is secondary. On the opposition benches they will do everything to keep themselves fresh as a reserve for the system.

In the meantime the disintegration of their positions will continue. The polarization of their forces between priority for the "materialist" security line on the one hand and the "post-materialist" self-realization line on the other will progress and so their supporters will also in the next few years provide the main reservoir for us Greens.

And yet Social-Democracy is only the first major political formation of the industrial bloc which is sinking into crisis. With the development of a Christian fundamentalism which is spreading now throughout the youth, through sections of the clergy and the intellectuals, even in German Catholicism, expressing itself particularly through the peace movement but also through themes of solidarity and ecology, there is something in the air which will not leave even the CDU/CSU forces untouched.

7.   The question for us is: do we want to advance or obstruct the new grouping of forces beyond the present right/left set-up which is running itself into the ground and offers us no real chance? We will obstruct it if we continue to orient ourselves towards a "majority against the right", in the same boat as the SPD, even if this is under the formula of a "bloc of reform". To remain "left of the SPD" and at a distance from the rest of society would mean on our part simply continuing to argue over the division within one and the same 45 per cent of the population. And we would have to leave it to the SPD to bring people back from the CDU.

Instead, the strategic question after this election is how to achieve a direct transition from black [Christian-Democrat] to green. We shall not succeed in this if, out of disappointment with the results of the old and new radicalism which have failed to materialize, we retreat into a cautious reformism which strives after a minimum green consensus. What is needed is a new radicalism which openly goes to the roots of the ecological crisis and the crisis of civilization.

Instead of mocking at Helmut Kohl, we should take up the debate on what he stands for right at the grassroots, among those concerned with the conservation of values. By so doing, we shall find the language which will also touch the hearts of the conservative majority of the population.

We Germans have only ever had half-revolutions, but we were once a people of reformation. As at the time of Luther and Münzer, so today personal suffering over the lack of meaning in everyday life and disappointment with the old institutions are again entwined with the experiences of economic crisis and existential danger into a knot which can only be untied by a far-reaching radical change.

The new social movements which the Greens have now advanced into parliament are the harbingers of this reformation. And everywhere in the country the alternative forces are this time trying from the outset – as the Anabaptists in Münster once did – to remake everyday life so that (unlike in those days) a real reorganization of the political structures can come about. Both the prerequisite for this and the path towards it is for us to succeed in establishing the sovereignty of the people both internally and externally.

8.   For this some initiatives are now necessary to define our orientation as decided in Hagen and Sindelfingen, which still remains valid. We propose the following main lines:

8.1.   On the home policy front, our most important interest in the long term is not to attract a regular vote but to build up as autonomous as possible a network of alternative contexts of work and life which covers the whole country and offers support and perspective to all those who want to effect an exit from the formal economy or can no longer find a place in it. In parliament we can make some contribution towards maintaining the political and social scope for this.

Young people in particular, confronted with unemployment and most prepared for an experimental departure, need an answer which leads not only to transitional solutions but to a perspective for life. This can only exist in the development of a *broad commune movement* which also opens up more radical possibilities for the women's movement and provides hope for the reintegration of old people. We shall be failing in our task if we do not use the phase in which the capitalist industrial system is in long-term decline to create exemplary social facts. The commune is the germ cell of the social formation which will replace the existing one, the basic unit of the new social network.

Our Sindelfingen programme calls for the building of integral community projects in which all elements of the alternative way of life and production are brought together and integrated on the basis of an ecological cyclical economy, self-determination and decentralized organization. We call upon our friends to take the initiative in this without hesitation, and promise to assert our influence in as many ways as possible in order to secure suitable resources for making a start.

Our children's and youth congress planned for the autumn is being organized towards this perspective, since all alternative ventures, not least in the field of education, only have a real chance on the basis of an autonomous life which is no longer controlled by the state's social workers.

8.2   As the particular degree of military threat we confront is connected with the fact that Europe is divided here in our country and still partitioned between the victorious powers of the Second World War, we must summarize and accentuate our concept of nuclear and conventional disarmament, of withdrawal from the military blocs and of neutralization of the two German states into a Green Plan For Germany. Independence from the ambitions of other powers is the precondition for our really being able to start out along the path which we indicated before 6 March in the Sindelfingen programme: "Work meaningfully, live in solidarity".

8.3.   We had decided in 1983 to tackle thoroughly the status of the Third World, or rather the relationship between exploitative metropolises and dependent peripheries of the capitalist world system (this includes also the question of immigrants). Clarity on this question would contribute significantly towards a more precise statement of the starting points for our overall policy. In particular it would be clearer what international consequences flow from a direct orientation toward the existing social interests, expectations and values of the metropolitan sub-classes (right through to the middle income group) and a refusal to set the beginnings for a different society here and now.

In our Sindelfingen document there is a prelude to this debate but the discussion has not yet reached the grassroots. The relevant working party, supported by the national executive, was to organize a consultation session at which we would bring together as many people as possible who are active and interested both in theory and practice – not least immigrants themselves – in order to work out the practical consequences for which discussion should be carried out at the grassroots, and to create an overall view as to who from the district associations can be invited as a speaker.

8.4.   In order to raise to a new level the process of formation of political will from the bottom up, we must above all ensure that the grassroots receive information which is complete yet concise and clear, in other words impartially prepared, which can then be taken up by their decision-making mechanism. Within a Green media system which pays attention to the complexity of the issues, of the political levels (districts, states, national) and aspects (day to day policy, fields of work, theory or strategy) there must be an organ (for example a suitably improved *Grüner Basisdienst*) whose functions expressly include organizing the formation of opinion on current controversies and if necessary arranging ballots.

8.5. In connection with the open national delegate conference, the political image of the Greens is being discussed anew in the district and state associations. That is, in view of the situation after 6 March and in consideration of our responsibility to society as a whole, we are discussing once more our – sometimes unexpressed – assumptions and points of departure, the basic line of the programme statements and the ways of dealing with the public, the opposing parties, and the institutions.

The national executive and the national committee should form a group to bring together the concurrent results and set out the differences of opinion. On the basis of this the Saarbrücken Programme can be revised.[2]

If Only The Thing Was More Stable!

KOMMUNE: Sometimes one has the impression that the Greens are getting themselves into factions which thrive on fierce struggles and hold extreme positions on the solution of particular questions, while more or less failing to tackle the problem as a whole.

It might seem that two extreme positions have been adopted without there ever having been a genuine debate on the various aspects of the problem, even at the national conference. Perhaps what was at issue there was the strategic question of how – to stick to your terminology – one can effect a direct transition from black [Christian-Democrat] to green; but that doesn't solve the tactical question of how in the immediate future to seek a majority situation at the parliamentary level in order to win scope for the movement. I have no problems with the strategic concept that one must pay attention to developing a direct understanding with a considerable proportion of the CDU voters and that indeed this is the precondition for gaining a majority in favour of basic change in West Germany. But I have considerable reservations if you think that would solve the question of a tactical alliance at the parliamentary level.

BAHRO: You mean because I said in my propositions that there is no need for realpolitik or green reformism and so on, because in any case there is no possibility of exercizing genuine leverage in the Federal parliament?

KOMMUNE: Yes, among other things. I believe that the Greens, or the policies that are now described as green, must be in a position to argue with the conservatives, to weaken their base and to win people over from them, but I consider it vital that in order to gain scope for the movement one also attempts to solve the question of an alliance at the parliamentary level. And there I see no other possibility but to try to do it with the SPD. Now I got the impression that the people round Thomas Ebermann[1] simply stuck to this tactical position while rejecting, in fact not even seeing, the strategic question which you had raised, but that you on the other hand have totally neglected this tactical question.

BAHRO: Insofar as that was the case, it was deliberately left out of consideration.

KOMMUNE: Why?

BAHRO: Because I don't find it interesting. To talk about the tactical perspectives I expressed there, what I did was – how shall I describe it? – in view of the miserable wrangling that occupied the foreground, about setting up the parliamentary group and the relationship between national committee and party, I said: First of all in this situation the priority must be to establish a counterbalance to the parliamentary group in accordance with the demands of the grassroots. I said that it should not be controlled bureaucratically – in any case that wouldn't work – but that through the ideological case we put together we must exert an influence on the conduct and questions that come to the fore in the parliamentary party. I assumed the possibility that we might lose the parliamentary party, though not because all the people in it are bad. (There are of course some people in the parliamentary party with positions closer to mine and others with positions less close.) The danger lies simply in the structure. You have a machine with several cogs: first the whole society, this bureaucratic-industrial-corporatist bloc; then parliament which reflects the party structure and is in reality moulded by the government machinery; and then you have this little Green parliamentary cog, and those in it are so inundated with piles of paper that if they take the trouble to read it all they will in fact already be lost to us, even if they only deal so to speak with the modulations of the process. So I simply saw the situation in this way: what becomes of the Greens depends on what we make of the party. We didn't assess or evaluate the election result at all, and at first I was in favour of evaluating it, and then wrote my own evaluation into these propositions. But they were not accepted by the national executive. That didn't surprise me because nobody there wants to commit themselves to definite propositions. But the propositions did in fact have some influence on the preparatory discussions. That was the first tactical consideration. The second and more significant tactical consideration, which admittedly is connected with strategic matters, was that I wanted us to focus on a long-term perspective at the earliest possible opportunity after the election result, and I see 1987 as the long-term horizon.

I wanted us to regard the ecology and peace movement (and as far as the ecological side is concerned, I see something more fundamental at the feminist level) as a force with a hegemonic aspiration, though not in the sense of euphoric calculations as to how our percentage share will rise and we can hope sometime, somehow, for 51 per cent; even with this kind of majority you still can't govern, as Berlinguer correctly realized, but only produce a dead heat. I mean hegemony in the widest sense, as used by Gramsci, the predominance of a political concept, first of asking the right questions, but then of giving the best answers, answers which the majority of society can't just ignore, the active forces least of all, and with which the passive forces at least feel a friendly sympathy, in the same way as at present there are far-reaching passive sympathies with the peace movement. We must raise these questions as early as possible, and this means that we have to begin the unavoidable debate about them right away.

If only the thing was more stable! It must be said that the Hagen congress was not favourable. It was not good to have such a fundamental struggle so shortly before the election, and not to have any mediatory formulations. If we can steer a clear course next time, that can only be to the good. My basic position was that having entered parliament as a party of the left, we must introduce a rethinking process early on. We are reproducing the very pattern in which we cannot win. Thus at this level we remain a force which has no choice but to enhance another political force. So in short I wanted to eradicate any question of an alliance in the strategic sense – in the strategic sense, mark you.

There I actually prefer Johannes Rau[2] for raising the question of an alliance for professional groups, etc. instead of at party level. I no longer recognize the SPD as a subject which could be approached to join a bloc of reform, because half of the forces behind it did once want to reform things, but no longer want to do so. Just like the CDU, they want to maintain things as they are, the only difference being that they want to maintain the "German model" in the Schmidt variant and the others want to maintain it in the Adenauer/Erhard variant; the second of these is the more fundamental level, which is why they have been given the job. This is why I didn't want to pose these tactical questions, which doesn't mean that I want to negate them; I just see no problems there, even at the national level. We need to vote with the SPD on particular issues where we happen to agree, but not to negotiate with them. If necessary we can also vote with Ignaz Kiehle[3] if he puts forward anything sensible concerning the EEC agricultural policy. The point is that we haven't yet sufficiently clarified our image for the majority of the population to be clear as to what we are, whether or not we vote in a particular case with the SPD and in another with the CDU. We must make clear that this does not affect the fundamental things we stand for, but rather that what we are doing is realistically, pragmatically and reasonably to give preference to the lesser evil at any given time on a specific concrete issue. To put it differently: if you pose the question in a tactical way it obscures the fact that the basic packages and containers which the parties offer for election cannot be amalgamated. The SPD package and the package that we have – above all, what we should have, I must add – cannot be combined. In a certain sense it is grotesque. It was the Greens, not the SPD, who had in their programme a 35-hour week with no loss of earnings for lower and middle income groups, the line which has now been taken up by the trade-union federation. That's really a joke. Looking at things overall we must get to the point where it is clear to the whole society what the Greens stand for, and that this is not affected by temporary association with this or that individual development in environmental politics or any other realm. And, to take an extreme example, this is totally lost in the way that Joschka Fischer[4] understands politics.

KOMMUNE: But was it not a problem that both at the national conference and in the whole discussion so far you have directly linked the question of establishing the Greens' own image and developing such a power of attraction among the whole population that you even succeed in breaking up the conservative basis of the CDU, with the assertion that the question of a "green/red reform bloc" has been settled by the election of 6 March? Certainly if one conceives of a possible parliamentary alliance of Greens and Social-Democrats as a red/green reform bloc, it looks as if this would be a *strategic* alliance through which the necessary social changes could be implemented. I agree that it is settled in the sense that this reform bloc as an alliance with the SPD cannot exist in the strategic sense and because the question of parliamentary majorities is not decisive. But at the national conference – and you must have noticed it too by people's reactions – the question of how to develop a perspective which really does include large sections of the population, including the conservatives, was lumped together with the statement that the question of parliamentary unity with the SPD is settled. This can also be seen by the fact that many could not conceive of it in any other way than that instead of a tactical alliance with the Social-Democrats you would establish an alliance with the CDU.

BAHRO: But that is the bourgeois media's pattern of perception which many of the Greens have adopted. Anyone who only thinks from one election to the next can only think tactically. Any sense of the underlying social dynamic at work is totally absent from these considerations. As I see it, everyone in the party who has gone through the past few years with us, who remembers that before the election there was this confrontation between what one might call fundamental opposition and social reformism, and yet now interprets the issue as if I want to make some tactical combination with the CDU instead of with the SPD (which I was always opposed to in any case), must think that I have forgotten what I said three months ago.

KOMMUNE: But one has to consider the reason for this. I don't think it's simply because people accept the patterns of perception of the bourgeois press, but more because during the last parliamentary election one important tactical question was real for a considerable part of the population, namely: how to prevent a reactionary government? And not only that but also: how to achieve a constellation of forces which might under given circumstances make it possible to put forward solutions to problems along the right lines, for example on the question of the arms build-up?

BAHRO: I have never considered such a majority to be possible.

KOMMUNE: Why?

BAHRO: Right on the eve of the election I published an article in the *Tageszeitung* in which I showed that the most we can expect from the SPD, if anything at all – i.e. a half passable attitude on the question of the arms build-up – will be if it is with us in opposition to a minority CDU government. My judgement of the SPD has always been as I just said in Hanover: Vogel would also have signed at Williamsburg.[5] I don't think that any of the things which are important for us can be done with the SPD. As for fitting filters into factory chimneys, we can do that just as well with Zimmermann as with any other candidate of the ruling bloc, perhaps better. By that I don't mean that the CDU is better, but that the conservative party – organized, political conservatism, the people who are steadfast in NATO and bound fast to capital – can carry out measures which after all are in the interests of the capitalists as a whole – to put it in conventional terms – more easily than the SPD. At this level of our ecological issues I see no need at all to cooperate with the SPD. In reality I see only one single area where this differentiation is of interest to us, and that is in home affairs, I mean on the question of civil rights. The SPD has never been a socialist party, but despite all the limitations imposed by its étatist and autocratic manner (even without an autocrat) it has traditionally been the democratic party, at least comparatively speaking. More precisely, it was not so much based on the authoritarian character structure. That is the only difference and the only place where one might speak of alliances in this tactical sense, or of an area where there is a sort of connection which is important also in our strategic considerations. But otherwise, as far as the policy of repairs to the eco-system is concerned, this is imposing itself on all political forces. Anyone in government here must as it were take into account the interests of society as a whole and see how the interests of society as a whole can be smuggled through the power complex. Ministries are ministries, no matter which minister is in charge of them. As for the question that you raised at the beginning, i.e. that I put this at the strategic level while others only want to deal with it at the tactical level, my impression is that this appearance of a tactically different treatment is in reality connected with a far-reaching divergence on the strategic perspective. That is only covered over by the impression you have picked up.

KOMMUNE: But then these strategic differences, which we ought perhaps to discuss now, don't come out at all, because one can't simply leave the field of tactics to the so-called practitioners of realpolitik. You yourself said in your paper that the question of an alliance with the SPD at parliamentary level might perhaps arise in 1987, but no longer with the Greens as junior partner and dependent variable. The problem seems to me to be that one can't get round this parliamentary level, but there again the question arises as to with which forces – and they are after all organized as a party – you can clear the way a little for radical change in society.

BAHRO: While there's life there's hope! But in fact we are faced at present with a Grand Coalition, it doesn't matter whether *de jure* or *de facto*. Until the political-psychological relationship of forces is fundamentally transformed, with this parliament you can only pursue a policy of ecological repair to the "German model". In that case it doesn't matter whether we are in an alliance or not. Our very presence exercizes pressure either on the CDU/CSU or on the SPD to steal particular points from us – which is to be welcomed. I can't see that there is a question of a coalition as such. Whatever the outcome of the 1987 election I still wouldn't harness us together with the SPD. Why should I? If I have won over a CDU voter, why should I want him to vote for the SPD? So that he wobbles to and fro?

KOMMUNE: Not at all. Let's take a look at the opposite position. This is basically a parliamentary one, and openly represents the view that the Greens – put quite simply – will take a bit away from the SPD and the SPD a bit from the CDU and in this way 51 per cent will be reached. This is in several ways both strange and erroneous. First, the Greens cannot be an independent force vis-à-vis the SPD if they only concentrate on reaching their full electoral potential and don't try to develop a perspective relating to society as a whole which reassembles the forces involved in the two big parties. Second, a majority can never come about in that way because in fact the SPD will not be in a position to draw away any significant forces from the CDU. On the key questions the difference is not so frightfully big, but most people don't believe that the SPD has any plan for getting out of the crisis. To that extent I consider it to be completely erroneous. But on the other hand this doesn't settle the question of how the Greens, if they become a party that can show a perspective to the whole of society and bring together the forces for this perspective, including forces that were previously tied to the CDU as well as to the SPD – if they become this kind of independent factor, there is still the question as to how to create at least a little space for the social movements at parliamentary level before the year 2000; and also how to achieve some legislation on certain points, whether in the field of civil rights or on such questions as energy policy, closure of nuclear power stations, etc.

BAHRO: The point is, where in all that is there the need for an alliance? I don't see it. The concept of an alliance is related to containers – it means taking either one or the other container and combining with it ourselves. We needn't turn down any legislative initiatives, on the contrary, we can hurry them along. If Späth[6] proposes the correct thing, or at least the relatively more correct, because he happens to be in power, or any other politician, what is to prevent us from throwing our weight onto the scales? I think we will be much more effective if we don't make ourselves dependent on the question of whether the SPD or the CDU or anyone else will be put out of government because of our vote.

KOMMUNE: I thought that the Greens' position before the Federal elections was a half-hearted, lazy compromise – that is, this line of toleration towards the SPD. That wasn't at issue in this election. What was at issue was the government, from the electorate's point of view. That could be seen from the opinion polls, too.

BAHRO: The voters weren't at all stupid in realizing that this red/green combination wouldn't work.

KOMMUNE: One of the reasons why it wouldn't work was because the Greens for their part raised it in an extremely stupid way. They didn't ask: What do we want to achieve in the long term, and how can we set the course now in the short term? If only they had said: Such and such are the decisive points and we will struggle for an appropriate government along these lines. The situation in Hamburg or Hesse can't keep on going with these toleration tactics, it'll fall to pieces. These tactics leave the initiative to the others. By keeping within this perspective of toleration and just saying that we will tolerate what is most correct in any given situation, whoever happens to be behind it, you are completely ignoring the question of a majority at parliamentary level and therefore also the question of forming a government.

BAHRO: It is not the same thing at all. It has nothing to do with toleration. The discussion about toleration referred to a particular government, and what I am saying is that on any particular issues we can support the option that seems most sensible to us and that by doing that we can lend impetus to the whole thing.

KOMMUNE: So you are completely distancing yourself from the question of parliament.

BAHRO: I am basing myself on the standpoint that it is not something on the agenda for us; that we are not candidates for office with the authority to lay down guidelines and that the difference between Schmidt and Kohl is not considerable. From the perspective of our present programme that is a difficult thing to say. What I mean is – I did say this once somewhere and was generally misunderstood – supposing the SPD really wanted to get out of the missiles decision and the CDU also wanted out – just supposing – then it would be easier for the CDU than for the SPD to withdraw, just because it does have a firmer anchorage in the whole power system. Nixon was able to recognize China and in France Mitterrand expects sacrifices from the working class that they'd have sent Giscard packing for. That's how it seems to be there.

KOMMUNE: Let's leave it there for the moment. You say that we must now achieve something positive. That refers to the movement. The movement must now develop certain practical forms of production and life, not merely describe them in words, but practically test cooperative/communal types of production and life. That is the decisive question for the immediate future. I agree. But the Greens as a party have another function. As opposed to the movement, the Greens are also in my view a parliamentary party and in any case it's only through parliament that they can keep certain paths open and – as you say – build in certain constraints. But they must therefore also behave differently at this parliamentary level from the movement, and they can also get involved in certain issues that the movement doesn't need to, indeed must not, get involved in. If the Greens are a parliamentary party and if their particular function for the movement lies in this role for the time being, I don't believe that the Greens can avoid the question of government, which is what always matters to people in parliamentary elections. The voters are not bothered about parliamentary configurations as such but rather about the question of government: who is going to *do* this or that in the next four years in government?

BAHRO: And should we then teach them this question is

important by playing along with it? Are we to teach them that it's important whether the SPD or the CDU is in power? That's what it would mean.

KOMMUNE: Otherwise why do you stand for parliamentary elections at all if it doesn't matter what is done there?

BAHRO: You are saying that orientation towards parliament means that we are interested in participating in government, and in the question of government.

KOMMUNE: Yes, that's what parliament's about. What else is it about?

BAHRO: When did the SPD start to govern? When things were at their worst, with Friedrich Ebert.[7] And why was it in parliament before that? In all the years of the rise of Social-Democracy was it geared towards participating in the German imperial government under Wilhelm? Was that why it was in parliament?

KOMMUNE: Of course not, but if you draw that parallel, the first difference is that at that time the movement developed much more within the SPD than is the case today in the relationship between the movement and the Green party. The second difference is that the pre-1918 regime was not a parliamentary one and that the question therefore presented itself in a different way. I don't think you can so simply transfer labels like "talking shop" or "just a platform for the class struggle" to the present-day parliament.

BAHRO: Yes, "platform for the class struggle" is an outmoded concept. But I still think it's right to call it a platform. Perhaps I can say how I see the problem.

First, I wouldn't formulate the issue very differently from you. But it's a question of how the thing is evaluated. Yes, I would say the Green party is definitely the most conventional branch, as I always say, of all these movements, partly because only certain people from the whole field of the movement get mixed up in this particular process and shut themselves up for four years in those concrete silos where those who enter cease to live. In this respect it is specialized.

And then there is the question of what we do there. Look, insofar as we abide by the rules there, in however "alternative" a way, we are participating in nothing more than a pseudo-ecological general overhaul of the "German model". Maybe we'll still manage to save part of the German forests and so on, that is, things which reassure the population, so that in principle we can still preserve here a model which is in fact insupportable for humanity as a whole. As long as we are zealously participating in various legislative initiatives, nothing more can happen. That is, we become an instrument of relief and even in some respects a final injection for the sick patient. And I am saying this only because it is necessary to be realistically clear about this matter, not because I believe we should be purists and not get involved.

And I see this first of all at the level of legislative initiatives on ecology and tax policies and all those things; there I see us as completely functional, just as the workers' movement – they have since succeeded in subordinating it – was functional. At the parliamentary level we should concern ourselves with warding off danger, as I see it, with the question of gaining space and time, with defending our room to manoeuvre, for instance opposing efforts to dismantle the welfare state and the rule of law. We will defend that – by the way it seems to me to be important for us to learn to distinguish between state and law in a certain respect. For example, I think that the West German constitution is not the worst one. Particular things that we got from the Anglo-Saxons after 1945 certainly belong to the best elements of political culture, things worth defending and things which we need much more than any other forces do. In that we are simply engaging in politics which can still be interpreted as protest and resistance – but at the same time I can say that none of this political level will remain for the total process. The fact that we have prevented some things, protested, resisted, is not going to bring about any new society, but what is then in practice decisive is whether this together with our role in parliament really makes us the organ for building what I would call the *ordine nuovo* – I prefer the Italian expression because it already has a good connotation. And the problem is that we can only remain the organ for something like this if – and this was actually the point – we do not accept this specialization suggestion that Dany Cohn-Bendit[8] is making, by saying if you are a parliamentary party then please don't be anything else. I find that totally wrong.

Then there is the danger that we will reduce ourselves to a role of emergency brake for the system and so to speak of merely reproducing the room for resistance; coming out of our homes every two years to demonstrate against this and that industrial and military madness and show that they haven't been able to make things completely watertight. That is too little. The point is whether we consciously see ourselves as an organ for ensuring that in this field something positive happens, and if that is the case, then our main function – it can be seen most clearly in the economic sphere but it is also valid for social and legal policies – is to make sure that we no longer concern ourselves with redistribution at all these levels inside the system, but rather redistribute out of the system. That means that we get hold of and release economic, legal, political and social support for this new beginning, and that instead of dedicating ourselves submissively to the approaching fifth Kondratieff wave of industrialization we make use of the present trough to found the beginning of the new civilization, a change so deep that one must speak of a break with basic European patterns of behaviour. That is more than the final and most definitive fulfilment of the principles of the French revolution. It goes beyond everything that we have discussed in our various basic values commissions. For liberty, equality and fraternity are all defined on the basis of this structure of individualistic competition. Formerly I myself very much internalized the way that the impetus for emancipation in Beethoven's symphonies is power-determined, the assertion of individuality in competition with others.

That is the point as I see it, that in practice we carry out this redistribution. And the main level of redistribution – which is where the function of a platform is particularly useful, more important than all economics, politics, social matters and so on – is psychological redistribution, or in practical terms that by the input that we make into public opinion we create an output of energies, of psychic energies, from all the old structures. In the latest issue of *Der Spiegel* they mention how workers' morale has deteriorated, not only because of the famous spongers on the conveyor belts – but (how can anyone enjoy it when here too, not only in the GDR, investments last ten years and then are no longer up to date because, thank God, there are so many restrictions) who can still find satisfaction in some kind of construction? Let us help to dissolve the system of values – by the way, I consider it important that we no longer talk so much about smashing it to pieces.

On the rational level – this seems to me to be the strategic difference from the others, there being psychological things behind it which have to do with the whole problem of being a minority and the fact that the left has always been defeated – at the rational level what it is about is: should we actually welcome the disintegration or should we rather lament the split in society?

Doesn't the Socialist Bureau[9] – and in this the whole of the left is virtually united – tend at present to complain about the split in society which is allegedly being pursued by big capital according to some sinister plan that doesn't really exist? For it is happening fairly spontaneously, of course with a bit of help. It is not Kohl's strategy to split society and thus build up as many marginalized counter-forces as possible, which then become dangerous. True, there is much to be gained from it, simply because the priority is to accumulate capital for investments, and it has consequences. Blüm[10] is not there simply to deceive people, in other words when they say they are a government of the centre they are expressing a strategic interest. They don't want street battles here. They can't afford such things in the metropolis.

In my view it is a completely wrong decision for us to resist this disintegration. They want us to help with repairs. As a whole, our immediate programme – I'm not criticizing individual measures: the individual measures in the Sindelfingen programme will in most cases probably be correct, but the context it is fitted into is precisely along the lines of an overhaul of the "German model" – will function as a restabilizing force. The only place where we will hurt them a bit – and I'm not at all sure whom this will benefit in the end, because the investment strategies will in any case not come off – is by preventing them a little from accumulating capital, by fighting the dismantling of the welfare state.

That is of course good, every mark that one can deprive them of is better invested anywhere else than with those who will make concrete out of it. But this basic orientation of ours, which inclines towards reformism and gradualism and to these repair strategies, is in the most general, world-historic sense actually social-democratic. And so I would be in favour of our entrusting ourselves to disintegration, not asking how we can restore those who drop out back to their old status – a slightly worse one because there's nothing else for it – but rather how we can create for them the status of a new, different society? And I admit that this doesn't provide the answer for every individual who gets into a personal crisis. But what we do is important. Let's take for example the woman bank clerk who, as I heard recently, has at the age of forty no longer any prospect of getting back into a job. During the first few months that she's dealing with the problem of no longer being a proper person because she hasn't got a proper job, we might try to convince her that if she makes a great effort and if we struggle hard she can get back behind her counter again; but we could also try to handle this psychological crisis in such a way as to make her think "To hell with it, what would the next thirty years of my life have been like, what would have been the point of everything continuing in the same old way, at work and at home, and our marriage is really boring too. Isn't there a chance of building another way of life?" And at this point we begin to face the question of power; are we in a position to divert resources in the broadest sense? That affects everything, it goes from economics to therapy and more than – better than – therapy. And the legal circumstances are the middle of it.

KOMMUNE: The problem remains of course that even the question of diverting resources presupposes parliamentary majorities.

BAHRO: Yes, but parliamentary majorities in what sense? After the CDU won in Berlin it wasn't accidental that there was this discussion about public money. And why? I remember the election posters in Berlin. I can't remember exactly what was on Weizsäcker's,[11] but in any case what was clear was that he was promising the citizens law and order in Berlin. And Vogel's posters had the slogan: A Strong Hand For Berlin. That's what he wanted to be, then. So they were basically both talking about the need for order felt by the average Prussian Berlin population. I don't believe that street politics are what the majority of the Berlin population wants – at worst it would be, I don't know, 13, 15 or 20 per cent who want a violent solution and just like our stone-throwers at the other extreme enjoy riots because they satisfy their aggressive potential, as a substitute at least. Then the police have to take up truncheons. But the majority of the population want order in the city in the normal sense and don't want to break each other's late-Roman heads over the latest grain that Augustus or whoever else it happens to be has got hold of from Africa or wherever. In that case our real dispute could be whether it is really better to try and succeed through street battles and whether those people are right who argue that we are actually relieving the burden on the system by guiding people in the extreme case into rural communes. In my contributions to the discussions in Hagen and Sindelfingen I perhaps brought the subject round to rural communes rather too simply; we can also conquer parts of cities, or rather not conquer but appropriate and cooperate with sources of supply outside. You know, if they decide on middle-class programmes, it is because there is a certain lobby for them. We are also a lobby. Let us exercize pressure. Let us play the same game. When they see how it was in Krefeld, how it was with the Frankfurt runway,[12] how things are going everywhere, if you don't want that to escalate – we have here, in the form of the *ordine nuovo*, a constructive offer, if you like you can even call it jobs. We don't recognize it as such. But you can call what we are doing that if you like. In Berlin in any case there are already eight thousand for whom the job centre is not responsible. I can't see any reason why that should work better with the SPD than with the CDU. I don't see that at all. It is just a simplification to see the CDU only as the party of big capital. There are psychological and ideological structures in it which would actually permit us in a certain respect to shift the confrontation from one between minority versus police, where we have to deal physically with fibreglass tanks and steel water-cannon and whatever, into a confrontation which is so to speak much more on the really cultural plane; whereby we introduce our lifestyles into society and then have to deal with people instead of police. People will certainly react at first with outrage and close up their character armour. But things keep working on inside them; this strategy is much more productive than battles with the police. At Hanover, in the commune discussion, a woman related how in the country too they are taking a long-term view and how peaceful relations prevail with the village population there. Of course I don't know how radical they are in their lifestyle. Let us get close enough to the people and achieve an anchorage there so that the police can't come between us again.

KOMMUNE: Or at least only with difficulty . . .

BAHRO: Now on the level of social forces: at the beginning of the squatters' movement in Berlin there was some sympathy amongst the general population. At the moment the aggression of our own forces stands in the way of our making the best use of that. I am arguing that we should reconstruct ourselves in the broadest sense. The Hanover conference received this idea more sympathetically than the Greens at large, because it was presented to them more in context. But what the Bavarians then said, one after another, starting with August Haussleiter,[13] was: Don't deprive us of the concept of an enemy. Zimmermann's perjury has been upheld by the court, and I still want to be allowed to call him a traitor. My God, what kind of perspective is that! Looking at the basic problems around which the Green programme is being organized – by which I mean what is being organized around the base of the ecology and peace movement – I have the feeling that the interests involved are so fundamental that they make us into an organ of society as a whole.

KOMMUNE: Let's just go back. It is certainly true that a large part of the left would not be able to go along with Marx in saying: "The crisis is developing splendidly"; and that your way of seeing things, if you like, is more Marxist.

BAHRO: Seriously, I do consider my mentality to be more Marxist than that of a lot of other people here, even if my theory is perhaps no longer Marxist.

KOMMUNE: There is certainly a lot of moaning and groaning on the left about crises and splits, which only shows that what exists as "the left" is in many ways closely attached to the status quo. Otherwise one could say: "The crisis is developing splendidly: problems are manifesting themselves in a new way, people are beginning to think differently about themselves". Instead, for the most part fear predominates, and this whole business of a struggle against the right is in two respects fairly unproductive: first, it isn't true that the development could be correctly described as "fascisization"; and yet if the crisis is as deep as it seems to be one can't get by merely with the idea of prevention. But what I would be interested to know is what is the relationship between this building of the beginnings of a new society, that is the *ordine nuovo*, and parliamentary tactics? What is the relationship in general between building the beginnings of a new society and the state? What will the transition be like?

BAHRO: To put it in conventional terms so as to make it comprehensible, I would see it almost on a par with the way the socialist countries (when it still seemed that's what they would be) formulated their concept of foreign policy: namely to secure peaceful conditions, favourable conditions in which to build themselves up. We have the problem of creating zones liberated from the industrial system, whose consequences are all understood to be exterminist. This is a twofold problem. There is a security problem, which is why we are joining the political merry-go-round – i.e. how do we safeguard space for ourselves? But the main question is, of course, what are we going to build there? With the main emphasis on the building of a new psychology.

KOMMUNE: But that only relates to the first phase. Obviously, in the first phase it is a case of trying to build the beginnings of a new society and to safeguard these beginnings; while also developing relations of peaceful coexistence which would be favourable for the new society because it has a greater power of attraction. But as soon as the new becomes a threat, the question starts to pose itself differently. You're not always able to control how the old society or the ruling class will react. To keep to the same example: the Soviet Union was still armed.

BAHRO: This is where the analogy with the Soviet Union really ceases. In the metropolises the only thing possible is a non-violent strategy. That is explained in the political formulations of Gramsci. Perhaps we must as a precautionary measure imagine the conditions under which we are open to attack and avoid precisely those. A commune-type model would not function either economically or politically in a mainly aggressive way. It must attract people essentially because the people who work in the new context of life are more attractive than those who still have to commute on the underground. I believe that the question of power in the violent sense does not arise in cultural transitions of this nature. Even in ancient Rome, though the question of power was first raised by the Spartacus rebellion, later on it was no longer a matter of power in the sense of who will overthrow the emperor? He was only followed by the next emperor. Nothing came of it. But finally the whole thing crumbled away and a new system came into being. The way I see it is for us to create from below in a particular way an alternative institutional structure, via a non-antagonistic path; and to bring about a new institutionalization, for which we also obtain consent, indeed for which consent is obtained for us because of the inability of the existing system to pursue policies of salvation; in other words they can't save the forests and the only things they can think of for security are armaments and the like. If you draw a comparison, you can see that after 1968 the nature of consent changed completely: now it is only negative and passive. So I believe there will also be tolerance towards local structures, the principle of subsidies and so on, as they call it. There are a lot of other forces that will come to our aid. For example, 250,000 copies of this book by Franz Alt[14] have already been sold. This is precisely the sort of instance where Gramsci told us for goodness' sake to stop staring at the armour-plating on the machine. Of course, in theory the Yanks could have destroyed Vietnam, the Russians Afghanistan and the Shah all the Shi'ites.

KOMMUNE: There seems to be some misunderstanding here, because it's not the question of power I'm trying to get at.

BAHRO: Protection against intervention, you know, that is the point – when I spoke of appeasement up until the year 2000 this is the perspective I meant. Because many of us think in such a short-sighted way that all they can think of is: well, do we want to adapt now? And then Joschka Fischer was complaining about the traditional costume we put on to enlist support in Bavaria. Maybe because he is doubtful about a total perspective in that direction. Because he can't conceive of anything else except that we should keep a reserved seat on the political merry-go-round.

KOMMUNE: What I was talking about was not the question of power but the problem of how the transition might look – since you want to retain parliament and the state during this whole phase of building up commune-type structures. Or do you consider that, so to speak, the old structures would remain, new ones arise and the old ones at some point or other become quite empty? That is one point. The other is that, since in society itself a whole range of development possibilities are politically blocked, the question still naturally arises for the beginnings of a new society: what can you do to support such a development in the face of parliamentary majorities and government policy? What I am trying to get at is that even if one considers that the decisive point is the building up of one's own structures – and I agree with that – this doesn't settle the question of parliamentary majorities or the question of forming a government, i.e. of also doing things "from above".

BAHRO: Again, the way I see it would be for us to seek temporary majorities for the things that are important to us. If we want to get something out of it, we must of course concern ourselves with the general budget, the situation simply requires you to retain an overall view of the thing. In that area there are certainly no differences of opinion. The problem is really the perspective with which we participate, i.e. whether our perspective is to maintain the welfare state and to prevent or correct the worst environmental crimes, which makes us just an auxiliary engine for the repair policy – without necessarily criticizing individual points – or whether we pursue everything from the point of view of how we can construct this new thing. I see our chance above all in the fact that sooner or later this expansionist model with its tenfold consumption of materials and energy, linked to the world market and the material world market structure, will simply not function any more and a phase of contraction for society as a whole will become imperative. Actually my idea is that in practice we shall really contract the whole economic process – if one starts from that – into local conditions of production, that exchange outside a 50 kilometre range and at the state, European and world level, etc. will be minimized and that the world market will perhaps decline from 100 to 1 and the national market from 100 to 10, so that just as formerly people used to trade with far-off places for luxury goods, now too they will trade only for special materials which really have to be exchanged. Of course in certain specific cases the exchange will be on a bigger scale. But the point is that simple reproduction, upon which everything else must rest, should not at its core be dependent on the market. Thus if you organize the reproduction of the community and its means of production on a local basis (the two are not at all identical, but come much closer to one another if one manages to get the emphasis there, I mean to produce it in the life process), then the central institutions will be relatively dependent on this basis structure, at least in comparison to now. Then the main question will not be whether parliament is restructured, abolished or newly constituted or whatever, but – perhaps it really will turn out one day to be a parliament of soviets without any turbulent campaign having taken place. Perhaps that is presented a bit too harmoniously: I just mean to say that when history shifts its emphasis to the field of cultural revolution and the building of new social relationships, actually to the restoration of associations, then decisions don't come about as a result of the struggle for political power in the direct sense; whatever happens in the way of street battles and police intervention are unpleasant side-effects of the process.

KOMMUNE: But at same time there are obstructions in society itself, and not only obstructions caused by politics, simply by the exploitative relationships of capitalism, which produce quite definite constraints for the members of this society. I can't imagine it being so harmonious, this exit from society which spreads quantitatively bit by bit; I don't believe that such commune-type developments will come about in the form of specific models and be able to develop a power of attraction in society as a whole. The majority of society are unable to live in the relevant conditions and to tackle the building up of such life processes, simply because the capitalist process of exploitation controls the whole society. The mass of society can't even get their daily bread without selling themselves to capital. I agree that today one can't conceive of a radical change in society without social development itself having already created some indicators for a new type of production, by which one can see the way ahead. One can't start to build up cooperative communal production after the revolution: on the contrary the revolution begins as a radical social, cultural change, and indeed not only in the mind but in fact, with the building of new structures. But one may ask whether conflicts would not arise at an early stage between these two societies which exist in one, conflicts which would end in such a way that these new structures never get beyond being a model; there is also the danger that they will run themselves into the ground or be absorbed. The whole thing depends in any case on their continually receiving new influx and on new forces always arriving on the scene.

BAHRO: Well, we know that we don't have a guarantee of survival even for this afternoon. Who could guarantee that we will succeed? But the background is after all that this capitalist exploitative structure as a whole is running up against barriers – external nature; external proletariat, i.e. the population of the Third World apart from the elites; internal proletariat, i.e. the population of the developed countries outside the power structure – in each case that section of the population which is not entrenched. After all the process of exploitation depends on the influx of living labour, whether directly or indirectly, it is only human beings who maintain it. Thus if it becomes less and less satisfying and fewer and fewer people want to do it, if management is no longer enjoyable, and on the other hand this policy of a certain reunification of human beings with means of production and land is tackled – that is what we want, i.e. the progress to free wage-labourer actually to be reversed.

KOMMUNE: Are you serious about reversing? It is actually a contradictory formulation if you talk of "reversing progress".

BAHRO: I have said positively "Yes": reunification of the human being with the means of labour, or actually with the conditions of production, means of production and land – the separation from which is relatively late from a historical point of view. In the Big Machine, or to speak less mysteriously, in some big combine with ten levels of management which is connected to the world market through its whole structure of production and sales, through research, and which has branches in various cities – in an organization like that there can be no removal of alienation, or self-management and all that. What will aid us is the fact that we are standing with our backs to the wall, that the boundaries are there, simply that now for many reasons this contraction – as against the former expansion – is historically on the agenda on a material as well as a psychological level, which means directing energies inward far more than into making things. The big computers obviously don't do it, they are optimistic right up until everything goes wrong. At all levels it is becoming obvious that this process of expansion is coming to an end; that contraction is now on the agenda, as at the end of the Roman Empire. For that is the route from these military emperors to St Benedict.

KOMMUNE: You are drawing a pretty strong analogy with Roman history or rather with a particular interpretation of the fall of the Roman Empire, i.e. Raith's interpretation.[15]

BAHRO: I was always well up on the Romans. I've seen Roman history as a model for a long while, I referred to it several times in *Socialism and Survival*. Raith's book only confirmed what I'd said. Johan Galtung wrote something similar about the analogy between our epoch and the fall of the Roman Empire. Because it's simply a case of a total formation collapsing. The Marxist hypothesis was: one of the classes within the formation, the second industrial class, will displace it. In reality even the genesis of capitalist society was not brought about simply by the bourgeoisie, but this bipolar formation arose as one of bourgeoisie, towns and free workers, and it is this formation as a whole which is being demolished, which must be demolished. Thus far the comparison with Rome, where it was also like that.

Something has just occurred to me by way of explaining this whole SPD/CDU business. Because of this bisection of the political forces (if we leave aside the FDP for the moment) somehow people think automatically in terms of these two parties. Especially on the CDU side the two parties don't interest me; what interests me is the population as a whole, with the accent on the fact that in the present situation the population are in general conservative by inclination. And I directed my attack against the SPD because conceptually we are trapped by this party and not by the CDU.

KOMMUNE: That also follows from what you said in Hanover. In your speech you said that around 75 per cent are conservative and if we want to bring about a radical change we will only be able to do so if we attract a considerable part of this 75 per cent to our side. So far so good. Only of course the term "conservative" doesn't convey a terrible lot.

BAHRO: There is really a problem in this term. Even in the term "value-conservative". All the values we are dealing with here come from this European context. The pattern of thinking behind them is the one I developed in chapter 11 of *The Alternative*. There I start from the premise that there is an absorbed and a surplus consciousness and then I subdivide each of these again. But the basic thinking is that all people in society except extreme cases have a share in all these levels.

I'm not trying to define people as CDU-voters or SPD-voters but to look at how we can actually penetrate this consciousness. Naturally I want to get at the spot where there is a surplus, where the consciousness is not completely bound, and hope that from there one can, in traditional terms, make conquests in people's minds. So that the power relations within human beings change. Fred here, who is on a visit from England, has a brother in Munich. This morning he told me quite by chance over breakfast about his brother's wife, now middle-aged and bound up in typically Bavarian middle-class ways, perhaps lower middle class, I don't know. He always thought of the wife as conservative, Catholic and so on, but to his surprise she voted for the Greens. So for example particular motives functioned differently in that case. Some relationships shifted, without the things which had always made her vote for Strauss suddenly disappearing from her head. That I wouldn't maintain. In my view this is precisely the means of access which Gramsci taught us.

KOMMUNE: One problem in your analytical approach is connected with the fact that, if I have understood correctly, you have totally abandoned the concept of class.

BAHRO: No, not as a concept. Look, if we have a situation which fits what Marx said – as in the case of Rome, which is always important for me – where it can only end with the ruin of both classes, where there is therefore no class which can act as agent of what comes next, this doesn't mean that there are no longer any slaves or slave-owners. But if you orient yourself politically to the class concept you must have high hopes that it offers a way out. And that is the point. I see that capital and labour do in reality collaborate in order to maintain this dreadful formation. In practice I see that what used to be called proletariat and capital function in a similar way to the power blocs. They are both industrial classes which hold us fast on this merry-go-round. And I have to halt the merry-go-round and as far as possible divert forces away from it. I must neither attack nor support people as capitalists and workers but say, what you are doing is increasingly defining yourselves as human beings as part of the formation that needs to be replaced.

KOMMUNE: But that is only the case so long as the workers are functioning, as they must, as the labour-power commodity. In that sense they are naturally completely tied to the system. But the question is, where does the negation of this system begin? Does it begin with those who are compelled to function as labour-power or does it begin with those who operate as the functionaries of capital?

BAHRO: That is the same question as where does disarmament begin, with the Russians or with the Americans?

KOMMUNE: I see.

BAHRO: One must understand this as a system where in practice class struggles, as you can see empirically, have only served to move the system further in its own direction.

KOMMUNE: But the emancipatory tendencies and forces don't all develop evenly, they develop among particular strata of wage-earners, they develop in particular generations, social and political generations of workers. I think that you have correctly opened up the question of how we can win a majority for what we want, but you have as yet scarcely answered it.

BAHRO: My proposition is not about the interest of the workers as workers, but as people.

KOMMUNE: But in that you're no different from Marx. After all he only says that the interest in human emancipation. and in being able to attain self-realization as a human being arises or can arise among wage-labourers or wage-earners precisely because their *human* essence is negated.

BAHRO: If you take a look at E.P. Thompson's *The Making of the English Working Class* you will see that the early working class actually functions in a populist way, that is, they by no means orient themselves to a perspective of emancipation through the valley of wage-earning, but defend themselves in practical terms (machine-wrecking is only one aspect of the whole thing) – so that what they do directly want is their complete liberation as human beings, and it is only in proportion to their becoming so to speak faceless numbers that the question is narrowed down to merely preserving the interest of wage-labour as the most important and organizing the struggle around that, whereas previously, and presumably it was still like that in Germany at the time of Lassalle, the thing was the other way round.

KOMMUNE: So you have the phase of the working-class movement which you describe in its emergence, where the workers
defend themselves against being reduced from relatively broadly
developed individuals to the wage-labour commodity and appendages to machinery, and functioning as such. Then the dumb
pressure of circumstances, once established, proved very effective, and succeeded in restricting the workers largely to their
interests as wage-earners.

BAHRO: Up to a certain point in time, and that has passed.

KOMMUNE: Exactly. But in view of the movements which are
currently developing, why should one not assume a new phase of
the working-class movement in which the individuals who make
up the working population begin to cross this narrow horizon of
interests and question the whole relationship again as human
beings?

BAHRO: But this is a working-class movement whose whole
course has led into the bourgeoisie. In these rich countries its
perspective was to attain the bourgeois way of life for itself too,
that is actually to climb up into the patterns which the average
bourgeois would still have found quite good in the last century.
So, precisely if one keeps to the Marxist description, labour and
capital are correlative in connection with this formation. How
then should the working class, especially as it has been politically
pacified in the rich countries and since a working class can't be
formed through unemployment . . . I can't see how that works. I
see simply that in the crisis of this total formation, as at the end
of the Middle Ages, the forces should rather structure themselves
in a populist way. So my ideal is Thomas Münzer.

KOMMUNE: But perhaps the forces of the working-class movement can develop in a populist way again precisely because
wage-earning is almost universal and because universal wage-
earning, even where it has been forced on a section of the
workers, produces the social base for new populist movements.
Everyone or almost everyone can be addressed again on this basis.

BAHRO: But surely not on the basis of being wage-earners. You
are right in your description, though there are still important
differentiations among wage-earners. But that would mean
reverting to sharing out the cake.

KOMMUNE: No.

BAHRO: Look, on the issues upon which we are mobilizing now
they are not being appealed to as wage-earners.

KOMMUNE: No. Perhaps the mistake lies elsewhere, in that one
assumes that the fundamental interest of wage-earners is the
question of wages. That is probably not correct, or only correct at

a certain phase of the working-class movement. The fundamental interests are precisely those which are negated by wage-earning, the human interests, such needs as are now expressed in the ecological question, the questions which kindle the peace movement. But it is not by chance that the peace movement and the ecological movement are movements of workers and not inter-class movements. They are working-class movements which are however not formed around the wage issue.

BAHRO: If workers are 85 per cent of the people, couldn't you just as well say that these are movements of people who have all the hair on their heads? Especially since people also participate who are not wage-earners. For example, self-employed authors. Does this point matter in terms of whether one is for or against the missiles? If you look at it statistically it may well be that business people and the self-employed are less involved, but I just don't believe that is the appropriate way to define the subject. If you define the movement sociologically – I am saying this just by way of illustration – those people are most correct who represent us as some combination of the new middle class and certain sections of young people who have not yet been definitively classified. But I wouldn't want to hold that against you. That seems to me characteristic only for our recruitment. But the movements are not an organ for the particular interests of these classes and, on the contrary, this stratum which is being formed is going into battle – or at least to face the water-cannon – for common interests which actually affect the whole of society.

KOMMUNE: I wouldn't dispute that the working-class movement has become a part of the system and forms a bloc within the system, in the sense that it has managed to adapt the workers to capital as wage-earners, and whereas formerly they had resisted becoming that, they have nevertheless become it and have reconciled themselves to the role of being wage-earners.

BAHRO: And certainly that cannot be the subject of moral criticism. We have to acknowledge that this was the path of history.

KOMMUNE: This phase of the universalization of wage-earning, once it was established, also produced a particular form of working-class movement, whose beginnings were already recognized by Marx when tackling the problem of social-democracy. This phase of the working-class movement has been bequeathed to us by the Second and Third International and the various Communist parties; they are seen as identical with the working-class movement, and those paths of emancipation have failed. Where I differ is that by concentrating on this one phase of the working-class movement you want to ignore its whole history as an emancipatory force. As wage-earners the workers belong to the system, that is of course true. But the question is, who negates capital and wage-earning? Who else but those whose human needs are negated by capital and wage-earning?

BAHRO: But that is really still the same as with the hair. It is not open to challenge. If you talk of a majority and don't mean the wage-earners, 85 per cent of the population, where does that leave your arithmetic? Naturally the majority comes from the wage-earners because among other things people have the characteristic of being wage-earners. But this class characteristic is precisely one that now works as a retarding factor in the historical process, tying it back to the structure of the system – you just said so too – so, the point is not that I no longer want to say that they are wage-earners, but that if we want to intervene we won't win them by addressing them as such. In that case the skilled concrete worker, if I address him as a wage-earner, must demonstrate against the squatters. It's not a question of denying that this class structure still exists, only that it functions conservatively, in a way that conserves the system in the widest sense, and that the ways out are being formed via quite different sides of the subject.

KOMMUNE: Certainly wage-earning functions conservatively if it is accepted and in this respect also moulds consciousness.

BAHRO: We must break this mould instead of reinforcing it by addressing them along those lines.

KOMMUNE: But that would already be a social-democratic approach, to use your term, to address the workers as wage-earners and say, you must establish and preserve yourselves as such in the existing society.

BAHRO: The question is, if we actually have the guy in front of us: Perhaps he has two hours free each day. Should he devote this time to the trade union or to something else? If he doesn't do anything else I admit that it would be better for him to get involved in the union. But the active spots for getting out of the whole mess lie elsewhere. That is simply the rear. He should use the little finger of his left hand to stop the union getting out of control. But his energies should be elsewhere.

KOMMUNE: But you are leaving the trade unions as the biggest associations of the workers completely to social-democracy. The fact is that the most enlightened forces in the working class, by which in practice one can nowadays only mean the trade-union movement, are battling with the same problems in the unions as the Greens elsewhere. They are not active in the unions just to defend their existence as wage-earners, and just like Marx, believe that the unions are completely failing in their job if they restrict themselves to this.

BAHRO: Trade unions and trade unionists are not of course the same thing. So long as they exist and so long as people gather together in them, that is the place where subversive work must be carried out, but against the industrial system as a whole. That means also against the basic interests of the workers insofar as they are the second industrial class. Seen on a world scale there is the following problem. People never like it when I talk about colonialism. The balance of power between the classes internally is more or less fixed. So if the cake here is this big, the segments that I can get in the distribution struggle are fixed, they can be shifted only by millimetres. And if, say, the overwhelming number of wage-earners are entitled to 60 per cent of the cake in the distribution struggle, and want to have more, then the real fundamental orientation emerges when you consider the global context, and it becomes a question that they can do best if the cake increases and gets bigger. If it gets smaller things become more critical. I recently heard Volker Fröbel talking about this.[16] He has already defined the issue in terms of 300 years of struggle for and against market forces. I say, yes, against market forces insofar as we are trying to gradually abolish the law of value for wage-labour, rather than by getting more out of it than we are entitled to according to the definition of value. That is the political impact which the trade unions have succeeded in having, together with the increase in the price of labour and all the other things that capital enumerates for them. But the market as a whole is the uncritically accepted prerequisite and trade unions can't go about things any differently. Thus in the present historical constellation I cannot be simultaneously trade-union oriented, in the strict sense, *and* for the dissolution of the world market and the rebuilding of society on a commune-type basis.

KOMMUNE: I would formulate it differently. If one acknowledges wage-labour as a basic fact that one doesn't want to call into question, one can't be in favour of the radical change of society which is to overcome the annexation of labour by capital. Perhaps you should explain in more detail how in your view things stand with industry and the industrial system. As I understand it you don't want simply to throw the whole of industry overboard.

BAHRO: In the Middle Ages even the mills were called industry.

KOMMUNE: Granted.

BAHRO: So this level of form, wage-labour and capital, is after all not so decisive. For a long time we have acted at least superficially as if this level could be treated by itself. As if one could do away with what is capitalistic in accumulation and basically accept accumulation itself. After 200 years people are so imbued with all their habits, with the logic of buying, selling, market problems and so on, that they go along with every mental twist of capitalist calculation. I am not reproaching anyone, but what everyone agrees on is that the cake should be as big as possible. The only question is whether it is better now to shift the dividing line between the segments a bit this way or that with a view to enlarging the cake.

KOMMUNE: The question of the bakery has hardly been raised, that's true. What is it like and who is baking what for whom?

BAHRO: They go along with the optimism about the ability of the system to function as a whole. We really must distinguish between the historic role of the trade unions and the unions now as a place where people meet and where of course you have to have discussions. Maybe there is a contradiction in our work as facilitators, in that we must destroy the myth of trade unions, but not their social role. Especially as there are important interests that want to confuse the two. Obviously this risks a whole lot of misunderstandings, but I have the impression that many on the left in the Green party have simply not thought through the many questions of principle which are involved in this. It really struck me that it is the very understandable and natural need for protection as a minority which is calling the tune in the left-green mind. Without the trade unions and without the SPD, what a hopeless, forlorn little bunch we are!

Kommune, *July 1983*

Dare To Form Communes

Ten Propositions on the Line of the Social Alternative

1. Our peace work, all our efforts to ward off danger, which bear no postponement, still lack the basis which could support them in the long term. We are living on the very foundation which we want to use part of our surplus energies to do away with. Not only in our daily work, but also in a lot of what we do politically, we reproduce or at least indirectly confirm the deadly context of our civilization. We still haven't removed the pivot of the carousel. We still have not really begun to produce the soil of a different culture, a culture of peace. So long as we fail to find the way to that, we shall remain fighting a hydra which each day stretches out more poisonous heads towards us than we are able to cut off. And we ourselves will have to reproduce daily our aggressive will to do this battle. It is time to become positive.

2. The challenge we are seeking to answer is not that the system is functioning badly (economic crisis, unemployment, etc.) but rather that it functions at all. The crisis is the most hopeful thing about it so far, for it offers us a chance which we can and must use.

   We know that there will not be full employment again. In the EEC as a whole 25 per cent of young people are unemployed and in West Germany 15 per cent. We should not simply confirm even adults, elderly and old people in the belief that everything can be stabilized back into the accustomed ways. But seen from our point of view it would be reactionary to want to create for young people work, apprenticeships, a training which sets them onto the largely pointless and above all fundamentally wrong life perspective of wage-labour in the capitalist industrial system and its accompanying bureaucratic and service sectors. They need immediately at least a new and different context of life which they can shift into to complete their socialization.

3. The left is reacting superficially – in a merely political way – and in the last instance conforming with the basic consensus of West German postwar society, to the decline of the traditional social structure, by interpreting this as a reactionary act of will by the right. From this viewpoint we hear laments about social division and warnings of its consequences. These are not without substance, but basically fruitless. Even the conservatives will not

want to carry marginalization in the metropolises to extremes –
insofar as the social question is concerned – and for our purposes
its essence is not grasped if we reduce it to the aspect of relative
material impoverishment. What is declining above all is the
general consensus around the "German model", even the "European model" as it has previously existed. This is a matter of a
split in consciousness of enormous significance, in the course of
which larger and larger shares fall to us – and in the most diverse
minds. We cannot welcome the psychological decline and oppose
the economic one. We must make up our minds to take the total
process positively in order to make the best of it, and also
consider our contribution to the solution of the social questions
on the basis of this new starting position.

It is pretty absurd to use the fascist threat to justify sticking to
the old strategies of crisis aversion, which in the end will not stop
the increase of unemployment. We don't by any means want to
fall into the arms of those who continue to practise these, and
will simply lend them our assistance from case to case, to avoid
falling into the temporal gap between too swift a decay of the old
safeguards and too slow a build-up of the new. It is important to
keep a space free for ourselves and to gain time, but more
important still is what we are doing it for and that we conserve
our energies for constructive things. Nothing is left after demos
and protests. And a political crystallization between armed power
structures and sections of the population which have been
declassed or are threatened with being declassed, i.e. the "brown"
[fascist] peril, becomes probable precisely if we do not in good
time counter the irresistible decline of the ruling structures, their
"expulsion of superfluous human beings", with the attractive
beginning of a new order.

4.   The decision in favour of a commune perspective assumes
a considerably longer path than the "march through the
institutions",[1] and envisages a much deeper reorganization than
any which is possible via the state. Under the Damocles sword of
the Bomb, and looking at the clock with its hands pointing
almost to midnight, we still trust that we have time, in the end by
refusing to let this be determined by mechanical clockwork. We
dare to make an experiment, not ultimately for the sake of this or
that particular commune – although we won't move so easily as
from one shared apartment to another – but for the principle of a
life beyond the currently valid norms and career paths of
civilization.

Moreover, we recognize in a relatively autonomous basic unit
of social life which is no longer economically expansive (self-
reliance) the only chance in the long term of tearing up the roots

of the East-West conflict and above all of our opposition to the Third World. With a pinch of salt one might say (and indeed with the accent much more on the cultural than on the economic-technological aspect and with regard to the seeds of human community which are still present there), that the path of reconciliation with the Third World might consist in our becoming Third World ourselves. The existing techno-bureaucratic structure here can in no way be reformed in such a way that the rest of humanity could live with it. If we allow ourselves to be guided by the fear of "poverty", we continue to apportion naked misery to the others.

Yet however far we may be led by the insight that communes are the main way to uproot the exterminist peril, deeper seated still is our motivation by the psychological reward which we promise ourselves from the accompanying self-transformation. We build on the fact that the commune organization is anthropologically favourable, or – in comparison with other arrangements – corresponds more to human nature, among other things by avoiding both the neurotic-making family and the alienating big organization, while the inner pressure to conform can still be balanced by sufficient external contact. It is also the social form which most readily permits the control of social power.

5. The commune is the basic social form for a new, more economical way of life (a "domestic" way of life, as it has been called). Its purpose is not the production of means of subsistence – whether of the agrarian or industrial type, whether in the country or in the town – but the reproduction of the commune-type community. Economic efficiency is not negated, but subordinated to ecological demands and above all to the development of social relationships and the self-development and transformation of individuals. In the ideal case the commune network is socially so strong that all material and institutional infrastructure on any but the local levels remains dependent upon it, instead of the other way round as formerly.

Historical and recent experiences show that this produces a structure in which the feminine element permeates the regulation of community affairs from the bottom up; within a large organization and with the prevailing type of rationality and division of labour women's liberation is impossible.

6. Externally, too, the function of the commune is not primarily economic. Neither are job creation, taking the burden off the welfare state, producing food, etc. its purpose from the point of view of society as a whole. But among other things it also does all that. Since in this respect it represents a constructive alternative to the crisis of the society of labour and the danger of

an escalation of violence which is unfavourable in every respect for our objectives, there is the prospect of winning public support so that we can divert aid from the formal sector towards setting up a commune-type mass movement. The fact that such means would reach us principally via the state is in itself no counter-argument, since the resources concentrated there belong to society, as whose organ we are acting – especially as most of these resources are otherwise deployed either directly or indirectly in a destructive way, in order to continue the present overall course. The achievement of conditions under which any type of deforming state control is out of the question will depend on the social power relationship. The autonomy of the commune movement is the highest priority.

The subsidizing of commune-type beginnings will appear more or less significant from completely different standpoints in the traditional political spectrum. It is by no means a foregone conclusion that the possibilities under the present CDU government should be fewer than under the previous one.

But financial support from outside will not be ultimately decisive, though it can make many things easier, especially as we are faced with the disgraceful price of land.

The means will be found, especially as people from moneyed circles will get involved. Where insurmountable difficulties of "primary accumulation" for the new way are seen, it will generally be because people are thinking of an additional area without abandoning their previous basis of existence. Here there will naturally be many kinds of transition. In principle, experience shows that particularly in this matter the motto applies that where there's a will there's a way.

7. The real alternative which the commune poses to the industrial Goliath is not of an economic but of a cultural nature. The subordination of economics to living is only the first condition. Basically we are talking about a system of values which is new for modern Europe and also modified in comparison with medieval Christian Europe.

The Judeo-Christian version of culture, including the Indo-Germanic predisposition upon which it is built, needs remodelling. The problem lies at the level for which Johan Galtung coined the concept of "European cosmology". By that he means the deep structure of the ideology or world-view, i.e. the psychosomatically fixed patterns of behaviour which have been handed down to us, for example the drive for expansion to the ends of the Earth, and the Olympian principle of absolute competition for more, faster, higher, better, etc., without which we would probably never have attained our capitalist efficiency.

If we take a look in history at the foundations on which new cultures were based or existing ones essentially changed, we always come up against the fact that in such times people returned to those strata of consciousness which are traditionally described as religious. In order to be at all capable of a new definition of their culture, and thus of their behaviour, they must find a practice to dismantle their previous psychological structures and be socialized anew. Psychotherapists sometimes go part of this way, but it could hardly be completed by the individual man or woman without reference to those horizons which were symbolized by people like Christ or Buddha.

8. With such a horizon the alternative reaches back to historical experience which modernity – particularly where it calls itself "left" – has systematically suppressed, so that it no longer even has any direct familiarity with it.

Almost one and a half thousand years ago the Benedictines gave the new Western culture emerging from the collapse of Antiquity not only a very significant economic impulse, which at its peak involved up to 30 per cent of the population. Above all, they guaranteed the cultural synthesis of the new order which was current at that time, on a meditative basis – hence "pray (first) and work" – upon which the whole social radiation of their practice was dependent. The intellectual impulse from the monasteries which is acknowledged in all historiography was essentially a spiritual one. It came into being by people getting involved in communicating so intensively with "God" as the epitome of our transpersonal, generic essence which ultimately originates in the universe, that they found their own true selves beneath the rubble and the character armour of their socialization – the energy source of their charismatic effect.

We need a new Benedictine order. It can only flourish in a socially effective way within a commune-type framework. At the moment, those who must come together in it are still divided up into religious (and sometimes also pseudo-religious) sectarianism on the one hand and political sectarianism on the other, and one of the most important reasons might be that between these two poles the load-bearing social centre, the real context of life, is lacking. Certainly, for a preparatory phase in which the model is crystallized, separation or dissociation from the remainder of society will outweigh association with it, that is internal contact will outweigh external. (In this connection our Third World debate is to a greater degree than we think also about our own alternative to "development".) Without a retreat at times there will be no transformation of ourselves and no radical influence on the general consciousness.

9.   This new Benedictine movement will be different from the old in at least the following two respects, both of which concern the break with the foundations of patriarchy:

The spiritual culture will not be linked to a repressive monotheistic idea of God, which stems from oriental despotism and is designed for a hierarchical church. On this point the Judeo-Christian tradition must be broken. Happily Christ himself breaks out of this line at the deepest level of the image of him which has been handed down.

Social organization will not be linked to the separation of the sexes and sexual oppression, which corresponded to the Near Eastern and also the Hellenic origin of Christianity, a tradition which Christ likewise seems partially to have broken with.

"God" will be for both sexes simultaneously male and female, in some respects more the one, in others more the other. Community life will be based on the natural equilibrium between separation and communication of the sexes, and will give space to the uninhibited development of sensuality and sexuality.

10.   For the beginning it comes down to one thing: that there should be some initiators (men and women) who make a personal decision, begin by preparing themselves and a project and gather around them a circle of fellow strivers. When, if not now, would the time be ripe?

Befreiung 27, 1983

Why Communes?

European civilization is admittedly not the first to move into a general crisis, or rather it moved into it a long time ago (as the two world wars demonstrate). But never before did the self-destruction of a culture drag with it the physical destruction of its own vehicle, indeed the vehicle of any culture whatsoever, together with the anthropological substance of its biological foundation. This is what now threatens. And it is our *total* culture, including its achievements, which works "exterministically", i.e. which is destroying on a massive scale things human, animal and vegetable, and threatens to eradicate the last few million years of evolution.

It is therefore no longer at all justifiable to go on analyzing whether there *can* be an alternative outside and beyond this death-dealing structure. In reality, because of people's interest in being able to stick to what is familiar, it is usually presupposed in a circular way that there *cannot* be, because the given system is perceived as all-embracing and omnipotent. For those who have recognized that there is no chance of salvation within the systemic logic at work up till now, the problem is quite different. Even faced with the most stringent proofs, the only thing that remains for us is to rely on the possibility of error in the analysis and deliberately try something like the famous planting of a tree in the face of the announcement that the end of the world is coming. A new *credo quia absurdum*.

In quite different phases in the development of cultures, particularly of course in periods of crisis, attempts have been made to form communes. In the last few centuries the impulse that emanated from this has usually led back into the mainstream of expansive civilization (for example the pioneers' communes in North America that stole from the Indians, or the Israeli kibbutzim). What communes mean in a particular epoch depends on the epoch itself. If I now expect something different, I am starting from the assumption that the logic of expansion and of the accumulation of capital is losing its force because it is coming up against external limits and devouring its sources. In this respect the earlier attempts at communes in modern times were premature as attempts to break out. But analysis of historical communes will not prove that nothing else can be expected now either. The very impact against the limits, the ecological crisis, exterminism, create new conditions.

The reason why I have in my propositions referred mainly to the Benedictines is that the Christian communities were an answer to the *total* crisis that went before. In Europe the collapse of the Roman Empire is the only event which can be compared in dimension with the present-day crisis of civilization. This time, on a world scale, the inhabitants of the metropolises (of the "West", the OECD or however one wants to describe the centre) stand faced with the task of liquidating the empire, of doing it for their own sake and in their own interest instead of leaving it to the periphery.

The Benedictines – to take the most obvious beginning for the whole – represent the one historically influential, culturally creative commune movement of our history. Monasticism, which found its material embodiment in the cloisters (whereas the orders were its inner principle of form) characterized medieval Western culture (which then also declined with it) like no other institution. This experience is now relevant once more, no matter how incapable the form it took at that time is now; monasticism as such has long exhausted its culture-founding impulse.

The prospects of such a commune movement, which now seems to me to be urgent in order to reassemble and radiate this kind of creative impulse, are not at all affected by how much scope can be diagnosed for the development of an *alternative economy*. If it should fail because of this, that would rather prove that the task which I see for it was an illusion – or that it has not fully made up its mind to take it on or has dropped back from it again.

When a civilization as a whole moves into crisis, naturally its economic structures are affected, and – something which the "economites" among the economists inevitably overlook, because human motives scarcely play a role in their expert understanding – not only at the edges but at the core: the economic elites become tired. What is the sense of counting up the revenues and the number of people in the "formal sector" against the mini-amounts outside it, if the normal carousel is at an increasing pace catapulting people onto outside tracks and finally off it altogether? Yet for this line of vision the saying may well be true: "If you have ears, then hear." The pseudomaterialism of normal science does not yield the right perspective.

With regard to the next form of society it is of little significance what share of the total amount of labour and goods is organized by the centres where the spiritual state of mind for it is modelled. At least in the transition from Antiquity to the Middle Ages it was not at all a question of organizing the whole of society into communes; the monastery was not meant as an economic microcosm to be indefinitely multiplied. Its "service" as forerunner related to the inward arrangement of the feudal world. Thus monastery *economy* – although sometimes also exemplary as such – was above all significant insofar as it supported this particular social function of the monasteries.

Even if today for example the extended discussion about "self-reliance" and the necessity of reducing the expenditure and burden on the environment of each "unit of needs satisfied" indicate strongly that the reproduction process for the satisfaction of basic needs must everywhere be contracted into small units – that is not the subject here. It is even less so insofar as the bottleneck for a transition on a massive scale to a kind of "contractive" (in contrast to the present expansive) mode of production by no means consists in the fact that the resources, including land, do not exist or would not be available!

That could be tested if the psychological dispositions for a centripetal lifestyle, i.e. one directed inward, were in existence beforehand – in both the individual and the collective conscious and unconscious. Naturally these would also be developed by the owning classes, who after all will not be left untouched by a really all-embracing cultural crisis. The problem of access to resources would then resolve itself to exactly the same extent that the inner "ground" is prepared.

Anyone who with regard to the transition from one social formation to another, even from one civilization to another, remains fixed on the resistance of class interests – which certainly must not be denied in its relative weight – only shows that they have no idea at all of how a dissolution of such total structures can come about. Especially as never yet in history has the subordinate class of a dying social formation or civilization victoriously founded another world.

In such times of world-historic transition particular class and strata interests are more likely to be negative and retarding factors, working together towards the common ruin of the parties in struggle. The differentiation between the creative forces and the forces of inertia does not take place economically or sociologically but rather psychologically and in the last instance religiously (anyone who wants to misunderstand and refer that word back to "church" may of course do so).

To be more precise, it will always be the creative forces who articulate their practice in religious terms, because the forces of inertia in the social psyche have no access at all to the sources of renewal in the unconscious from which the resurrection of culture springs. Nowadays people usually talk of "spirituality" because this word appears less loaded than "religion". It doesn't actually make any difference.

We should cast off our fear of words, and rather bear in mind an extremely important difference *within* the meaning of religiosity and spirituality. The suspicion of traditional words is justified insofar as all higher religions are creations of a consciousness which was already patriarchally moulded. (Even if women had a part in them, this was rare and mostly as subordinates.) This patriarchal character is expressed above all in the one-sided orientation of energy "forward" (expansive, progressive, etc.) and "upward", toward world appropriation by masculine conquest and toward heaven (away from the Earth). As opposed to this, feminine spirituality tends rather to be directed "backward" and "downward", toward the origin in the mother's womb and the Earth, nature.

That *contractive mode of production* will only be possible if at least a slight dominance of the feminine element is achieved in human spirituality. Luise Rinser[1] spoke recently – in front of soldiers! – about it being time that men should accept the era of the anima – i.e. men should submit to the feminine part of their own nature. This seems to be a condition of salvation. It does not mean a permanent reversal of the power relationship between the sexes, but it may well be important for a transitional period, in which the male-masculine state of mind is still dominant, to give women as much influence and power as possible in formal terms as well.

Here I come to the problem which I mentioned in my introduction, based on the assumption which follows from the foregoing, i.e. that the only purpose of commune-type communities today would be to develop the spiritual foundation from which a biophile culture beyond our suicidal patriarchal civilization can feed. After a constantly renewed dispute in the preparatory group on this commune question, which revolved around the power orientation of the masculine consciousness – and naturally not least of my own – Dorothea Mezger[2] wrote me a letter closing the matter for the time being. She starts from the premise that even in the concept of completely integrated large communities and an eco-village – as in the Green Sindelfingen programme – there still lies the temptation to continue along the masculine-expansive path.

She wonders "whether it might not be more important, instead of planning a new society, to heal the existing one", not by means of reformist repairs but through a practice which to a certain extent emancipates itself from society's normality within the existing society, not set up as a kind of tent city before its gates. She speaks of "forming base communities, ashrams, opening up our homes to each other, meeting on particular days or at particular times for common spiritual exercizes and prayers". "The new society will not save us but the old will destroy us if it remains as it is. The real change can first take place only within. If large communes are built now, an infinite amount of energy will be put into them which should actually be devoted to spiritual development."

"Would it not be better to create small units and let them grow together . . . Surely it cannot be so difficult (I tell myself), instead of organizing a gigantic commune, for people to get together every day from 7 to 8 am or from 6 to 7 pm or every Thursday evening, etc. for common spiritual exercizes, throughout the country. Either everyone by themselves or in visits to each other. Eating together, etc. Such an obligatory or uniting practice creates a consciousness of mutuality and strength, as it was perhaps with the early Christians. Naturally such a thing must be begun with extreme caution, for people are rightly put off by the way many religious practices are used as instruments of dominance. But the strength to somehow continue can only come from this."

I don't want to try to clear up everything that seems contradictory in this, even for myself personally. In any case, I don't want to answer glibly that one way (the large commune) and the other way shouldn't be posed against each other, that they could rather complement each other. They *are* different ways, at least opposite emphases, different strategies, if you will forgive the word, and behind them lie different subjective states and also different assumptions about the path of history, in the end too different attitudes to the world. Are we permitted to want *to bring about* the future? Will not the building of a counter-world withdraw libido, to use the Freudian term, from the transformation that is due, the shifting of emphasis from the masculine to the feminine spirituality? Shall we not repeat once more the pattern of activity of Western civilization (in which the course the monks were predecessors, preconstructors of that which now exists and which is destroying us, as one can read in the works of Lewis Mumford among others)? The large commune is still, as ever, a Faustian undertaking, isn't it?

I previously stated that we should accept this Faustian inheritance of ours, should reprogramme the energies which from Bernhard of Clairvaux to Beethoven had been invested (psychologically) in expansion, for withdrawal from all conquests and empires. Perhaps that is too hastily thought out?

Nonetheless I think we shall have to accept one thing: even the feminine-ecological alternative will have to be *made* – the other society will have to be *built* and building will have to take place *for it*. Incidentally prehistory teaches us that the building of huts was originally a women's activity. In reality I presume it won't be a case of "not doing" and "not making" but of priorities: should we start again by immediately founding a (new) order, just as we are? Will we not then face the threat of being trapped again, only this time a little farther away from the old structures than all the other repairers and reformists? How can the precedence of the feminine mode of behaviour, of the mode of contraction and of humble instead of power-determined dealings with the world, be anchored *first* in the spiritual disposition?

Lao Tzu, the old master who in his search for a way back into a feminine culture recommended "doing nothing", "letting things happen", instead of "making", was not against the building of huts ... In any case in our own preparatory group we had reached the point where it might look as if the commune was from the start a patriarchal organization. In particular, are not certain attempts to bring sexuality and eroticism out of the prison of the nuclear family, which on the surface appear quite legitimate, in fact subliminally misogynous and exploitative of women when taken in connection with the usually masculine charismatic leadership which frequently marks in particular the more successful commune-type undertakings? Has not the fixation on "dealing with" this particular sphere – even if women continue participating in it with complete self-awareness – in fact much more to do with the masculine than with the feminine? Do not certain efforts to eliminate the patriarchal hostility to pleasure, to break up the character armour etc., depend all too much upon the very thing which is being combatted?

Even if it is emphasized by men that women too can play a charismatic role in the commune, that will not always be the case. Should women join communes at all in which men dominate or one man is the "man of God"? (If God is "the whole", then it cannot be completely represented without a "Goddess".) Posed differently: should men now put themselves at the head of a commune at all, however much they feel a vocation to do so? Elisabeth Otremba said to me in the preparatory group that once I had admitted these questions for myself, I ought to refuse.

Dorothea Mezger sees a possible solution in forming within communes separate women's communication and influence structures, and always in decision-making allowing the right of veto to the female "half". From the approach of Jungian psychology and its interpretation of "individuation", one could conclude that – at the head of the communes, if there is such a thing, and in general – loving couples should represent the human-divine unity, in which case the management of social affairs would be much more likely to fall to the woman. Here I can only leave that all open.

What seems certain to me is that we must heed the warning against the flight into activity simply in order to avoid confrontation with ourselves. Do not let us throw ourselves right away onto the forge of big projects. Above all, let's begin not externally, but internally, with the formation of a common spiritual practice, with the search for and testing of appropriate undogmatic and non-sectarian forms for this. Then we should not first have to be on the look-out for an *objective* but for a local context and naturally for a room in which we could meet regularly – or, following on from what I said before – two rooms, in case the women find that necessary.

That would mean we should not give in to the mood which has been spreading in the ecology and peace movement, that it is five minutes to midnight, that we have no time. At least we shall not gain time, but lose it, if we plunge ourselves into founding the material thing. Just a reminder once more of the monasteries: at the time they were being founded on a massive scale this was preceded by long phases of accumulation of spiritual force – sometimes in the community, sometimes even in the hermitage. What matters is the necessity of starting along the path, of not using the pause before a "founding fever" as an excuse for inner tardiness, for postponement, or hesitating to take the trouble with ourselves.

We can build on this, and indeed after repeated historical experiences.

The accumulation of spiritual forces, the association of people who create a common field of energy which confronts the old world with a new pole of attraction, will at a particular point in time which can't be foreseen exceed a threshold size. Such a "critical mass", once accumulated, then acquires under certain circumstances a transformative influence over the whole society, reorganizes the collective pattern according to which people in that society act in combination. That is this time all the more probable and could happen all the more quickly as the exterminist message is written ever more forcefully in flames on the walls. Maybe the very situation will arise which Hölderlin saw when he said: "God is near and hard to grasp. But where there is danger, the force of salvation grows too." And another man, the young Marx, had for this eventuality hoped for "the lightning of thought to strike the naive soil of the people". Perhaps the time is nigh.

In America There Are No Cathedrals

Rajneeshpuram, Oregon, 29–30 August 1983

TAZ: Have you often been invited here to "drop your mind", because it is only a hindrance to you?

BAHRO: Yes, constantly.

TAZ: Did you manage to do so?

BAHRO: For some moments. Then it is very meaningful, and that is enough. In general I have no intention of losing my head. Perhaps many people have to jump from the functional mind and the social role directly into the opposite extreme, for a while. I have always let my head work intuitively on the significant things. I don't need this absolute "getting lost" as an enduring condition.

But the success of the commune here is not conceivable without this "drop the mind" which brings the sannyasin into the mood of childlike geniality which is practised in the meditation therapies.

Insofar as the mind (unlike reason) is only a functionary of the existing society and its Big Machine, it must be rejected. And after all this childlike condition is not an end in itself, it is only a means – and this not for the success of the commune, but for self-transformation.

The sannyasins are induced to drop their old character structures to a large degree (on this point you can refer to Wilhelm Reich) and to create a kind of free internal space in which something new can happen. Nobody knows in advance exactly what – this openness is important. Only from truly liberated energies can a fundamentally different society be created. You can consider what Mao might have meant by praising "blank sheets". In the case of Rajneeshpuram, at least, what is demanded is not that some leader should write something on them, not even Bhagwan, but simply that something should "happen". When Bhagwan mentions "happening" when speaking of Heraclites or Lao Tzu, it sounds like Hegel, only in ordinary language, anyway quite dialectical.

TAZ: But to me it seems that here again the means is asserting itself over the end and the dialectic remains on the level of ideology. In practice Bhagwan is the leader, and his pupils don't want to go out into the world but rather to him.

BAHRO: The word "leader" can mean many things. For Germans in the case of Bhagwan it creates a false context. He seems to be a pointer rather than a leader, or a set of pointers which converge in a particular direction. The leadership, which in the commune as a small society is quite obvious insofar as the concrete, practical things are concerned, comes rather from the circle which surrounds him (predominantly female, incidentally). Likewise this almost obsessive search for a home comes from the sannyasins themselves. The very being of Bhagwan attracts them as the light attracts the moth in Goethe's "Blissful Longing", which begins: "Tell it to no one, only the wise man/Because the crowd will just cast scorn/I would praise the living/Which yearns for death in flames" ... Who he really is will not in the final analysis be proved by whether or when or how he pushes them back into independence. The commune as such may then break down or not. It depends also on the standards which one applies. After the departure of the leader, in any case, only a heretic – from within or from without – who overturns all the structures can give such a scheme continued life. More important, if not the sole important thing, is what happens to the people who pass through here? And one cannot disregard what they bring with them. Almost half the people here are Germans. Naturally, the inclination to flee from socially produced atomization, from being abandoned and forlorn, into totalitarian structures does not disappear when a person changes from a Communist group to Bhagwan. It must first of all express itself in the commune, lest it should be suppressed. You cannot ignore a totalitarian trait, like the notorious drop of tar which can spoil the taste of the barrel of honey. But how to handle this reality?

One of the most significant principles of Bhagwan's meditations and also of his commune is catharsis. That is: not to suppress but to work out even that which is dark in you. Just as in the meditations he has designed, which are perhaps his most inspired inventions as far as the outside world is concerned, it is obvious that in the commune too there is at first some darkness.

TAZ: In your conversation with the "party newspaper", the *Rajneesh Times*, you didn't mention the psychological mechanism of self-subjugation. Who would you blame for that?

BAHRO: There were a lot of things I didn't talk about, because other things were more immediately important for me with the limited space ... "party newspaper" – I suppose you are right. The experience which the commune most reminds me of is North Korea (though despite many parallels, the charismatic leaders are less comparable). Two years ago I said I didn't want to judge North Korea from outside. It is quite different if one is involved in the thing oneself, as I was in the GDR. That does produce a right to judge. As far as I am concerned the experiment which Bhagwan is undertaking with a part of the metropolitan intelligentsia should by no means be disturbed or hindered. It also seems certain to me – as in the case of North Korea – that the initial judgement which the Western critical spirit automatically passes here will in the long run prove mistaken.

TAZ: Bhagwan exploits and reinforces the need to surrender of those who come to him . . .

BAHRO: He transforms it. What matters is: for what purpose? That is a wide field, because two very different levels intersect here, in very "humble" consciousness. On the one hand there is the regression to childlike dependence. In the courses I have attended here that is brought out in order to get beyond it. But the English word "surrender" which you are referring to is understood here in the sense of voluntary dedication, without which there is no love. What is abandoned is the "normal" social precondition that mistrust is so to speak the first civic duty. After all Bhagwan claims to be like Lao Tzu, the true wise man who does not "do" but "lets happen", and who does not want to be praised. Not everything here corresponds to the wisdom of Lao Tzu's book *Tao Te Ching*. But in any case this is not a country anyone is forced to remain in.

But I want to point particularly to the level which your question is aimed at, because it seems to me to be the more significant. In European culture it doesn't actually occur: the relationship between a master and his disciples. What is written in the Christian gospel about it, for example concerning the apostle John, scarcely occurs in European practice. Let us just wait without prejudice to see what this brings. In Hölderlin's *Hyperion* there is the cry: "But one who is a human being, is he not more than hundreds who are only parts of the human being!"

TAZ: Masters live on the fact that their disciples forfeit their individuality. At least Bhagwan demands that: people without biographies, without social ties, who live in the here and now. There is something there in the European tradition which I wouldn't want to sacrifice.

BAHRO: No more would I, but your question misses the point. Of course there are some overly pious sannyasins here (and, more dangerous, also some with sectarian arrogance). In the workshops I have not experienced anything which could take any strength or anything worth preserving out of my biography. The basic thought of Bhagwan is certainly radical: Everything in the biography, in the social ties, which chains us to the overall pattern of the existing culture, should fall away. It's a question of clearing the internal building site for another culture. The principle is right. I am just not in favour of its being made so absolute. For European culture in the end there must apply what Christ said of the Jewish traditions: "I have not come to abolish but to complete".

TAZ: You are proposing commune projects for West Germany. Are there aspects of the Bhagwan commune which you would definitely not recommend further?

BAHRO: I don't ask myself that question because nothing at all depends on how I answer it. Rajneeshpuram is something whole, whose unity lies in the extraordinary human being without whom it would not have come into being. Someone who is different from Bhagwan can only found a different commune. It is not planned by the method of combining traits which please everybody. I myself for example have no car mania. Thus a commune which I take a lead in forming will have a different kind of screw loose.

In Europe, and particularly in West Germany, we must work in small areas, for example no more than 0.5 hectares of land per person. And we cannot live too far away from the rest of the population. What I envisage would first of all be externally distinct from the "Indo-American" design here, it would so to speak look "Indo-European" or "Sino-European" (because, as I said, I love the *Tao Te Ching*). In reality it's a question of something inward. In America there are no cathedrals and no music which came out of them. In Europe nothing would work which did not promise also the reappropriation of these buildings and this music, which marked the culmination of our culture. Georg Deuter's archaistic sacred music for Bhagwan is good, but it must not occupy the garden in which the individual *Kantilene* of Mozart blooms.

It seems to me that we have to overcome in a positive way something that exists in two of the great figures of European culture, who stand more or less at the beginning and the end of the era of cathedrals and great music – Bernhard of Clairvaux and Ludwig van Beethoven. Bernhard (after whom the Alpine pass is still named) was a mystic, monastery reformer, crusader, all in one. Both were representatives of the European spirit of expansion in its most distinguished form. If only we could regain their intellectuality and their militance, but for withdrawal from all the conquered territories, the colonies and empires of all kinds.

 When I reflect on what should come, I think of the line from Joachim Fiore to Thomas Münzer. You can find out about both quite well from Ernst Bloch's work *The Principle of Hope*.

Joachim had in mind that after the Kingdom of the Father (the Old Testament), and the Second Kingdom in which human beings still need a mediator, i.e. Christ, a Third Kingdom was already coming, in which the Spirit of God should, so to speak, be poured evenly over all. All equally near to God. As a political concept that would be "mystic democracy". Later on, secularized, in the classical and romantic era, Shelley called it the "republic of kings". Hölderlin celebrates it in the poem "The Oak Trees". I would not like to go back beyond that.

TAZ: And will you end on a more specific note?

BAHRO: Simply that I would not make any preconceived plan as to how everything should be formed externally, but must find the people who want to try such a thing with me. The understanding of what we actually are and what can emerge from us, what we are like, is the actual preparation.

This conversation for the Berlin Tageszeitung (TAZ)
was conducted by Klaus Wolschner

Withdrawal From the World is No Solution

GRÜNE INFORMATION: In the German edition of the *Rajneesh Times*, the newspaper of the Bhagwan followers, you are quoted on the occasion of your visit to Rajneeshpuram in Oregon as saying that for you this commune is at the moment the most important place on Earth. For us in West Germany that sounds very strange and hardly comprehensible. Does this commune project in Oregon really have such an outstanding significance?

BAHRO: I can begin with a counter question: That is, do we really seriously believe that the parliament chamber where the Green group now sits is a more important place?

When I said that, I was simply basing it on the fact that I have not seen anyone who more seriously pursues his contribution towards transforming and saving the world, as he understands it, than I experienced there with Bhagwan Shree Rajneesh. On the other hand it is presumably also clear from my *Tageszeitung* interview that his commune did not appear to me as the immediate solution which could guide us here at home.

But the principle is important. I believe that transformations can only come from the transformed; I mean transformations which lead out of the usual framework. From Bhagwan – admittedly he is not the first and not the only person to teach it – you can in any case learn what a central significance self-transformation has for the transformation of the world.

Again and again in history human beings have emerged who have radically trodden a path forward through their own person. Usually reports about them have exaggerated, saying for example that Christ was the son of God, and in the case of Bhagwan his sannyasins maintain that he has absolutely no ego at all any more. Those are the processes of absolutization, but there have been people like Christ, Buddha and Francis of Assisi who have been serious about themselves and practically made themselves "whole". Do we not often think of ourselves as a heap of broken people, who nevertheless want to mend the world?

GI: So you consider the way of the Bhagwan followers to be more important than the beginnings of the alternative movement. This would seem to at least partially throw into question the significance of the Greens in parliament and their serious concerns.

BAHRO: The alternative movement is stagnating because it has no spiritual perspective. With a parliamentary group it is the same again. I do not doubt the seriousness of our people in parliament. It's simply a question of the level at which fundamental change can begin. Approaches like those of Christ and Buddha also contain in an indirect way the intention of becoming political. Especially with Christ it is obvious to me that this is at the same time the most radical political approach, more far-reaching than anything that we normally understand by politics. Deep-seated change in society presupposes a different subjectivity.

If you look at ancient Rome and take Cato at the time of the republic, he was like Reagan, he finished every speech with the sentence "Carthage must be destroyed". And in this he stood for the majority of Roman citizens. If you then look ahead 700 years, you can see with Benedict, the founder of the monasteries, the tremendously deep change in subjectivity which had taken place in the meantime.

That is the most fundamental process by which civilizations are founded anew.

The Green party is becoming more and more conventional; I am not at all saying this out of disappointment, but simply that it is almost bound to be so. If nothing happens outside the parliamentary political work, we shall not get any further.

Bhagwan starts from the assumption that between now and the year 2000 the decision will be made as to whether humanity "leaps", i.e. develops a new perspective, or whether it commits suicide. I consider this diagnosis to be correct. It is an appeal to his followers not to be lethargic, to gather together sufficient force to be capable of the leap and to help others achieve it. To be sure, many orange people are only looking for a daddy and a nice new home. The growth in size of this movement is at present also detracting from its quality.

GI: Bhagwan is a leader figure. In comparison with him the mass of his followers are a movement of nameless people. Your treatment of this leader cult seems quite uncritical. The considerable amassing of capital is also a problem. In Hanover the Bhagwan people have for example bought up the biggest discotheque. There one might ask where the train is heading.

BAHRO: Let's leave the church in the village. They accumulate in order to extend their influence. And it works. In their Berlin disco I felt better for several hours than I have done after ten minutes in the few normal ones I've looked into. The accumulation of capital which threatens us is happening elsewhere, on another scale and with different results. At the same time it's not for me to defend these commercial activities.

With regard to my experiences in Oregon itself, I have consciously refused to perform the ritual of criticism. After all, you all know better than I do what has to be rejected in this. A "right-on" leftist has ready-made responses to that. I too consider ,Bhagwan's Rolls-Royces a wrong symbol, though I am amused by the criticism of these cars which assumes there is a difference of principle between a VW and a Mercedes, or that one would make progress by "giving the money to the poor". What I see is that Bhagwan is legitimizing technology as if it were not in the process of winning the race against him. And he refers negatively to Gandhi, holds up against him a "yes" to wealth, as if material self-limitation in the rich countries were a matter which can wait because it will at some point appear spontaneously when everyone has had enough of consuming.

As to the leadership – the issue is more complicated. There the perceptual pattern of your question is not correct. My access to it comes via Wilhelm Reich. You must temporarily entrust yourselves to the therapist. Bhagwan's practice (therapy with a spiritual perspective) is the basic model of Wilhelm Reich. Reich starts from a tripartite structure of human energies. On the surface they function in the sense of adjusting to everyday demands. Beneath that lies everything which we have accumulated since childhood in the way of defence mechanisms, etc., and beneath that again lies the biological nucleus. This is life-positive, it must become prevalent again. The second is the negative layer. Wilhelm Reich speaks here of character armour, of our barriers against the energies of the biological nucleus.

A Buddha is somebody who has managed to throw off this character armour. You can also understand Bhagwan in this way, though he does not represent anything at all godly in our usual sense.

This character armour is presumably also the reason why people resort to ready-made phrases when they have to react to something unaccustomed. A Buddha is somebody who has managed to dismantle the system of defence as defined by the past, who therefore has conquered the fear of injury. According to Reich the energies that you need for a full life are confined within the character armour. They keep on going into stereotyped reactions and are not freely available for what is appropriate *now*. Even if it sounds strange to many people, I think that the radiation emitted from the love of a Buddha is something which many had hoped for in vain in and from the Green party.

Bhagwan's role is in any case not that of a leader in the Hitler style, who achieved his goals through rubble and ash, and thus played politics with the character armour.

What it means for someone to be Christ is a totally different question. This is not in the sense of the "son of God", but somebody who has achieved complete access to his own nucleus and can react with love. Love does not mean at all that you have to be caressing all the time, but that the quality of the energy output is life-positive. In the context of Asiatic philosophy such a person is a master and not a leader in the sense that we commonly understand it.

To me personally Christ is nearer than this Asiatic tradition because the principle of responsibility towards the world is more marked in the original Christian tradition – as opposed to the Church and to Christianity. Luise Rinser has written a wonderful book on this.[1] There the Christ, the master figure is more manifest than in the gospel. There is a real and deep difference between subjecting yourself to a leader and Peter, Andrew or John following Christ. I would not write off as authoritarian leadership the act of entrusting yourself to somebody who is a teacher.

The people whom Bhagwan mobilizes are a potential force which should not be underestimated. In West Germany alone there are 50,000. Certainly I have said clearly that I don't think the Indo-American cultural form existing in Rajneeshpuram is a solution for here. Here it is more a question of the remobilization of the Christ tradition. I mean this in a general sense and not in the restoration of various doctrines or dogmas. It is a matter of getting back to the biological nucleus. As we need to fundamentally tackle the causes for this character armour, it is important for the life-positive aspect in the Greens to come out more strongly. A political party which is nothing more will be trapped.

GI: Could we come back more to German conditions, and above all to the Green party. You have spoken of the mass character of the Greens. As far as the Greens are concerned, that is far-fetched. The problems of an active base which is still too small indicate rather that the party is currently stagnating.

BAHRO: As the party of the alternative "scene" – as Joschka Fischer evidently imagines it – the Greens are bound for a ghetto. There are obviously people among us who assume that we have a particular clientele that we should represent in terms of the usual struggle of interests. This is doubtless a real aspect and taken in itself not to be regarded as negative.

When I speak of masses, I mean parts in everyone's consciousness. Here the attempt to withdraw from the system has a variety of crystallization points. On the one hand there are these neo-religious movements, and then the other kind of sectarianism is politics, first of the left, and now Green politics. By themselves the 30,000 Greens will achieve just as little in the Federal Republic as the 50,000 sannyasins. I don't want to reduce it to these two poles, there are also other poles. Of more interest are the 10, 15 and 35 per cent shares in the consciousness of the rest which aim at something new. More people than we perhaps believe have begun to recognize that what the Greens symbolize (rather what they symbolize than what they say) may well be right.

In addition to the sannyasins there are thousands of people who follow the other new religions or even the old ones in a new way. And don't several of those who wheel out their ready-made phrases against the sannyasins spend hours, if they can afford it, with a psychoanalytic or similar group? There they are dealing with the same things that Bhagwan is dealing with. People who stick to psychoanalysis may become further distanced from where things have to go now, because it operates completely on the ground of bourgeois individualism.

What we are experiencing now is that more and more people are crumbling out of the concrete, at the moment for limited periods of time. To this extent even the psychoanalytic path is progress . . . Since this potential force, even if it is growing, is for the time being still a minority, it can always be dismissed as sectarianism. The sannyasins depoliticize themselves primarily because an absolute switch-over is more comfortable, more enjoyable. But a whole series of people are beginning to come back to politics in a new way because withdrawal from the world on a neo-religious trip is also no lasting solution for them. What I would like to support is the politicization of this psycho-scene and the spiritualization of politics.

There are after all situations where you have to give a speech and there is nothing inside you, but you reel off what has to be said. Everybody notices that there is actually no power behind it. And if I use the concept of spiritualization it is meant in the sense of Wilhelm Reich, that in this case you have 100 per cent of the possible energy behind your utterance. That can also be silence.

GI: A central problem of this approach seems to us to lie in a comprehensible translation. The sensibility of many Greens is differently developed. More than a few old Social-Democrats and Communists who are now with the Greens are today once again trying to push this approach onto a sectarian track. It is also becoming easy for many from the traditional left to make fun of this important approach if for example you use examples from religious history.

BAHRO: That is not a real problem for me. When I think of our congress in Hagen, where people in the Green party echoed the CDU allegation that I wanted to see 5 million unemployed – many want to misunderstand and many evidently can only misunderstand. My speech in Hanover was completely unambiguous, but despite that some people simply wanted to hear that I was intent on an alliance with the CDU. I don't want there always to be a tactical stage inserted, this stupid question of "How shall I tell my child?" The dilemma is simply that nearly all concepts are already occupied. If you say "religion" people straight away think of the catechism, authority, etc. You must also be able to bear the moment of misunderstanding.

Our left is often like the Roman intelligentsia was in those times; the sceptics, stoics, etc. spoke with the same ridiculous arrogance about all the obscure sects which appeared in imperial Rome. The Christians were only one among many other sects. In reality retreat is often the first step forward. For anyone who has passed without a break from a Communist party into Green politics, it might have been better if they had first become depoliticized for five years.

GI: Inside the Greens there is another level to the problem. Our many town and district council representatives have their small daily struggle inside and outside the council chambers. That also shapes our external image. They are frequently so heavily involved that they do not concern themselves with the approaches that have been discussed, or only marginally.

BAHRO: For many individuals, and for many of the forces we depend upon, the Greens are also a trap. I mean this above all insofar as the beginning of a new culture is concerned. The problematic side of a parliament-oriented party was given real attention only at the beginning. On the political-cultural plane the old is winning through. A whole series of people want to tread the old Juso [Young Socialist] path again. The political model of the Greens is really different, but this march through the institutions as Joschka Fischer envisages it with 110 per cent of his energies, however idealized, can only end up in a left-liberal policy. No matter what is written in the programmes.

On many points we will certainly emit good impulses. It is quite right to want to install filters in factory chimneys. The direction this leads in, however, is away from the cultural revolution. Certainly I'm not yet giving the thing up for lost. For me the project of the Green party in connection with the alternative movement can only survive if it succeeds in drawing together the human capabilities which express themselves here in political activity, there in neo-religious activity, and in many other things which lie between these two.

Naturally nothing will come of it if one sees it as a mechanical process, and it needs a "place". That I see in the commune-type communities which will emerge. On the other hand there will be no zones liberated from the industrial system if we don't liberate the consciousness for them in advance.

In this respect, the economistic debates as to how much we will bring onto the scales by way of output, in comparison with the dominant economy, are ridiculous. To remain to some extent materially connected to the market is not the worst thing, so long as your main energies are not oriented towards it. If alternative only means seeking a niche for yourself in the system, that is too little.

GI: The green-alternative movement is at the moment concentrating very much of its energy on protest against the deployment of the new missiles. On the other hand we have a growing movement of people who sit in their temples and oases and at least give the appearance that this development does not concern them. We have tried this autumn more than ever to move people to active, non-violent resistance against the threatening nuclear holocaust. Here there is a considerable gap between what we have practised in the course of the year and those who have taken themselves into a conscious "withdrawal from the world". How are we to count upon these happy people?

BAHRO: Are you sure they are making no contribution? And if we don't succeed in our fight against the missiles, will that be primarily because they were missing? Nonetheless that is just the point I am making. I was in Rajneeshpuram, but also in Bremerhaven at the blockade and in Hamburg at the demo. We need many people who avoid both sectarianisms, the political and the spiritual. These two sectarianisms can only be overcome in the long term if there is a process of the centre which as well as self-transformation also includes participation in local, national and international resistance actions. This framework I happen to see as commune-based. Naturally we must also understand the "economy of time". Everyone mustn't do everything all the time. But I would have seen a sense in it if the 50,000 sannyasins, or many of them, had been at the recent actions wearing their own clothes. Some were there anyway, but mostly they put on a green parka for such occasions.

This interview for the Lower Saxony Grüne Information, 1983/20, was conducted by Jürgen Paeger and Uwe Brennecke

We Need a Lot More Empty Space in Our Minds and in Our Feelings!

BAHRO: The community of three thousand souls is something I copied from a poster. There was an illustration of a Hopi settlement, and the text said the Hopis believe that three thousand is the upper limit for it to remain human. That's why I called it that. What I meant by it was at least this much: experiences, insofar as I have absorbed them, show that if you base the thing on a small group level you just get the usual group dynamics, the apartment-sharing kind of communities which then disintegrate again. There also seems to be empirical research showing that people are much more likely to find the communication they are looking for among a hundred people than among fifteen. Evidently the space there is too small and you have no alternative if a relationship goes wrong or something like that; and in any case even for psychological reasons people need larger communities than would be best for a three-hour discussion meeting.

Thus you need a larger social framework, then people can keep out of each other's way, and that is also very important. If you also now consider the rationality of reproduction . . . I mean, in the monastic communities of those days there were nothing but men of at least eighteen years of age, and the problem of reproduction is considerably simpler to solve (even if in the ideal case they don't exploit anyone occasionally) than if you have a full society with children, old people, etc. and the whole rearing and raising goes into the economic calculation. I am wholly in favour of rationality or rationalization on the premise that you don't do away with work, that is with activity; thus I wouldn't say that the problem lies in the microchip as such. Although there is the problem of the extent to which the foundation stones have to be centrally manufactured. But a society with its main emphasis on community and commune will surely permit itself some infrastructure. That must result from the type of community that they need. But as I see it people won't go back to a zero division of labour, there will be a humanly surveyable division of labour in order to provide themselves with food, clothing, etc. This people's commune idea wasn't so bad after all.

KOMMUNE: And perhaps it will then also be bigger – well, it seems terribly small to me, but now to something else. The idea that you put forward at that time was: here we have communities which have exited from the system, which develop parallel to the existing structure and which then build up their own interconnections. The question is whether this should not much rather take place – and indeed must take place – within the present structures if it is to become a perspective for the masses; so that what I call a cooperative/communal mode of production or what you call a community/communal way of life, emerges only after an extended process of conversion.

BAHRO: The real problem is that the greater part of the infrastructure and production we have now doesn't actually deserve to be replaced. Do you realize that we shouldn't really be providing for amortization but should for example let the motorways fall into decay, one after another. That's what I mean by distributing out.

KOMMUNE: Well, you could certainly let a few fall into disrepair.

BAHRO: Sometimes the question is posed like this: so you want 30 million out of our 60 million to starve tomorrow by sending them to the countryside along Pol Pot lines, which is inconceivable in Germany. I think that these commune-type things are so to speak the germ cells of a new society, whether or not the situation is really like in the Middle Ages, as I wrote somewhere, where they effected 30 per cent of the economic reproduction process; nonetheless they essentially determined the total formation – who could say how that will resolve itself in detail, who above all would claim to know what relations would transpire between simple reproduction at the base and that at higher levels? Maybe I am overestimating the opportunities for contraction. For the moment it's just a question of the principle: to establish simple reproduction and to test what is necessary in the way of central structures from the point of view of such a society. I can imagine that it would look very different from today, above all that this whole transport and communication network could be much reduced and might perhaps be cut back to communication of ideas. At present we tend to believe that every citizen of this Earth should pay a visit to all 171 countries in the UN – that's roughly how it looks from the point of view of the metropolises, or of the Roman citizen of today. And that's simply not possible, so in that respect too I'm talking of contraction.

I would think that certainly some generations, two or so, will be needed in order to create these foundations for peace. Two

generations is the minimum, according to the research undertaken into the cultural assimilation of immigrants. And this
minimum is also a maximum, because the time pressure from the
dynamic of capital accumulation is so great insofar as the
ecological crisis and all that is concerned, that it is fairly likely it
will run out at the lower limit required for such a historical
process of transformation and all that is necessary for it.

KOMMUNE: You have said before that we need to reverse the
progress to the free wage-earner. Now one aspect of this progress
is that the wage-earners are divided up into quite a few spheres of
life, are fragmented, also that they develop very many relationships and that, even though mostly driven by capitalism, they
develop a considerable mobility, also develop needs, even though
these are of course as always bound up with constraints. And so I
simply find it very difficult from the point of view of the
development of the individuals and their needs to imagine that
such a cooperative/communal mode of production can be
developed within a framework so narrow as seems to be
conceived in your communities. And that all spheres of life can
be organized there. You sometimes take as an analogy the
Benedictine monastery. But that seems quite inappropriate to me
given the way in which individuals have developed, and that
there is also progress in this development.

BAHRO: The Benedictine rules have a section about brothers on
journeys. I want to say two things about this. The first is by way
of correction; I restricted that a bit afterwards to the question of
how the advance towards the free wage-earner could be reversed,
but my more general framework was really the reunification of
human beings with their conditions of reproduction: Marx has
shown that the whole of economic history is actually the history
of this separation, and Marx's plan is to reverse and do away with
this separation. Besides, to emphasize the point, I have a certain
sympathy for the model of Lao Tzu, which is admittedly too
summary, that though adjoining communities are within sight of
one another, yet the people of one grow old and die without
having any dealings with the other. You don't need ships and cars.
That is a contrasting picture, it's not a case of actually putting it
into practice, but of the rational nucleus of it, of the pointer
which is contained in the thing. With three thousand people each
individual in this particular community is available, that is
people can replace each other, and there will be no rule that there
have to be exactly three thousand and woe betide if there are any
more. What it is actually about are basic structures.

KOMMUNE: But how can one link that to the exit from the
industrial system? Perhaps we ought in any case to explain that a

bit more precisely, exactly what is actually meant by industrial system, whether it is technology . . .

BAHRO: What I mean by it is the whole thing as it has evolved and as it is now. The computer economy presupposes all four Kondratieff waves of industrialization and so it will be too with the rest of the world. They will go through the automobile phase while we here move on into some kind of material-saving set-up. What I mean by industrial system is a whole which sweeps us along with it, and if this whole stays more or less as it is I have no hope that the microchip will ever benefit any commune-type interest: it will just serve Big Brother. But if we succeed in founding society anew, individuals won't suddenly forget all the knowledge that they had, simply in that case there will no longer be any use for the knowledge that *only* serves to make a nuclear bomb. That can gather dust, nobody needs it, and then a selection will take place as to which knowledge, which technological process is significant, from the standpoint of a community which is no longer defined by production, so that production can be organized to be as fit as possible for human beings. Maybe it will turn out that a human being needs on average two hours of physical work per day. It must be regulated in such a way that rationalization and everything becomes dependent upon the main question as to what are the best conditions for a human being to be as happy as possible.

KOMMUNE: You are often accused of wanting to go back to the Middle Ages, and so on. If we were to take it seriously, this return to the Middle Ages – even in relation to technology, productive forces, etc. – then there would be the danger that this community of three thousand souls, which I am now using just as a symbol, would be completely devoured by work. What I am getting at is that it is precisely a further development of productive forces and the fruits of labour which will be the precondition for decentralized structures of production and life to be at all possible again with the present-day population structures as created by industrial society. We should discuss that in more detail in relation to the Third World because in the Third World a development of population is going hand in hand with the industrial society without this industrial society itself being developed. That seems to me to be a specific problem there, with the result that a return to the earlier possibilities for reproduction is no longer possible because that would in fact presuppose . . .

BAHRO: Because we have cut it off . . .

KOMMUNE: But also because the population structure is not like that any more. You can't simply say that they should return to their earlier reproduction methods nor can you say either that they should simply catch up along our path. But even so a considerable increase in the productivity of labour is necessary in order for this population – and this also applies here – to be able to live and not be totally absorbed by work.

BAHRO: I don't think that is right. This whole way of looking at the thing still somewhere contains the productivist flaw.

KOMMUNE: Well, perhaps so.

BAHRO: You know, there are these articles on Stone Age economics. Since humanity is still in existence one can deduce that they managed by working just four hours, or to some extent not working at all in the sense that it cost sweat and trouble which was felt to be negative; in other words, that it was a life activity in the broadest sense. The path has actually always been that the deeper we got into civilization, the more we worked.

If you consider what has happened in the course of the last hundred years, such a multiplication of productivity and such a small reduction in working hours. We are chasing ourselves to death in the superstructure, the auxiliary sectors, the repairs field, the state machine, the bureaucracy, militarism, and so on, we are putting so much work into it. If we were only to apply the currently possible level of labour productivity to smaller contexts and stop building the big machines, the war machines and everything relating to government palaces, everything connected with maintaining the structure as it is now, then we could manage with considerably reduced material expenditure. I don't believe that would be such a problem. For example just to provide the population of Latin America – in north-east Brazil, for instance, 20 or 30 million people live in this region – with the means or conditions, which have been taken away from them, for producing their food locally once more, is after all possible. Even in the Middle Ages they were able to build towns, they were able to organize crusades, they could afford luxury, the ruling classes. And the peasants in the Middle Ages – I read somewhere recently that roughly half the working days in the year were religious festivals.

KOMMUNE: Agreed, capitalism began after all with an extension of working hours.

BAHRO: I don't know, perhaps we're relying there on a logic which has also to be revised. You know, when we talk of the Middle Ages, the psychological problem is that we have a concept of progress which is orientated towards volume of production and technology. So when you look at the Middle Ages, from what standpoint is it dark? If you are expansion-oriented – I picked this up from Galtung – a drop in growth is a cause for pessimism. If you are contraction-oriented, then growth is a cause for pessimism.

KOMMUNE: That's where the difficulty lies. Certainly growth in the sense of an arbitrary growth of economic values, any growth whatsoever of use-values, is not the issue. But the question of growth in productive forces to let the springs of cooperative wealth flow more abundantly, as Marx put it, is a problem.

BAHRO: And now the question is, what productive forces? If one takes Marx's early writings, the *Economic and Philosophical Manuscripts* where he focuses on this question, then the wealth of human sensory nature is seen as the product of the division of labour, thus in practice of the wealth of satisfactions which are produced. But what was not solved at the time, and up till now has still not been solved, is the problem that this wealth is also produced for individuals, that it is so to speak social wealth which is filtered only through a few very privileged households, so that the English aristocracy is accustomed to go riding in the park. The real question now is to take Buddha and the life of Marx – I don't want to weigh up which was better, that can be left, but at least I would not say that the life of Marx is somehow to be preferred to the life of Buddha, seen as a whole. Or better still let us take Engels, who understood better how to live. I don't know whether you know that man in Frankfurt who has just left the Bhagwans, Rahimond Teube, or Rainer Teube as he was previously. He must have been a leftist beforehand, he is actually still a Marxist. So, he is trying to process this Indian philosophy for our understanding here, and indicates that the nub of this whole question is that they have a practice of internal activity which is dominant in relation to their practice of external activity – only the dominance is at issue, not the one or the other.

I quoted once in an essay Goethe's lines from *Faust* Part Two, where he says that "What's beyond is barred from human ken/Fool, fool is he who blinks at clouds on high."[1] What is meant is that an able person should be looking round here. Thus the perspective is one of reclaiming marshes. How do I conquer territories, many millions, and so on? That is a civilization.

Good, I don't want to get rid of it, I simply think that the problem is whether we are not far too fixated on seeing the whole of human development in terms of self-realization. Mumford shows this among other things in his book *The Myth of the Machine* [2] – if you read it you wonder whether the essay by Engels on the role of labour in the transition from ape to man is quite so correct. It seems that this cycle of realization to produce knowledge does not necessarily demand a type of practice in the sense of direct manual interposition, but that they had a tremendous amount of knowledge about nature in the context of picking berries and gathering mushrooms, etc., and could for example distinguish conceptually between 57 types of green, where the distinction was not made by means of an experiment. Our concept of practice today is an experimental one. That is very relative. I think that can no longer be geared wholly to material expansion, because the Earth is finite.

KOMMUNE: You spoke of the Stone Age economy. If one takes the concept of industry quite generally, that was an extremely extractive industry or an extremely extractive mode of production, which in practice lived on the wealth of nature and appropriated this wealth of nature as it was, but did not develop nature itself and did not modify it through the mode of production.

BAHRO: No, it was still in line with biological equilibrium.

KOMMUNE: But it is not possible to return to that. Certainly elements of this mode of production can be picked up again but a return to such a mode of production under our conditions – and I know that you don't want that either – would just not be at all feasible. That would lead to the complete ruin of nature.

BAHRO: You know, our mental block, what in the last instance I mean by productivist, is not so much the express orientation towards expansion, which is an additional factor if you take for example the last 35 years of capitalism here, but that somewhere we have fallen into a specialization of our evolution such that we define society through production. Above all, that we ask what the next mode of production will look like in that sense. Marx was always right to be cautious when depicting what would come later. At the same time I can see that one is forced to join in the speculation a bit, because that is also a human need.

I wouldn't want to be purist, but I also wouldn't pay too much attention to how correct the prognosis is as to how people will then produce. It is clear that production will take place, but somehow it has changed from being a condition for the continued existence of society, to the point where it is actually the purpose for which society is organized. We always run immediately up against the problem as to how things will be done technically, which instrument may be discarded and which not. What I mean is that it's definitely not a case of saying – apart from obvious things like nuclear power stations and the automobile – that individual objects should be banned, because they grow on the tree of evil. On the other hand you can't say either that we will carry out a selection now and decide which are the good things and which are the bad ones, because if you want to keep all the good fruits you can't throw the whole tree into question.

KOMMUNE: Perhaps it is also the case that capitalism is a society of development through and through and has no other purpose than the mere development of production.

BAHRO: The accumulation of all material products as capital. This expanded reproduction is the pattern of the whole.

KOMMUNE: Maybe such a development society in this sense is outmoded, has fulfilled its historical function and has no further purpose, but nevertheless it has created a stage of development from which certain perspectives are possible again or have become possible for the first time. Possible again, insofar as there is certainly a whole lot of inheritance from the various preceding formations. Possible for the first time, just because capitalism has produced a stage of development where needs which were previously ruled out come together and can be satisfied. You once wrote that one should reverse the whole direction of development which has been pursued since the late Middle Ages and the early Renaissance. I find that extremely problematic, wrong, because I am of the opinion that without this development all the things that we are thinking about now would actually not be possible as a societal perspective.

BAHRO: I'm not sure about that. For example you know, because the automatic course of the accumulation dynamic simply keeps shoving money in front of us, that it is now so to speak materially meaningful and necessary. Is this not to a great extent Hegel's "bad infinity" that we are moving towards? In a similar way Fourier once questioned the degree to which some 19th century lady was happier than Madame de Sévigny because the latter still ate off earthenware plates. I don't know whether many things are not going in this direction. Some things have also been lost along this path of progress. If you reflect from the point of view of opportunities for happiness, then what actually matters is the suffering on the one hand and the gain on the other if you change your habits. There again is the question as to whether we want to define it so much in terms of these external things.

Take for example the Amerindian cultures. The average tribe member was more a human being than the average worker is now in the present structure. What I mean is they were more flexible, stood in complex relationships in their particular circumstances. If there were a hundred people who constituted the tribe or the unit, then each had a function in the context of the whole, in which they were somehow irreplaceable. Whereas today that has been reduced to three people, plus perhaps two work colleagues. Seen societally that is already total anomie, as Durkheim calls it. What I meant there was that – certainly I am formulating it rather provocatively – we should be prepared to entertain the idea that in the last two hundred years evolution has gone wrong. That does not mean that in this process of evolution things have not been done which taken in themselves seem to be achievements and in some contexts perhaps might remain so, but that the overall development is leading to a point where the technological sphere will overwhelm the biosphere. It is that serious. If for example you take the history of Israel and consider it from the viewpoint of the destruction of the temple, then too you can say that something went wrong with the whole, and that with regard to all the structures which led to the destruction of the temple a correction was necessary.

Human beings are still the same as they were ten thousand years ago insofar as the genotype is concerned. Why then should we define them with regard to the last two hundred years as being dependent like ants upon the anthill or like tortoises upon their shells? We must at least be prepared to think of ourselves as independent of this whole technosphere, that is not dependent upon this whole configuration. People don't need cars, telephones, railways, and all that . . .

KOMMUNE: But they have them now . . .

BAHRO: Yes, I don't mean that all this has to be done away with because they don't need it, but only . . .

KOMMUNE: They mustn't be defined by it . . .

BAHRO: Otherwise we have practically built alienation into our horizons in advance. And constituted inescapability before we have tested it. So now we need a lot more empty space in our minds and in our feelings. Hence Thoreau's view, which fascinated me already when I quoted it in *The Alternative*: "Every superfluous possession is a limitation upon my freedom".[3] That has generic significance.

KOMMUNE: But what is superfluous? That can't simply be decreed. The problem is that on a mass scale nobody now would like to change places with the medieval artisan, for example, and that it isn't easy for them to change either.

BAHRO: That's not the problem. It's not a case of changing places with the medieval artisan. Thus when Illich worked out for example that we only travel by automobile at 6 miles per hour . . .

KOMMUNE: I have my doubts as to the correctness of that calculation.

BAHRO: Back to the increase in labour productivity and the small reduction in working hours. What I saw in the GDR in the mid-seventies was that they wanted consumption to double by 1990 and the struggle was for not increasing the use of materials fourfold for this doubling but only by 3.58, through specific savings on material. And that's how the whole caboodle runs. So that in reality we don't create more satisfactions for ourselves with more labour.

KOMMUNE: One of the problems is that capitalism can in any case only reduce the working time per product. Otherwise it has the tendency to increase working time for the whole of society – indeed it must do so because how else can it achieve an expanded reproduction of values? – and it has also the tendency to prolong working time for the individual and not shorten it. So that the shortening of working time per product is necessarily linked with a constant expansion of the production of goods, which for better or worse must also be use-values in some sense. What I am concerned about is that this completely one-sided tendency to shorten production time per product is simultaneously a condition for society not to have to be devoured by work. The concept of work as it has developed today, where work and other activities are completely separated from each other, may perhaps not have existed in the same way in earlier societies, but even so to a considerable extent they fell apart in the reproduction of human beings as natural beings. The ability to reduce the working time per product which capitalism has quite one-sidedly driven forward, connected with the tendency to increase working time for both society and for the individual worker, is simultaneously a condition enabling working time for society and for the individual to be shortened and potentially for a completely different use to be made of time both by society and by the individual.

BAHRO: That only appears to be so. In reality the case is that the extent to which we have to have possessions causes these gains to be devoured again.

KOMMUNE: In this structure, in this capitalist society.

BAHRO: No, is it only the capitalist structure? I indicated before that I am of the opinion that a correction is needed right down to the anthropological base. There is a point where the development of the human species has taken place in such a way that the greater part of surplus consciousness, this brain surplus, this anticipatory symptom, has gone towards material expansion for reasons of compensation – not in the psychological sense, but in the sense of compensation for things which would otherwise prove to be deficiencies of adaptation in the species. I think it has gone in this direction, that this is the logic which still underlies the level of productivism, and I could imagine the whole emphasis being shifted from this journey outward to a journey inward. That we could work much more with the inner forces. But some qualifications are also necessary. Buddha, and later Tagore, right up to the present-day Zen people, have been extremely rich in subjectivity. The West is defined much more by the external, by the object. That was also useful as a balance or counter-weight to the Indian way. But when the overall perspective of material expansion ends, we must be prepared to ask whether gains cannot be made in this other dimension from which we are being fundamentally kept away by the way in which our time-table is structured.

That once occurred to me. The Bhagwanis had invited me to a discussion with them in the International Congress Centre.[4] The discussion was about "dropping the mind". What would be meant by it. You can imagine the chief architect of this building. He has his school years behind him, then his years as a student, then the years in practice, and then the years when he built the hall there. That's how much life goes into developing this ability to abstract. So that his whole physiological frame, his method of energy consumption, is programmed to be nothing but the functionary who builds halls like that in society. That is fairly typical of what we are doing here. Is that a full life in comparison to that led by someone who takes the Yoga path in India and sees the focal point of realization there? One shouldn't pose the one against the other exclusively. But if the prospect in the present direction is in reality closed to us, in contrast to what Goethe was still able to say one hundred and fifty years ago, then let there be the chance to take advantage of this other dimension.

KOMMUNE: The difference lies in also seeing the possibilities which have been produced by what you have described as the wrong way. What Marx meant by the all-round development of the individual. Now naturally through this development today the individual is not simply developed all round but only as far as is possible . . .

BAHRO: In *The Alternative* I was still quite positive about it. Insofar as so to speak the cognitive orientation is concerned. The problem is that the mind is only an eighth part of human consciousness, that is the mind which goes in this direction. Somebody told me that recently, I don't know how scientific that is. Eight is just a street number. The mind is only one of the forces which the human being consciously deals with. Our culture has gone completely along this path, and Marx was in that respect simply a Cartesian as far as civilization is concerned. Taken in itself it need perhaps not even be downgraded, but the rank order it has must be redetermined. And in any event its share in the timetable must be reduced. We simply can no longer concern ourselves so much with pursuing just this one dimension which has to do with making things. For example, an engineer who has studied shipbuilding must actually want a whole ship to be built according to his design. That's simply not possible. That is not multipliable. But there is no enjoyment in always constructing just one part of the ship. So somehow you develop the tendency that you would like to be the chief engineer of this battleship there at the ICC. That is the tendency contained in that. This prospect must now be frustrated. One must frankly wish for things not to continue like that. That is what I still criticize in Mike Cooley,[5] that he always starts from the assumption that the worker must remain a worker and the engineer an engineer, and that we just have to convert to more acceptable products. That is not radical enough for me in the context which we are discussing here.

Kommune, October 1983

The Third World and Us
Conversation with Johan Galtung[1]

GALTUNG: A concept of development must have at least four components. These I call development of the human being, development of society, development of the world and development of nature. Let us say therefore the personal level, social level, world level, natural level. And you can formulate the ways of looking at the problem relatively easily. I'll take first the natural level, that is ecological balance. This has to do with the complexity and maturity of nature. Then to the personal level. Fundamental needs, they are partially material and partially non-material.

BAHRO: In other words, you don't understand by that simply the celebrated "basic needs"?

GALTUNG: Not only those. I mean by it also the possibility of attaining a state of identity with the world and with what is otherwise called the transpersonal or God, with the meaning of life, and something that has much to do with freedom. That you have possibilities of choosing, that it is not only possible to drive or listen to the radio but that you also have the material at your disposal to enable you to make spiritual journeys.

Then the social level. There the participation of the population and the autonomy of the country, so that the country has scope, seem extraordinarily important to me.

And then world development. Here I actually see two conditions: that one country does not transform others economically into its peripheral zones and that a country does not have defence forces at its disposal which are intended for offensive use. Those are for me the most important aspects of development. Culture, economy, social structure, international relations are all included in it.

And then comes the question of what we do in our countries in order to realize this. I believe that I have four or five preliminary answers to that. The first is of course anti-imperialist politics. The most important thing to do here is at home. And this is actually negative, i.e. not to diminish the scope of other countries through aggressive economic policies, non-intervention. That is number one. Number two is to create the scope for self-reliance, self-sufficiency to become the main pillar of economic policy. In this I actually exclude the whole idea that we must produce for the developing countries. The developing countries must produce for themselves. As a basic principle, this means that in general it is madness for a developing country to make raw materials available to us. They should do something with these themselves, either independently or in collaboration with each other, that is as South-South trade, not South-North. If this is problematic for us, that is our problem. We must find a solution for it, and the best solution is in general a green economic policy at home.

All the same I must say that if the developed countries make available 0.7 per cent of their gross national product, it would be madness to turn it down. But there should be two conditions. First, that development aid really does contribute towards satisfying fundamental needs, without restricting autonomy. And second, that the words "development aid" are done away with and a concept of symmetry introduced, so that it is made clear that people from developing countries can show us what is wrong with our own societies and what we could do better.

I think this money could in general be used for infrastructure, for communications structures, not always between centre and periphery in a developing country, but between periphery and periphery. For if you build a road between the capital and a provincial town you are always improving the prospects for the centre of the country to exploit the whole country. But if you establish a good connection between periphery and periphery that is in general not bad.

BAHRO: Then the question would be, how can that 0.7 per cent, insofar as it is available, reach the periphery by channels other than via the metropolises.

GALTUNG: That is the problem. One element is very important for me: that cooperation should not only be seen as a government to government issue, but that local communities in a developed country and local communities in a Third World country should make contact. We have had good experience of this in Norway, for example. There are exchanges of teachers and such like between local communities. In general it works much better than between governments. Here you can discuss ways of looking at periphery problems because periphery problems are more or less the same in the various countries.

I find it doesn't work with very different models for countries of the First and Third World. There are very many reasons for that. For me it is not universalism or so to speak an ethical generalization which is decisive, but the assumption that people won't succeed if they attempt to pursue a policy which is very different in their own countries from that in the Third World countries. You can see that.

For example I have among my material the most important Norwegian project: fishing in a village in South India. It has been going on for thirty years and is now a complete scandal. These are the achievements to date:

1.   There is less protein than before. Why? It's obviously more profitable to export top-quality fish than to catch fish for your own country!

2.   The fishing community's standard of living is worse than before. With the modern trawlers they have introduced an upper class, and these weren't the original fishers, but came from other castes.

3.   Terrible conflicts in the general fishing community. Trawlers have been set on fire, there have even been murders.

4.   There are no more lobsters, etc. because everything has been ecologically exhausted; and

5.   Japan has said that the fish have become too expensive and they don't want to buy any more.

BAHRO: Exactly what has happened with the "green revolution".

GALTUNG: Exactly. I have a particular interest in this project because I followed it as a researcher when I was a very young student. At the start everything goes well. The trawlers are so nice, so modern. When everything goes well the Norwegians leave the project to the Indians. Then the Norwegians go away and start up a similar project in another community. Then it goes downhill for the above-mentioned social reasons, not because it has been taken over by the Indians. But the Indians say, if they are not social scientists, that the Norwegians should come back, because it was so to speak the golden age when the Norwegians were there.

At the beginning of the 1960s I and many other people argued that what was needed here was intermediate technology – we didn't have the word for it then. And we did research on it. There were actually two questions: First, how do you catch the fish? This can be done for example in catamarans speeded up by aerodynamic sails, so that it is a bit modern but not using oil, etc. Then you must have a method of storage, so that the fish doesn't have to be consumed straight away. The freezing method they used is guaranteed to make it more expensive because it has as a precondition the existence of a freezer chain complete with refrigerated vehicles. The only consumers for the Norwegian fish in India are the people who have refrigerators. That is 1 per cent of the society at a maximum. There are other methods. But then the following problem arises: The Norwegian development aid agency knows nothing about catamarans with aerodynamic sails or alternative methods of storage. So we couldn't be experts on these.

I always take this as an example because there were absolutely no profits for Norway from this project. In this sense it was not a capitalist project. It was typically missionary, Norwegian, protestant – a project of conscience.

BAHRO: So our colonialism is much more than simply siphoning off profits?

GALTUNG: Much more, precisely. That is a problem. But then there is another problem. And here I must say that I am in favour of the Chinese policy. I'm not wildly enthusiastic about it, but I find it interesting. If you satisfy fundamental needs, then you have a population who are healthy, well educated, who have homes and in general relatively good food, if nothing brilliant. But there are in the world so many nice, beautiful things. And people hear about them, so what do you do? One possibility is to imbue the population deeply with ideology, as in a monastery, so that they are brought up to do without all the beautiful things. That is one possibility.

But I don't believe that is possible for 100 per cent of the population, without compulsion being involved.

MENDESES: But that would also mean an isolation of the people, total isolation.

GALTUNG: You would more or less have to build walls. Or inner walls. It could also be an inner isolation. I understand the Chinese method as follows. We have two problems. There is a problem of growth, we should like to have more things. And there is a problem of distribution, we should like to distribute the things better. They started with the distribution, in the countryside. Then there was a first period of growth, then a second distribution period, now we are in the second period of growth. My prognosis is that around 1985 it will come to a new distribution phase. You can't start with growth, it simply doesn't work. You get something like Gabon. I was there before Christmas. It is quite grotesque there, but also quite clear. A population of 600,000, with an elite of 5,000 black French people who speak excellent French and whose hearts are actually in Paris. They live in an air-conditioned chain, in their apartments, in their cars, and in their offices.

KOMMUNE: The Chinese path of development started in 1949, when the revolution was victorious. That was the condition for them to be able to start with a phase of distribution at all. To come to what Rudolf Bahro is fond of saying, solidarity with Nicaragua is all well and good but it is a relatively flat affair because it does not correctly reflect the relationship between metropolis and periphery. But the real problem is that development aid in the positive sense presupposes internal relationships in these countries which permit it. In the light of this you cannot criticize the left for considering it a central question to support the liberation struggles that are actually taking place, because these are decisive. Otherwise you are just going round in circles. For example the word "severing" conveys nothing. Who are the subjects of this severing process? What kind of internal conditions must exist in order to be able to sever onself?

BAHRO: I mean something else. If you are left, anti-imperialist, green or whatever else in a right-wing country, you can focus on what we should do with the 0.7 per cent and how you can prevent the ruling powers from direct interventions of a military kind. But by doing that you will change nothing in the total process of reproduction here which causes this peripheralization and causes the interventions. So the question is whether there is not time and again in this Third World solidarity an escapism in order actually to avoid making a radical decision for the centre.

If you, Johan, say that there is only one model of development, and the assumption is correct that this one here is not reproducible, where do you find a hold, what kind of logic results?

GALTUNG: I have a list of five strategies which I consider to be very meaningful in a developing country. Previously I used to concentrate on what we could do here or in Norway. I would like to enumerate the following five strategies for the Third World. The order is very important.

BAHRO: Strategies for us here at home?

GALTUNG: Actually they're also valid for us. But I am principally thinking now of the countries of the Third World.

1. A certain seizure of power by the population. How that happens is perhaps not so important. I don't say revolution because that is too limiting. There could be several methods. But there must be a break. Thus for example what happened in China in 1949.

2. A certain severing process. In general this must take place vis-à-vis *one* colonial power which is very important. Thus it is selective severing, not a total severing from the world.

3. A distribution of the factors of production. That could be a land reform. And something definitely has to happen with regard to education and health. It has to do with technologies and credit possibilities, etc.

4. Agricultural production. Food first. There are actually two

aspects, i.e. food first and then raw materials for your own industry. These should be produced by agriculture.

5. Industrial production. First consumer goods, quite simple things for the home, like crockery, i.e. all these little things that are so extraordinarily important. Then also the production of capital goods, i.e. means of production.

Finally 6. When the other points have been implemented to some extent, production for exchange. Here I mean South-South exchange as a priority.

The order is extremely important. If for example you start with severing, without a certain seizure of power by the population, then you have Equatorial Guinea, i.e. you can then get a terrible dictatorship. Completely severed from the whole world. For example Somoza could also have severed himself, that was in itself not impossible. Therefore seizure of power has priority, then severing, and then distribution. Agricultural production first, industrial production, and only then production for exchange. You might say this is somewhat doctrinaire. But if it works then you have at least achieved one very important thing, namely that the population do not suffer for material reasons.

By distribution I also mean the distribution of decision-making power, which has to do with committees, with popular participation. We should not use the words democracy or socialism, but think in more general categories. I see this as a spiral, always leading to new contradictions and new class formations, and then having to start again. You have to keep on doing it again.

So this model is applicable for West Germany too, i.e. again a certain seizure of power for the people, then a certain severing, partially now from the Third World. If the Third World severs itself, we must also sever ourselves.

BAHRO: We should first of all sever ourselves from America.

GALTUNG: Of course. First from America, but also from the Third World. And then start in West Germany with agricultural production. The proposition that we can't feed ourselves here is wrong. Of course it is possible. For me it is important to be able to construct a theory which is relevant not only for Third World countries but also for other countries. But it is a theory of spiral development, the essential thing is not that you do it once and for all. You have to repeat it.

KOMMUNE: Johan Galtung said before that one must generally try to create green structures, a green culture, which at any given time presupposes a seizure of power by the people, so that something can be done along those lines. But then the question is no longer simply "to sever or not to sever". One could even say that the severance strategies are still completely subordinated to the logic of the state, for it is usually thought that the state severs by monopolizing economic relations.

BAHRO: I should like to know what we are to understand by severing. That is, we can understand it as Huber[2] sees it or as it appears from the Third World: that after the seizure of power a certain state power is constituted which is in a position to set in motion such a process of severing, for example a monopoly over foreign trade. But the process which the severing refers to would be capital accumulation, the world market as a material process, which in practice keeps on spreading these alienated European super-productive forces over the whole world.

GALTUNG: I have here a letter from a very good friend in Iran. It's about all these things. I should like to quote something from it. You asked what severing actually is. Actually it is relatively clear what it is. The first indicator is the trade statistics.

BAHRO: According to your theory the first act of severing is the Islamic revolution as deep ideologization.

GALTUNG: You have to have that. I actually can't see how you can go through the programme here without a deep ideology.

So, my friend writes: "In a certain sense this revolution was just like the environmental movement, in that people knew clearly what they didn't want to do but we had no idea of what we should do now. But after many experiments we have come to the realization that technology is and remains the main factor. And that imperialism can penetrate us in various shapes and colours with the aid of technology. So we have to develop our own technology. That is the main condition."

He was in prison because they weren't quite sure that he was really Islamic, partly because he had lived in the West for too long. Now he works with solar panels, biogas and a lot of these things. He reports that it is not possible to develop anything at a community level to make yourself independent. He also says that there are fewer persecutions now.

BAHRO: Fewer than before?

GALTUNG: Yes. But has there been a seizure of power there? In a certain sense there has.

BAHRO: Certainly.

GALTUNG: And at the community level there is dialogue between leadership and people. It is not at all democracy in our sense, because the organizations are different. Here I should like to leave it open. It can't work without dialogue, consultation, etc., but does it have to be a parliament? My friend says that dependence on imperialism has all possible shapes and colours. Therefore democratization can also be transformed into a method of rule.

BAHRO: So the constitutional form says nothing about whether the people have any say?

GALTUNG: Exactly. Now my friend has been appointed as an expert in intermediate technology. He sees this as the key point to development. Here good old Marxism is shown to advantage again – that there is a certain primacy of technology, not in the sense that they thought in East Germany, but in the sense of independence, local communities, not too specialized. Technologies that can be understood and controlled by the people themselves.

BAHRO: If you talk about our being able to sever ourselves here – as an idea – then in any case you are starting from the assumption that you don't share 'all these arguments about the Third World having finally to starve and all our cultural and other help being in vain and they won't be able to get our currency any more and everything will be much worse there . . .

GALTUNG: Not at all. That is all deceit. You can see that quite clearly if you know for example how land in the Third World is used in order to grow flowers for our countries. They take the land away from the peasants and grow flowers there and sell them here. But when I speak of severance it is clear that a severance without these five or six points cannot be successful. The precondition is that something should happen in the First World countries at the same time.

BAHRO: What do you mean by precondition?

GALTUNG: If for example we drink less coffee then they will grow less coffee in Brazil, but if they grow flowers instead of coffee and we then buy flowers, it turns out to be more or less the same thing.

BAHRO: What would you think of the argument that the people in the Third World certainly won't gain anything if I leave the slice of sausage off my bread here.

GALTUNG: Actually I agree with this argument. I believe that people who assert the opposite exaggerate our role as a causal factor. The real causality must lie in the Third World countries. They themselves must develop their independent policies. I believe Iran is doing that. Nicaragua is doing it.

BAHRO: You think the fact that for example we import protein from the Third World for animal fodder here will sort itself out?

GALTUNG: It will sort itself out. That's exactly what I mean. But I think it is naive to believe that if we drink less coffee anything will change in Central America, Colombia, etc. And I consider it to be an expression of the way that even on the left people are still working with the same old causality, i.e. that we in the West are the centre and they are the periphery. Thus the causality emanates from us, we are always the source of the causality. And actually I find that a bit imperialistic. We perhaps exaggerate our own significance as a causal factor. That's why it seems so extraordinarily important to me to do everything to prevent interventions.

BAHRO: I remember a kind of sudden insight I had. I was in prison, that's perhaps why I took it in more. They reported how Fidel had been speaking at the Non-Aligned Conference in Havana. That was summer 1979. He had come out with his lament that people in the Third World imagined the good life as being like life in Washington, London and Paris. This causality really does exist. Naturally there is also some interaction in it. But where does the vicious circle start?

GALTUNG: Yes, the vicious circle doesn't have a single point where you could break it. That's always the way with vicious circles.

BAHRO: But if you were to cut it?

GALTUNG: A policy of beginning in a so-called developing country with the satisfaction of fundamental needs and autonomy must arise from that people and that country. And our task is not to stand in the way. But it can't begin here.

BAHRO: What options would we need to have if the connection from periphery to periphery was to have a chance, if we don't want to stand in the way?

GALTUNG: There I would go through all the German trade statistics, to see where we are dependent on the Third World for raw material, etc., i.e. what we must do differently in order to be less vulnerable ourselves if it comes to the point where the Third World countries say we will use this ourselves. I would do that for two reasons: First, in order to protect ourselves when our dependence becomes almost catastrophic – oil is already an example – and secondly, in order not to promote those forces which lead to intervention, even to military aggression if you have not prepared yourself.

BAHRO: The way you formulate it, this is a concept which could also be applied against the propaganda of the ruling interests. It would not be an altruistic argument for the poor people in the Third World, but a self-interested argument.

GALTUNG: I like that better. And I also find it less paternalistic. I would also say that on the whole causality will emanate from the Third World, as it was in the case of oil. And that this will happen again, more and more.

BAHRO: That is how it was at the end of the Roman Empire.

Kommune, *March 1984*

We are Defeated. That is Not Exactly Unimportant

Conversation with Johan Galtung (ii)

BAHRO: How far can a policy lead of taking up the issues here at the centre? Of emphasizing the dependence on raw materials and saying we should become independent? Can you see a point of access where one could slit open the belly of the beast? That is, this thing which simply keeps going under the aegis of the big corporations? You can't sell more than 26 million cars here, and then they start saying: Let's hope that in the meantime there are enough black French people around the world we can palm them off onto.

GALTUNG: But the black French people will usually buy Japanese and Far Eastern products. First because they are cheaper and second because they are better. They would be almost idiots if they didn't do that. I actually believe that we are here in quite a deep crisis. Our governments don't have the courage to see that and to admit it. The crisis is arising actually on two fronts; on the world market there are forces who are more diligent and in the Third World there are sufficient independent people who are at least rational enough to be good consumers, that is they don't buy our products but other people's. That has developed like an avalanche over the past fifteen years, certainly in the last five years.

BAHRO: So you think that Europe will be forced into contraction in any case?

GALTUNG: Just so. For me the Green movement is the movement of those people who have grasped that intuitively.

BAHRO: And take it positively. That is, we say yes to the destruction of the existing system of values.

GALTUNG: So we shall take advantage of the crisis to establish a better society.

BAHRO: Admittedly that is just what many Greens don't know about themselves.

GALTUNG: I give a lot of lectures to people in top positions in industry, civil servants, politicians, etc. That's what I do for a living. Generally I say to them: Suppose you divide the world into four parts, North and South and West and East, i.e. the First World, the Second (socialist) World, the Third and the Fourth World. Here we have the OECD, the rich capitalist countries. They are threatened by global mutual suicide through their confrontation with the socialist countries. From the Third World, from the South, they are threatened by independence and from the Fourth World, that is from the Far East, they are threatened by competition. Then there are various waves: first wave Japan, second wave the mini-Japans, thirdly the ASEAN countries and then the socialist countries of Asia. Then Australia and New Zealand as a recreation area and source of raw materials for the Japanese. That is a lot of people.

If we look at the rich countries like this, we see that they are threatened by exterminism, by being overtaken on the world market and at the same time by more and more independence of more and more people and countries. Then the situation looks relatively bad. And they have manoeuvred themselves into this corner.

BAHRO: That is to say, the threat from the Soviet Union is obviously something they have produced themselves. Actually the Soviet Union couldn't maintain its power as a political threat without the Bomb. The Americans could have done it without the Bomb.

GALTUNG: Partly out of racial contempt, they simply overlooked the competition that was threatening from South-East Asia. How could these little yellow people make something themselves? The problem with the Third World they have anyway created themselves, for here the whole problem of imperialism is involved. And behind the whole affair the Western deep ideology is involved.

BAHRO: The self-organization of tragedy.

GALTUNG: In my lectures for these people I then deal with the relationship of the First to the Second World, and the relationships of the First to the Third and of the First to the Fourth World as the three main sources of crisis for the First World; then of course the relationships of the Second to the Third and the Second to the Fourth World, and then the relationship of the Third to the Fourth World. The only relationship which is still somewhat unclear is the relationship between the Soviet Union and the Asiatic countries.

The Green attitude to the Third World is reasonable, their position vis-à-vis the arms race is reasonable. I consider that there is still a problem of security and that one should find answers to it. But I believe that even among the Greens people have somewhat forgotten the Fourth World. The crisis in the world system is actually not a crisis of the capitalist system. Capitalism is stronger than ever. The crisis consists in the fact that the focal point of capitalism is moving away from the First World towards East Asia. In my opinion the focal point has already shifted there. These people there have the initiative and are making things . . .

BAHRO: So you mean technological initiatives.

GALTUNG: Techno-economic market initiatives. In general people say that scientifically they haven't come as far as us. Maybe that's true. But in one direction they have come very far, namely: How does one make a new technology immediately marketable? They are very skilful at that and that is connected with science, because there the scientists work very closely together with the industrialists. Here they mostly sit in the universities. Here people insist that an invention is something individual. There it is always collective, nobody insists that Mr So-and-So made such-and-such a thing.

BAHRO: Would you go so far as to say that it is only a matter of this shifting of the focal point of capitalism? Or do you see this whole industrial structure, the expansion of capital, the whole world system, running up against boundaries?

GALTUNG: There is world power and there are regional and national powers. What is interesting is who controls world power. And I say that the focal point of world power is shifting towards Asia.

My analysis is very simple: In order to gain world power, one must produce high quality goods at low prices. In this the Fourth World is first. In the West we have high quality and high prices. The Second World has low quality and low prices, because they are subsidized. The Third World has high prices and low quality. The shift towards the Fourth World is something new. I find the quality there higher than here. For various reasons. We could now discuss the structural conditions for high quality and low prices. These processes I regard in general as irreversible. I believe the focal point will lie in Asia, not for decades, but for a century.

BAHRO: But on the assumption that the same process of industrialization which has emanated from Europe will continue with another long wave or two.

GALTUNG: Yes, but my assumption is also that the Japanese and East Asian mode of production is different from the one here. It is not quite correct for you to say the *same* process of industrialization.

BAHRO: So you say that the very Japanese who have apparently been best able to adapt to Western capitalism will have the greatest power of resistance in maintaining their own cultural model.

GALTUNG: To regard the Japanese model as an adoption of our technology only serves our own self-gratification. Once more, it has to do with deep ideology. In general Europeans are not in a position to understand that the Japanese proceed quite differently.

A little story. On my first day in Japan, in 1968, I met two people, the first of whom was later to become my wife. The second was a Russian from Gosplan in Moscow, that is from the absolute centre of the red system. We met in a hotel for foreigners and he said: "How nice to meet a European. I am so desperate. Can we go to the bar together and have a drink?" I was already in love with my future wife and not at all desperate, but I said: "Well, what is the problem?" He said: "Here there are only Japanese and Americans, so can we have a chat with each other?" So we had a few drinks. He had been there for two months in order to study Japanese capitalism. And his conclusion was that the damn Japanese capitalists were better socialists than the Russians. I thought that was nice. That was my first day in Japan. At that time I didn't understand how deep that was, very deep. And I must say that it would have been nice to meet an American who said: "These damn Japanese socialists are better capitalists than we are". But I have never met such an intelligent American.

BAHRO: You have tacitly assumed that if the Japanese take over it needn't have the same terrible consequences as if America continues to dominate.

GALTUNG: Not the same, but other terrible consequences. A conformist society.

BAHRO: But as far as dealing with the bounds of nature is concerned, how do you see that there?

GALTUNG: If you take my four spheres, that is, human beings, society, world and nature, then with regard to nature it is more or less the same. In relation to the world also more or less the same. They are trying to set up cycles in which all negative effects remain outside and the positive ones inside.

BAHRO: Does that mean that Japan is the worst for humanity?

GALTUNG: One might say so, because they are the most effective. But with regard to human realization and social organization there, they are quite different. That is, their industrial concerns and their social organization are quite different. And in both these realms they are superior. They have discovered things which are in general simply better. But the problem for Japan is that the numerous negative effects for the world and for nature bring about a certain reaction. And to some extent it is possible to imitate the positive effects, mainly for the mini-Japans and China, and the Japanese will be overtaken in their own wake.

BAHRO: Later on by China?

GALTUNG: No, not by China yet, but by the mini-Japans.

BAHRO: Aren't they too small?

GALTUNG: No, they are not so "mini", that's what frightens the Japanese.

BAHRO: So, you have been putting this accent on the Fourth World for about four years now, if I am right. Do you see in that any consequences for us here?

GALTUNG: That we are defeated. That is after all not unimportant.

BAHRO: But there are some people who want to resist with violence in the battle against Japan, as for example in the sense of the book of Servan-Schreiber in France.[1] And they would like our course to be: break the competition.

GALTUNG: I have discussed the scenarios in various writings, and what possibilities there are. One could build a wall round the First World.

BAHRO: The Roman *limes*?

GALTUNG: Yes, the *limes* again.

BAHRO: It didn't work very well before.

GALTUNG: It won't work this time either, because then we would be leaving the Third World completely to the Fourth World, which would penetrate it. The Fourth World is better suited to developing products for the black French people in the Third World. After all the Fourth World has a much greater understanding for it than the First. For example, the way that the Japanese won the contest for the new Indian car was fantastic. That is the Maruti. Even so we are talking about a market of 60 to 70 million, about 10 per cent of Indian society.

The next possibility is that people will try to wipe out Japan, for example with nuclear bombs. That is, something aggressive, less defensive. That will be difficult, because of the tensions between First and Second Worlds.

The third possibility is for the First and Second Worlds to try to get together. The scenario is: Ronnie calls Yuri up and says, more or less: "Hey, Yuri, don't you think it's high time to start working together. You've got problems with the Chinese and I've got problems with the Japs." I have the impression that that is the one thing the Japanese are actually afraid of. The Chinese have always talked about their collusion. I believe that the Japanese strategy consists of ensuring that the Cold War continues so that in reality no possibility of an alliance arises. It is in Japan's interest for the Cold War not to disappear.

BAHRO: Our Green strategy would mean, let the Japanese come, and in a certain respect, too, let the Russians come.

GALTUNG: But not for the Japanese to flood the whole German economy?

BAHRO: In the sense of letting them keep up the pressure out there in the world. We should only see to it that we can reproduce ourselves autonomously and relatively autarchically.

GALTUNG: Exactly: but we will no more welcome Japanese penetration than American or West German.

BAHRO: No, none.

GALTUNG: I am opposed to this Japanese idea that it would be best to leave television completely to the Japanese and so on, telephones and whatever. Just as I was opposed to the idea of Norway being the shipping agency of the world.

BAHRO: Yes, I am not at all of the opinion that all our shipyards should disappear. But it is just a case of reducing shipbuilding to the proportion that one needs, certainly, if we imagine a world market that is in any case reduced and where we no longer transport everything, cars, etc. back and forth.

GALTUNG: What I would like to see in the Greens is so to speak more global understanding. People do a lot locally but they don't think globally. That they could do better.

BAHRO: But that has primarily to do with the collapse of the global Marxist concept. Besides, if one acts locally, then naturally first of all one's being determines one's consciousness. At a very direct level the thesis is correct. Nowadays one hears even from traditional leftists the most vehement criticisms of the fact that one has a global concept at all. Global has in any case still the secondary connotation of the abstract.

GALTUNG: Somewhat elitist.

BAHRO: And anyone who even attempts to develop a total concept immediately comes under suspicion of totalitarianism. So there are a few inhibitions which come in the way of a global way of looking at things.

Naturally for a switch in deep ideology it would be of the utmost significance if people would accept that the focal point has already moved and that there is no hope of winning the war with Japan.

GALTUNG: The crisis is not that we have problems with the three other worlds, but that everything is upset because the deep ideology says we are the centre of the world. The others are all periphery. But that is simply not true.

BAHRO: So that would mean we would have to adjust ourselves in practice to taking more than giving in respect of ideology.

GALTUNG: Yes, I would say so and I would also say that we would be happier if we could change our deep ideology. I am afraid of one thing: If a people has only been used to being the centre and to the others being the periphery, and then sees that this won't do any more, then the natural change is to say: "Now we are the periphery and the others are the centre". I don't think that is a good change. The good change would be to say that we are all the centre, but we are different, and there is a possibility for coexistence among us.

BAHRO: In other words, a plurality on a world scale?

GALTUNG: A plurality, an equality. We can learn from the Chinese and they from us, etc. We can learn from the Peruvians, from the Incas, and they from us. And we can also say that it is not so extraordinarily important to learn anything, one can also develop oneself within one's own logic.

BAHRO: As far as the conflicts on all these lines of connection are concerned, that would mean in each case: unilateral disarmament.

GALTUNG: I don't take that so sweepingly as a formula.

BAHRO: In other words, industrial, technological, military.

GALTUNG: I have tried to express it in two formulae: first, that no country tries to draw another country as periphery into its own economic cycle, and secondly, not to have any offensive weapons.

BAHRO: You think that those two points are sufficient?

GALTUNG: I believe that these two formulae are very rich in content, but they are devoid of content if they don't penetrate into the deep ideology.

BAHRO: In the case of non-offensive weapons the formula is very concrete.

GALTUNG: The other is even more concrete.

BAHRO: But on the level of non-peripheralization it means that we must give up our whole technological and cultural dominance. And that is not so easy to achieve through measures of adjustment.

GALTUNG: Let's first tackle it, so to speak, quite economistically. There are six false relationships of exchange. You take out raw materials and send back waste; you take out liquid capital and invest tied capital; you take out people as migrant workers and you export goods; you take out products of research and you export tied, ready packaged technology; you take out half-manufactured goods and export ready-made products; you take out production techniques and export plant which is ready for operation. Thus you have a division of labour, and this division of labour is precisely that between centre and periphery.

In order to end this division of labour there is the "juche" model of Kim Il Sung, the Chinese "relying on one's own strength" and the Tanzanian "ujaama". And then the other possibility: to build up relationships in such a way that we are available to help you and you to help us, but we do it symmetrically.

BAHRO: Only that the first, the severance strategy, given certain changes in power, is at least relatively possible, as the Russians and so on have shown, whilst the mutual symmetrical relationships presuppose that the difference which is there does not exist and that there is not this pressure towards peripheralization.

GALTUNG: Yes, that is correct. So, between Norway and Sweden we have symmetrical relations. In the last century they were relations of dependency.

BAHRO: Dieter Senghaas has written a wonderful book, *Learn from Europe*. He compares the similar starting conditions of Denmark and Uruguay and has other such examples. Even Ireland comes out on the same side as Uruguay, so to speak. It turns out that beneath the economic and social factors which he investigates there must clearly be a predisposition in North-West Europe which wins through every time: so Denmark succeeds, Uruguay doesn't succeed; all the Latins, the Southern Europeans don't have the same drive, probably in respect of these special Viking virtues.

GALTUNG: Senghaas keeps trying to understand that all economically.

BAHRO: I think it has developed like this between Sweden and Norway because they both belong to these blue-eyed peoples. If you want to counteract the pressure towards peripheralization and attain symmetrical relations, then you are always first confronted with the question of whether the Viking can be transformed in the sense of his own psychology or whether he must be slain.

GALTUNG: I fully agree, but that has to do with deep ideology.

BAHRO: In principle that means that from our point of view we have no other access but this. This total structure which in the beginning gave rise to this centre and now defends it, can actually only go on working in the same way as before.

GALTUNG: But there are various types of people in this centre. For example, the Greens think differently in principle.

BAHRO: The Greens think differently.

GALTUNG: The Greens are more than 5.6 per cent.

BAHRO: Yes.

GALTUNG: And the people out there in East Asia are more Western than the people here. They are also better capitalists. That is also a problem.

BAHRO: It seems that the green factor is stronger now in the very parts of Europe which were more expansionist, that is in North-West Europe, or Germany, Britain, the Netherlands and Scandinavia, rather than for example in France. Because it is perhaps not so necessary there as a kind of antidote.

GALTUNG: But that can change, I find this so-called socialist phase in France particularly unfortunate.

BAHRO: But perhaps it was necessary, perhaps they are making complete fools of themselves.

GALTUNG: That is my hope, that they make big enough fools of themselves, these little Napoleons.

BAHRO: I don't see as yet how one can convert the preferences which arise from these various models now into a consistent Green economic and social policy. As yet what we do socially and in our economic policy continues to be at variance with our pious speeches of solidarity with the Third World. But how can one make any headway if in the case of any changes which are so to speak practicable one is always dependent on the SPD which still remains embedded in the old development logic?

GALTUNG: That one must do through constant dialogue with the SPD and not by withdrawing from such dialogue.

BAHRO: There is nothing to say against dialogue. It's just a case of whether we want to carry the state with us, not of breaking off communication.

GALTUNG: This is how I see it: the only possibility for a change would come through a deeper crisis. There I agree with you. I find Western civilization in general so arrogant, so terribly self-righteous, that it is almost incapable of learning anything. So the only possibility would be for the crisis to be even deeper. And there of course there are two variants. Either Western civilization starts throwing nuclear bombs around, or it starts looking for alternatives. And it is our responsibility as Greens to develop these alternatives. That is our historic responsibility.

BAHRO: And those must be targeted at the deep structure, the deep ideology.

GALTUNG: At the whole thing *and* also at the deep structure.

BAHRO: You mean a total framework, targeted not only at the deep structure but also at other structures?

GALTUNG: I mean that one must have an overall concept. But of course this overall concept runs the risk of becoming too totalitarian. And of people saying that we must change everything all at once. If you say that we must change everything, that is acceptable for 2 per cent of the population, but if you say that we could take small steps in this direction, that is perhaps more acceptable. I see it as a family of factors and that even small steps in the right direction do signify something, although they are intellectually not so extraordinarily satisfying. My philosophy of defence is also connected with that. Thus, a step from offensive to defensive defence is actually no small step. It is unsatisfactory for the absolute pacifist but it is a step in the right direction.

BAHRO: I'm not rejecting that, nor is that what I have written.

GALTUNG: No, you have said: I am not opposing your concept *per se*, but simply its being addressed to the peace movement. And there I agree with you, that there must be people who insist that we don't need the whole thing. In order to continue the dialogue.

BAHRO: So the Greens would not be the force to make the whole package of small steps into their main preoccupation.

GALTUNG: You might say that. But you could also do both at the same time, though for that you need an elastic brain. That is also a possibility. I think it is very important for people to say that we need a total concept. But one should also be thankful if things are moving in the right direction, but haven't yet gone the whole way.

BAHRO: If what you said about arrogance is right, then if one is content with the small steps this will have a regenerative effect on cells which are confirmed in the old arrogance.

GALTUNG: Maybe. They will say, now we are healthy again and now we can carry on, and get back to the real story, and that is the story that has us at the centre.

BAHRO: Perhaps it won't happen like that immediately, because it's no longer possible to get very far with that. But the process will have a retarding effect, because it constantly spreads reassurance.

GALTUNG: That could be so, but it could also be that in the meantime the international situation will change and things will move in the same direction, namely that the old politics of the First World becomes more and more impossible.

Kommune, *April 1984*

Notes for a Lecture on "Dimensions of Exterminism and the Idea of General Emancipation"

I want to give you an outline of what is occupying me most at present. Incidentally, the structure of these considerations takes up from the central chapter of my *Alternative* which was headed "The Present Conditions and Perspectives for General Emancipation".[1] It was this chapter that made Carl Amery[2] recognize me as a suspect ecologist when I was still locked up in East Germany. If you were to read it again you would see that I have not distanced myself very much from my starting point at that time, especially if you include the subsequent chapter on the subjective factor, on structures of consciousness as organizing forces of the historic process.

But there is one significant difference – among others, of course – which I would like to emphasize. At that time I had a onesidedly cognitive concept of emancipation. Appropriation of the social totality by means of rational knowledge and democratization of the conditions for this – that was the main road. I have begun to correct this, also in accordance with experience. My attitude now is not conversely a onesided critique of rationality, its rejection as such, a farewell to Descartes and the Enlightenment, but to overcome the separation and making absolute of the forces of reason, and the relativization of their leading position in the economy of consciousness.

To get to the point, that is, first of all to this terrible foreign word "exterminism". What is it meant to signify? The word doesn't exist in German. Edward Thompson derived it from a verb that originates in Latin. But the concept was already used by Gustav Heinemann in the West German parliament in 1958, when he refused to call the atom bomb just another weapon. He said it was a question of pesticides, this time with human beings being the pests. Mass destruction, eradication of plants and animals, after we have expediently declared them to be weeds and pests, is called in English, Spanish and French "exterminate", "*exterminar*", "*exterminer*".

The threat of the mass destruction of humankind, as expressed in atomic, biological and chemical weapons, lies in the very existence of these weapons and the way they are continuously being designed, built and planned for deployment. "Exterminism as the last stage of civilization" means admitting along with Edward Thompson that the logic of mass destruction of humankind has become the mark of the epoch.

This epoch began with World War I. At one time, weapons – when they still deserved this name – were in the last analysis tools, even if already murderous ones, initially for the killing of animals. With industrial progress which affected them like other tools as well, but always expressed itself first in better instruments of murder, they were developed ever more consistently along the line of the bold little tailor with his "seven at one blow".

Then with one load of dynamite hundreds could be killed at once, with gas thousands, with the first atom bomb hundreds of thousands. We finally entered the epoch of exterminism with Auschwitz and Hiroshima. Incidentally, apart from Heinemann there were others who realized this and expressed it over twenty years ago, for example Linus Pauling, Günther Anders, C. Wright Mills and Karl Jaspers. So the concept – unlike the word – is not a recent one.

But technology does not work exterministically only in its directly determined purpose towards mass destruction. Günther Anders in particular pointed out at an early stage that we could be participating in it through virtually every type of production. To generalize we need only to think of the murderous indirect consequences surpassing any use of the Bomb to date, as in the poverty and starvation of hundreds of millions of people indicated in the report of the North-South Commission edited by Willy Brandt, or the report *Global 2000* prepared for President Carter on the destruction of nature which endangers all human existence.

The concept of exterminism explains nothing. For a start, it only points towards something by adding up the sum of the interconnected dangers to make one single challenge. It is obvious that exterminism cannot be localized only in military means and their logistics. Wherever we look, disaster seems to be looming. And the thought imposes itself spontaneously that these are not plagues which are independent of each other and by chance simultaneous. In them there is a law, a force which is working against us. The symptoms only indicate that death must have lodged itself in the regular cycle which guides the development of our species. There is something at work which the cyberneticians call "positive feedback", a reinforcement mechanism of continuous self-intensification, as for example in cancer.

To talk in this connection of a "death urge" does not mean insinuating that "human beings" or "history" are seeking or striving unconsciously or subconsciously for doom. Insofar as psychology or psychoanalysis is relevant, it does not only concern the dark sides but just as much and perhaps even more the light and the lightest, the light of the Enlightenment included. Urge denotes to me an impetus, a driving force or a collection of driving forces which do not work by chance but at least in a guided manner.

Later on I will use a diagram to indicate a kind of multi-strata "drive" towards catastrophe, such that the cogs and the construction of this have to be understood in order to stop it.

I admit that this might sound like paranoia. But someone suffering from paranoia really does have a force against them. It's just that – for the present at least – it comes not from outside but from within. It is his or her own misguided energies, although the original impulse for the dysfunction comes from outside. That could be an indication as to the direction in which we should look. After all human beings – this is a triviality which so far no one has contradicted – are the subject of their history also as a species, not only individually. In the last instance the whole is the subject – that is, the body of the society in question at any particular time – and not only particular protagonists, whether persons or classes, institutions, etc. For none of these powers is as autonomous as it sometimes appears to be. Everything which looms as a danger to human beings (the social ensemble), everything which threatens them or it, is either their own alienated power or is obeying their alienated command. The central control rooms may be lords over death, but even they are not lords of the process which puts them in this position.

Arnold Toynbee, whose *Study of History* fascinated me when I was still in East Germany, summarizes his historical view on the fate of cultures as follows: "The destruction which fell upon a number of cultures in the past was never the work of an external cause but always happened in the way of a suicide action." And important for augurs in the centre, in the metropolises of a world system: "Should we not remember that . . . the ruling minorities are the original aggressors in the war between ruling minorities and external proletariats" (the East could also be included in this category according to him). This conservative historian makes all the Western critics of totalitarianism take note: "We must remember that the annals of this war between 'culture' and 'barbarism' are almost exclusively written by authors of the 'cultivated' camp. The classic picture of the external proletarian who brings his barbaric fire and slaughter into the pure sphere of a harmless culture is therefore probably not an objective representation of truth but an expression of the resentment of the 'cultivated' party when it is made into the target of a counter-attack which it has itself provoked."[3]

So much for now on the concept of exterminism *per se*. Now a new approach. In the title I have after all combined and confronted the concept of exterminism with the concept of emancipation. We are probably agreed that it is not merely dangers and threats to which we are now reacting with the ecology and peace movement. Actually the emancipatory drive is autochthonous. Naturally it is forced on by the danger of total catastrophe and combines with the urge for self-preservation.

In the final analysis we are not doing this in order to survive but we are using the most extreme provocation as a means to live or rather to experience, to discover, which is of course identical with giving a meaning to life. It is of course an imperative that there should be life, but this is why! If the question of survival now forces itself to the front, that alone signals what things have come to with us. And anyone who ever concerns themselves a little with history and has a sense that there too things happen according to laws, there too there is causality, will not find it adequate to blame such an outcome on the failure and the egoism of some class which happens currently to be hated. There are always people who are more strongly responsible than others, and those who live with them are always jointly responsible to some degree or other.

But what is at issue is something which lies beyond any weighing up of degrees of responsibility; that is another theme, if an important one, which I am not concerned with at present. Here I mean something which I call the "critique of human nature", because I think that we must discuss very thoroughly the reasons why with all the power of our knowledge we have got into this dead end of evolution. This is the question of those susceptibilities in the species which are exploited by exterminism and in which exterminism is inherent. Whether they also cause it is a second issue – I will leave it open. In any case there must be something which makes it possible. And perhaps we can overcome these susceptibilities.

Human beings are regarded as unspecialized, undetermined beings. Perhaps they can rise above themselves. In the GDR the poet Johannes R. Becher, about whom I wrote my dissertation, used to quote Pascal: "Human beings ceaselessly transcend human beings". Certain possibilities of escape, as it were, have already been individually tested, there have been some types of "quantum leap", so these are possible for human beings. I want to mention Francis of Assisi – to take someone who was not claimed to be the son of God. So far the historical pressure has never been so great as to produce several "quantum leaps" at once. At the same time the idea has never disappeared from history that at the end the target of emancipation would be located precisely in this. The fact that we have never been forced to undertake the great work upon ourselves has always had a firm hold on us. Now there is a compulsion as never before, arising from the nuclear forces which we have ourselves unleashed, from the ecological crisis which we have generated. There is in the Bomb and in *Global 2000* also one last chance.

But back to the theme, to the relationship of the two poles in the title. Exterminism and emancipation – I am reminded of two Hegelian propositions which belong together and which contradict each other. World history is the last judgement. And it is progress to freedom. For Hegel the first proposition was not meant so universally as it sounds, in any case not apocalyptically. For his last judgement led the spirit into the bliss of absolute knowledge. Naturally this final standstill of the whole works can also be thought of as a kind of death, but not in hell. And the whole proposition about the last judgement referred much more to the decline of particular civilizations, particular cultures which had fulfilled their tasks in the Great Plan and had exhausted their creative force, not to the – quite catastrophic – decline of civilization and culture altogether.

Seen in this way, the contradiction with the second proposition about progress to freedom was a relative one. The individual forms of life which grew old and died were really stations of a progressive process. It was actually inconceivable that there could be a condition of materialization, of realization, that is of the alienation of the spirit, in which phase – to some extent as objective spirit – it commits suicide. Even in the most extreme case the absolute spirit, in the abstract figure of God, remained the precondition or the protagonist of the last judgement and the apocalypse. And from the Apocalypse of St John to the Jehovah's Witnesses today, some 144,000 of the just are still supposed to remain.

For the moment we can say that Hegel underestimated in the way characteristic of his system the dead weight and the momentum which is produced when the spirit finds realization, particularly the human spirit in a second nature. The alienation which comes with this realization is supposedly removed by the fact that we recognize this second nature as created by ourselves. In a historical materialism such as that established by Marx there must from the outset be much more room for the possibility that the horse really does bolt, together with the rider; that the work of yesterday, dead labour, accumulated in the second nature into a technical and institutional Megamachine, becomes master of the living.

The ultimate general emancipation of human beings must confront precisely this tendency. No danger was ever seen in the amassing of quantity, in the accumulation of wealth as such, on the contrary what was needed was to remove from accumulation the shackles of the capitalist form, in order to create the material abundance that was the condition for liberating everyone. In this way something really did result which for a while looked like progress, even emancipatory progress: the welfare and social state for the greater privileged minority of world history – the lower classes of the metropolises, of the capitalist centre, Toynbee's internal proletariat.

Today we see that this process, whose emancipatory element must not be denied, runs counter to the most fundamental interests or requirements of three factors: of the external proletariat into which the majority of humankind has been transformed, of the external or first nature which is the basis of our life, and of the inner nature of our own first nature. Seen as a whole, the ever greater masses who have been drawn into the limited emancipatory process via production at an ever higher level, in the tendency to transformation of humankind into a working class, have at the same time entered ever more deeply into the shell of bondage.

It is above the entrance to the Megamachine which has emerged from this that Dante's words should be written: "Abandon all hope ye who enter here". Not only does it not liberate, it kills. You will not reach the summit of that heavenly kingdom on Earth in the short time till then.

The process of material expansion, the transfer of human progress and human evolution onto this main centre of gravity functions exterministically. In an extreme sense, the emancipatory process has been proceeding exterministically and self-destructively at least since the beginning of the modern age. And without reducing the whole issue to this one factor, I want to focus on the conjecture that this perversion of the progress to freedom has to do with a given component of human nature, that is with the power component of our consciousness.

Let us ask ourselves for a moment what has usually been understood by freedom, what we understand by freedom. I don't mean as a question of definition, but what was meant by it. We will scarcely ever find the will to freedom – this holds even for hopefully falsified parts of the evangelical texts – without the will to power. At all events, even Marx has to accept as a precondition for his concept of emancipation the same thing which begins the task of humankind in the Old Testament: have dominion over the Earth. In my opinion there is something trans- or pre-patriarchal at work, something which perhaps just permits us genetically to understand civilization up till now, which is patriarchal. There is an anthropolgial precondition, I did briefly indicate it, a basis for historical expressions of destructiveness. For the spirit is the original instrument of power with which human beings gradually rose above the rest of nature and confronted it. The change – at least as a possibility – is programmed in from the outset, probably in the principle of deficiency compensation. It is surely not only since the end of the Middle Ages – where Horst Eberhard Richter[4] begins with his "God complex" – that there has been a impotence/omnipotence dynamic in the human psyche. And the question is whether it has not also entered into our concept of emancipation. For example according to Fichte, in whose work it greatly impressed me long ago, emancipation requires the desire to "make everything which is non-Self dependent on the Self".

In other works, it is a concept of emancipation which is defined from top to bottom by power. I quoted a very similar definition from Marx in *The Alternative*.[5]

The power component seems to me to be one of the main lines, possibly more important than exploitation (which would then be a sub-function), running through the whole of history towards exterminism. If that is correct, it would follow among other things that we can only survive in conditions free of power.

All this does not mean that the acute immediate dangers can be directly removed through recourse to an anthropological dilemma. But we shall never be able to fill the cracks in the battlement in anything more than a provisory manner if they are caused by faults beneath the foundations. Then we should have to consider-ably revise our practice and our concepts of it. For example, the relations of production as we have understood the concept hitherto, relating to the uppermost class structure at any given time, are not the foundation. They are rather the storey directly under the top floor inhabited by ideology.

To review the issue once more, before I come as promised to the dimensions:

Exterminism is a particular point of view, in which world history appears from its possible end. This destructive, that is, self-destructive tendency has always been inherent. We remem-ber that Marx, for example, never failed to point out the circumstances in which productive forces were transformed into destructive forces, and that the concept of productive forces was conceived by Marx as relating to the subject, and had human beings at its central point. It is the running rife of this destructive tendency in human practice which compels us to think apocalyptically.

This time it is really not religious and psychological ideas of judgement that are at issue, even if there is all too much reason to include questions of self-determined behaviour in the discussion. The evidence shows simply the real danger of total catastrophe which results primarily – on the surface – from the incomparable range and the incomparable effectiveness of our technology.

Erhard Eppler writes quite correctly that it is "extremely doubtful whether our ancestors had a particularly fruitful relationship with nature". But "human beings simply didn't have the power to destroy nature to such an extent that they could thereby have endangered themselves. They had no mechanical saws . . ." not to mention nuclear energy.[6]

As never before in history it is becoming obvious that it is not only the tools meant for destructive purposes which function destructively. It is becoming clear that the concept of practice itself can no longer be understood as undialectically positive. Practice intervenes from the standpoint of a constantly limited knowledge into states of equilibrium about which we should need to be omniscient in order to be able to continue them unhesitatingly.

A practice of intervening in nature on a grand scale thus generally includes a moment of hubris. This is now coming to the fore and we are being compelled first to think of self-limitation before we continue to change the external world.

We have already sawn halfway through the branch we are sitting on and the saw has by no means come to a halt. It would be a great mistake to confuse the currently almost zero rate of growth which is the result of the economic crisis with the stopping of this saw [. . .] It is a thick branch, without a doubt. But the rate at which we saw, which in the last analysis means how many people each consume or place a burden on how much nature, can mean a difference of generations.

In this connection – despite a certain economic and even more so an étatist limitation – the observations of Herman Daly on a steady-state economy would be worthy of a closer examination.[7] In order to restrict the economy he suggests a method for limiting population growth, a minimum income and a maximum income for everybody and also apportionment of the expenditure of resources, all this under state supervision and sanction. Within these limits the market economy and variability in general are to be preserved. Whatever one thinks about the details of his proposals, we must come to an assured practice of self-limitation and to this end in any case divest of their sovereignty the "normal" excessive driving dynamics which lie in the accumulation of capital.

So much for the introduction of the theme, for the two main concepts. Now to the matrix which goes somewhat more into the particular aspects, into the dimensions of exterminism and of the emancipatory answers to it, as I envisage them.

Some Explanations on the Diagram

(In outline; no individual detail is literally all that important)

The dimensions of exterminism are not to be sought in the phenomena indicated in the third column, which are evident on the surface. It is true that the strength of the resistance consists in the fact that it develops in the unsurveyable output of the system, i.e. it responds to the open provocations. However, a strategy of warding off danger will remain controlled by the logic of the system insofar as it is actually reactive and may indeed possibly permit the individual activist to become conscious of the context of the provocations without making it into a theme. I am assuming that on this level we will not make a breakthrough but will only allow ourselves to be led on from one protest campaign to another, ever closer to catastrophe.

Since the plan assumes that beneath the exterminist tendency which appears on the surface there are a whole series of "essential" or "causal" layers – so that political practice could descend step by step towards them – I will come to the conclusion that the initiatives for warding off danger (which go from top to bottom in the diagram) must be met by a movement which works "from the bottom up". The new values may well have been provoked into the open by the dangers, however they do not have their reason in them, but much rather in the "radical needs" (Agnes Heller),[8] which are always there, but which can express themselves much more freely in the current state of decay of the existing culture.

The basic principle of the diagram is a certain application of the social formation concept (the column with the arrows pointing from bottom to top, which forms the centre of the observations). This application can primarily be traced to Marx who formed it consciously from geological and geotechtonic analogy.

Admittedly in his version the social formations followed more one upon another (in somewhat linear fashion, and according to an immanent dialectic, which taken strictly only applies for the transition from feudalism to capitalism) rather than lying one on top of the other (the older ones remaining beneath the upper ones). In this the Hegelian concept of resolution played a trick on him, leading him to maintain that everything essential in each older formation in turn became merged into the next, so that it was (theoretically) sufficient to resolve the modern contradictions in order to do away with all contradictions. In addition, Marx's scheme was Eurocentric – regardless of the "Asiatic mode of production".

The Marxian scheme is valid as far as it goes, i.e. starting from where I have put the "European cosmology". At this point my sequence of steps has a break insofar as in history no actual immanent transition exists from large-scale cooperation to Greek conditions, which emerge independently from the "military democracy" (Engels' concept for his "upper stage of barbarism") typical particularly for the Indo-Europeans. The link of the Greeks to Egypt and to Minoan Crete seems to a great extent to have been superficial. The concept of cosmology adopted by Galtung, in this case of European cosmology, is designed to sum up what was typical in Europe from the time of the Greeks with their market economy and object-dominating science up until modern bourgeois times (interrupted by the Middle Ages).

If I give this description an ideological accent, this results only from the intention to summarize. In fact the whole series of modes of production from Mycenae to today could be included there (even feudalism as an incubatory stage, similarly to Mycenae with the Greeks, is not outside this logic).

Galtung has characterized Europe cosmology (world view, but psychosomatically rooted) as *expansive* from the centre to the outermost peripheries, as regards the spatial dimension; as *dramatic* in the time dimension (from Paradise via the Fall, etc. up to a finale with redemption or damnation); as *rationalist-discursive*, one might say "binary", as well as deductive, pyramid-building from top to bottom in the dimension of knowledge; as *exercizing power* with human beings at the head in the relationship with nature; as *vertical and individualistic* (which together mean wolfish competition over rank) as regards the social ensemble, the interpersonal relationships; finally in the transpersonal connection as *orientated towards an autocratic personal God* standing dualistically opposed to the world, who controls everything and has the right of punishment as well as mercy. (As far as the knowledge dimension is concerned, Marx described it very well when he explained how, though leading first inductively from the concrete to the abstract, the way then

GENESIS via	FORMATION	Personality PHENOMENA	ATTITUDE ECONOMISM ETATISM	versus ECOLOGISM	RESPONSE	SUBJECT/PATH
Global Power and Competition for Affluence	Exterminism (Ecological Crisis) ←	*Teller* Nuclear Bomb, Nuclear Power Stations, Pollution, Obsolescence, Psychiatry, Hunger	Nihilism	Vitalism	Averting Dangers (Civil Courage)	Citizen's Initiatives (Protest, Opposition and Resistance to Specific Phenomena)
Industrial Revolution	Industrial System (Modern Megamachine) ←	*Schmidt* Arms Race, Destruction of Nature, Impoverishment, Periphery and Marginalization	(Vulgar) Materialism	Spirituality	New Age Values (Post-materialist Counter-culture)	New Social Movements (Ecopax, Women, Third World, Psycho-scene, Communes, Projects)
Great Transformation (Money, Market, Science), Absolutism	Dynamic of Capital (Competition or Profit) ←	*Rockefeller* Wealth of All Accumulated as Capital, GNP as Measure	Expansionism	Competition	Production for use, Communist Economic Formation	Simple Reproduction, Alternative Projects, Communal Living

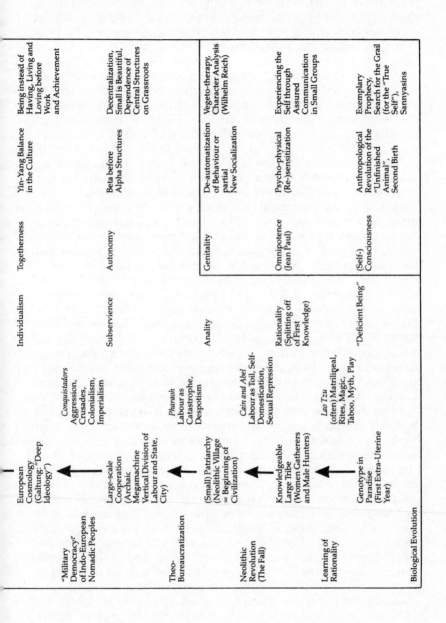

Stage / Transition	Societal Form	Emblematic Figure	Individualism	Togetherness	Yin-Yang Balance in the Culture	Being instead of Having, Living and Loving before Work and Achievement
"Military Democracy" of Indo-European Nomadic Peoples	European Cosmology (Galtung: "Deep Ideology")	*Conquistadors* Aggression, Crusades, Colonialism, Imperialism				
Theo-Bureaucratization	Large-scale Cooperation (Archaic Megamachine Vertical Division of Labour and State, City)	*Pharaoh* Labour as Catastrophe, Despotism	Subservience	Autonomy	Beta before Alpha Structures	Decentralization, Small is Beautiful, Dependence of Central Structures on Grassroots
Neolithic Revolution (The Fall)	(Small) Patriarchy (Neolithic Village = Beginning of Civilization)	*Cain and Abel* Labour as Toil, Self-Domestication, Sexual Repression	Anality	Genitality	De-automatization of Behaviour or partial New Socialization	Vegeto-therapy, Character Analysis (Wilhelm Reich)
Learning of Rationality	Knowledgeable Large Tribe (Women Gatherers and Male Hunters)	*Lao Tzu* (often) Matrilineal, Rites, Magic, Taboo, Myth, Play	Rationality (Splitting off of First Knowledge)	Omnipotence (Jean Paul)	Psycho-physical (Re-)sensitization	Experiencing the Self through Assured Communication in Small Groups
Biological Evolution	Genotype in Paradise (First Extra-Uterine Year)		"Deficient Being"	(Self-) Consciousness	Anthropological Revolution of the "Unfinished Animal", Second Birth	Exemplary Prophecy, Search for the Grail (for the "True Self"), Sannyasins

leads above all deductively from the abstract to the concrete of thought, i.e. the pyramidic deduction from top to bottom, which according to Galtung is specifically Teutonic in spirit.)

In my diagram the formations (dimensions of exterminism) are layers of subjectivity lying one upon another, I could also say they are "ensemble structures". Everything in history, even the most "material" products, presuppose human beings, are a second nature created by them. Marx knew that and wrote for instance: "Human beings themselves are the basis of their material production, as of every other kind which they perform. Therefore all circumstances which affect human beings, the subject of production, modify more or less all their functions and activities . . . In this respect it can indeed be proved that all human relationships and functions, however and in whatever form they appear, influence material production and intervene in it in a more or less decisive way."[9] But this was said defensively, and the focusing on production shows what he was most concerned with: If one could analyse material production and its relations in their totality, then one also had human beings in one's grasp – this being not explicitly his opinion, but implicitly at work. The same also appears in Marx and Engels' *German Ideology* but it does not show through enough in their theory: The relationships between the physical constitution of human beings and the surrounding natural conditions "determine not only the original, spontaneous organization of men, . . . but also the entire further development, or lack of development, of men up to the present time". And "All historical writing must start from these natural bases . . .".[10] Later they did not put that into practice.

From that point historical materialism has developed inconsistently. Put more exactly, and here for the first stage I can refer particularly to Carl Amery, three "stages of being" of nature do not come out adequately: the actual "external" nature right up to the biosphere in general (the earth as Gaia), human nature and the human consciousness as a simultaneously material fact. Lewis Mumford convinced me that Engels' famous essay on "The Role of Labour in the Transition from Ape to Man" (against which by the way he does not at all explicitly polemicize) is incorrect, that there is an initial process of brain development before the development of tools and that history, reduced to a formula, even if it is a simplifying one – and even materialistically interpreted! – is first of all psychodynamics. Anyone wishing to dispute that should first please read the first chapter of *The Myth of the Machine*. I emphasize this in the two lowest strata of the series.

In the Stone Age economy knowledge played a greater role than tools. And – not to go into more detail here, but only with regard to its meaning for the exterminist component – power based on structures of knowledge has played a greater role for the accumulation of wealth in the hands of ruling classes than vice versa.

In sum, I maintain with the ordering of these strata that there is an anthropological dilemma which goes back to the human genotype, which may perhaps not necessarily have to lead to the exterminist tendency gaining control but in any case influences it in a conditioning and facilitating way. (In passing, the Irish ecologist Michael Tobin writes quite explicitly of "patriarchy or civilization.")

I accept this equivalence, i.e. the patriarchal thread runs from there right on through to today. It is the most complex thing, a structure which is mainly objectivized in completely different relations than in individuals in the more narrow sense – women's liberation will certainly not be won by a gender struggle set aside from the class struggle, however inevitably features of that may appear. In the "response" column, the problem is indicated in the term "yin-yang balance" (Fritjof Capra, *The Turning Point* and Sukie Colegrave, *Yin and Yang*).

With this I have already reached the "responses" and with these also the subjects, or the ways to oppose exterminism. To come straight out with it: all the factors mentioned here, however they may be realized through a "division of labour", combine together to make up the strategy of the movement which can save. Warding off danger will not save. If we allow our forces to be absorbed at this superficial level and struggle so much against ever new exterminist conditions that we never get round to changing human beings, starting with ourselves – then we have no chance. Warding off danger through direct action is imperative for gaining time in the race with catastrophe. We do it for those (from the movement, for I am including this branch) who (temporarily?!) have committed themselves totally to the "search for the true self" (see for instance Fritjof Capra, *The Turning Point*, chapters 10 and, above all, 11), on the ladder from psychoanalysis via group therapy and existential processes (vegetotherapy, bioenergetics, gestalt, etc. – the concepts of the "humanist psychology" of Maslow and Rogers) right through to transpersonal therapy – which is no longer therapy, while even in the "existential" processes the tendency to a positive remodelling of the person already predominates, recognizable by names like "integrative" or "initiating" therapy.

The therapy concept here leads one astray – in the last instance. For first of all it is of course only too true what one can always hear people say who have started along this path without making it absolute: "I experienced that I was broken while we in the political groups, in the women's movement, etc. were mending the world." It seems perfectly obvious to me if I think of the Greens. We are a non-professional party. That means, our activists concentrate their free energy (outside of their work) more or less completely on the limited, intellectualist, and in addition competition-oriented type of practice which happens to be connected with politics "as such". We will not form any new society by doing that.

According to my viewpoint and experience we must start with the responses from "below" in order to work towards warding off danger. What modern physics (Jantsch, Capra, Prigogine, Weizsäcker), biology, anthropology, etc. now permit us to say in an "enlightened" way is that the "anthropological revolution" (Metz) of the "incomplete animal" (Theodore Roszak, the theorist of the American counterculture) could have something to do with a new "religious" synthesis in the sense of a "cosmic consciousness". "Second birth" goes back to (for example) Buddhism, but refers to the anthropological reality of the long dependence of early childhood (the first extra-uterine year according to Portmann), which generally seems to result in "power"-orientated compensations; to a generic state which anyhow proposes control of the environment as a solution to problems, and to the "dreamtime"-phenomena (the archetypes of Jung) which need reappraisal. Previously it has been taken for granted that figures such as Buddha or Christ, St Francis, etc. are exceptions. But possibly history will now have a continuation only if "humanity", that is at least for the moment larger minorities than in these well-known cases, succeeds in breaking out of the circle of Mammon, of karma or whatever the integral of the alienated forces of practice may be called. That would mean that we need a mass practice of self-appropriation, "therapy" (but not on this commercial basis which also presupposes anomie) with a spiritual perspective.

As for the method, that would have something to do with prophecy, and in the sense of Weber's sociology of religion we should have to make the distinction between "ethical" (his example: Moses) and "exemplary" prophecy (his example: Buddha – hence also the accompanying sannyasin concept). That is, this spiritual dimension would have to develop in commune structures which are at the same time complete units of reproduction, not only in the economic sense but much more in the sense of the all-round context of life. These social betastructures (Johan Galtung's terminology), "small" and "horizontally" connected, would then gradually (particularly if increasing

numbers of people attempt a "second birth", a new socialization)
subordinate the remaining "big" and "vertical" alpha-structures
– whose functionaries (using the word in its broadest sense)
would have their main location in the communes and – ideally –
would function centrally only from the socialization and new
socialization there.

The exemplary prophecy of Buddha is Asiatic – though Trevor
Ravenscroft has brought out a European variant in his book *The
Cup of Destiny: The Search for the Grail*, after Wolfram's (not
Wagner's) *Parsifal*, at least for the partial aspect of the "second
birth" (especially his chapter 7). All the higher religions – even
the Asiatic ones, although they are not so extremely yang-
oriented as the Near Eastern and Western ones – are patriarchal,
probably in this context directed towards desensualization and
"liberation" from sexuality. According to Ravenscroft's book, in
the search for the Grail this ascetic aspect, presumably as a result
of the connection back to the original Celtic basis (Robert von
Ranke, Grave's *The White Goddess*), goes back a relatively long
way, as also in Asia in many of the Tantric traditions.

I hope that all this makes it understandable why both for the
constitution of the subject and for describing the course to be
taken, I do not start from social structures, or more exactly not
from sociological and class differentiation. That doesn't mean
overlooking the fact that "recruitment" (to resort to that stupid
terminology) at present statistically begins with particular strata,
and on a mass scale with the young generation. But anyone who
starts off in the new direction does not do so in the name of his or
her individual interests (which do admittedly make themselves
noticeable as hindrances, negatively as in the case when Christ
"recruits" the rich young man), but in the name of his or her
general human, long-term and fundamental interests.

It is not true that absolute economic barriers stand in the way
of mass departure also from other parts of the body of society.
They are rather barriers of socialization and fetters of custom. At
the age of fifty one can as a rule no longer imagine an existence
beyond the family home. In any case not sufficiently to make the
leap. If hundreds of thousands were to decide, we could also wrest
the start-up capital from "society". The issue is becoming a
question of example, that is of the "exemplary prophecy".

Possibly the critical mass which is assembled in the self-
development complex (the six boxes at the bottom right-hand
side of the diagram) is not yet sufficient. For the strategies of
warding off danger (above) and of self-change (below) are still
divided from each other, and practised in a style which is absolute
– in the extreme case here the streetfighter and there the hermit

in a white empty room (instead of on a pillar). Even extremes may contribute something. But only the synthesis can have load-bearing strength, which presupposes that there is a social centre, a reliable association which one can trust in and where this strange anti-authoritarian image-neurotic individualism which once more reaffirms bourgeois society can gradually be polished into preparedness for cooperation and for the recognition of someone advanced as master for a part of the way.

Only in such communities and on the basis of interpersonal and self understanding (i.e. the six boxes at the bottom right) shall we achieve the backing for the capacity, the preparedness, the courage to break with the habits engendered by the Megamachine and to detach ourselves from the safeguards afforded by the state. "Liberated zones" in the world and "liberated zones" in the consciousness belong together. All those in a position to invent one of the technological monsters – from the Bomb to the International Congress Centre – have brains consisting for the main part of occupied zones. To this extent they are a particle of the Megamachine.

We must learn at least to subordinate all this technical knowledge. For that we need communities, communes in human proportions, in which there can be a scientific technology on a human scale. Microchips can serve complex reproduction in a relatively small commune of several hundred people, without life being determined by work. But the beginning lies not in alternative instructions for the use of this knowledge, but in a context of life which is emancipated from the Megamachine.

All the aggravation in the alternative projects – including such political projects as the Green party – comes from the fact that the monadic and frustrated personality structure in general enters in an unreformed state. The entry into a different society which is on the agenda in the metropolitan countries can only be achieved via a "journey to the interior". A policy of conversion must begin there. Of course we can for the time being set out alone along the path, the connections will then in any case be closer. People know and recognize each other more frequently, even now. In private conversations on such a theme nearly always something different comes out than at a conference. Probably we need, in order to lower the threshold of inhibition, a "materialist" concept of God (which besides I do consider possible). The individual departure to God – to regaining one's original self, to experiencing unity with the Whole – and the collective departure into the kingdom of God (it has historically many names) are two sides of one and the same thing, which in the final analysis only go together. Salute!

Fundamental Thoughts on the Crisis
of The Greens

After the previous delegate conference in Duisburg I resolved to resign prematurely from the national executive, and I have accordingly gathered all my contributions from Hagen to Karlsruhe into a 250-page booklet.[1] You can buy copies outside at the bookstall.

I am happy about this collection, especially as particularly after the economic and the commune papers I was often asked if I had finally decided against early resignation. My intention of resigning was based on the way that neither the national executive nor the other party committees above district level seemed to me to be the place where anything significant could be done to overcome the crisis in our party. In fact formal positions are more likely to stand in the way of this. I thought that if we fundamentalists wanted to save the Green party we needed to take a new run-up from so far back that we can't afford to waste our time in the mock battles which are so typical of the Green committees. Nothing is achieved by that. Personally I was also concerned to correct the possible wrong impression that my presence on the national executive might have in itself some meaning for the party line. "Bahro hovers over everything" is what Joschka Fischer was wanting last autumn; with his kind of realpolitik of course the party needs somebody for the Sunday speeches. I didn't want to carry on doing him that favour.

Change of Sides

But I want to relate how my Duisburg decision was triggered off. For me the most depressing moment was when we were applauding the American Indian. He spoke in the spirit of a text which most of us know, the speech of Chief Seattle before the President of the USA in 1855 is after all one of the few more or less mandatory cultural treasures of the green-alternative movement: "We are part of the Earth and it is part of us. The fragrant flowers are our sisters, the deer, the horse and the eagle are our brothers. The rocky heights, the luxuriant meadows, the body heat of the pony – and of human beings – all belong to the same family." The Indian at our meeting spoke on the assumption that these interrelations were "sacred" to us, he said that literally. We, partly out of a sense of duty, partly moved, applauded as if we *were* part of this bond, or were at least trying to be so. We were never so far away from it as at this dead conference in Duisburg. Without really knowing or wanting it, the Greens are changing sides; from the Indian to the President. That has nothing to do with political formulae, but with our political *culture*.

Because we can't make a breakthrough at parliamentary level on essential matters, we adopt the criterion of "feasibility" and "achievability". We are far from being radical on any subject, not even in peace politics. There "non-aggressive defence" rather than "living without arms" is becoming politically feasible. According to Marie-Luise's[2] report we have already reached the stage where our parliamentary group is putting forward proposals for reducing the military budget, instead of a total rejection. As if we would ever get a reduction in this way. For God's sake don't reject, not even the military budget!

We're doing the same thing everywhere, it's just that in military matters it is particularly noticeable. We are concerned for the government to support not the thriving, but the wilting branches of industry, so that a bit more is produced. We defend the steel works. We are not for a halt to all experiments on animals, but for a few more restrictions. We consider it important for the farmers to feed a bit more *German* grain to their cattle. The examples are numerous. Every time there are petty rational arguments for realism. And so we contribute covertly towards keeping the great death machine working, instead of at least spreading the message that it must be stopped.

Joschka considers it an argument in this affair that the world simply moves differently from how we would like. We should formulate what can be achieved. I ask him, why didn't he simply adopt that position in the missiles debate too? After all it was pointless to say "No". Every rejected proposal of ours which contains the WHOLE message is worth a hundred times more than an accepted one which just sets about correcting the symptom without intervening in the suicidal logic of the overall process. Moreover everything confirms that the policy of correcting symptoms is irresponsible, that it is not worth one iota but adapts itself to exterminism. I have explained elsewhere that the SPD is a party of moderate exterminism.[3] With Joschka Fischer and Otto Schily[4] we are becoming a "lesser evil" of the same type. And at least with Joschka Fischer it is clear how he has come to that. We should all realize that total catastrophe is inevitable without a radical change, without a leap in consciousness, but he considers only small steps possible. He doesn't want to tackle at all the very problem which gave rise to the Greens. And the small steps that he would like to take have nothing at all to do with the lifesaving mission of the Eco-Peace movement but with the specific conditions of reproduction of the countercul- ture, the protest movement, in short, the alternative "scene". We are to be one lobby amongst others. He just wants to ensure that we should be able to continue to act "rebelliously", in conformity with the wingeing culture of our clients.

For Joschka Fischer it was not the betrayal but the transforma- tion of Green principles which began in Hesse. According to his own logic, he is right. This starts from the assumption that, as you can read in *Der Spiegel* (1984/9), our whole society is united on the necessity of ecology, even the power-workers' union now recognizing economy and ecology as of equal importance. If someone is as "green"-minded as the power-workers' union it is easy for them to see Green principles at work in a budget tailored to reflating the economy. Joschka thinks that the Greens have buried their heads in the compost and haven't even noticed that everyone now considers ecology important; nor that the ruling bloc, unlike in Schmidt's time, presents itself once more classically divided into two; nor finally that the train to eco-industrialization, as taught by Joseph Huber,[5] the secret guiding spirit of the whole Green reformist trend, has long since departed.

The change in consciousness – and this goes deep into the Greens, Fischer with his power-workers' union is no exception – up till now amounts to the firm intention of reformist tinkering that changes nothing essential whatsoever.

The split in the ruling bloc hardly carries their rift deeper than the uppermost tenth of the consensus which calls itself the "common ground of all democracies", but actually means the foundations of the "German model". If at the moment the SPD is the first reserve for the system, then the attempt to commit us to a hasty reintegration into the right-left pattern ends up by making the Greens into a second line of defence.

Joschka thinks we overlook the basic fact "that West German industry is undergoing a massive restructuring process which has fairly quietly been taking place for years, hidden behind mass unemployment and the collapse of whole branches of industry". His concern is that we should in good time tag along in the correct and inevitable direction of growth, that we shouldn't arrive too late to profit properly from it.

Like Joseph Huber, his mentor, it doesn't seem to bother Joschka that this whole perspective is that of a metropolitan luxury class. Seen on a world scale the *whole* alternative scene in the rich countries, at least insofar as they are mainly bothered about reproducing their own conditions in conformity with the system, are just "in people", "trendies". If we build a new eco-storey onto our metropolitan industrial system here – and Joschka is covered by the notorious "investments in the future" of the Sindelfingen programme – we leave the whole of the rest of the world, degraded to the periphery, with the solid recommendation to first catch up with our auto-culture, the "good life" of Washington, London, Paris and Frankfurt.

In order for the Greens,. firmly set on parliamentarism, SPD alliance and compromise, to be fully equipped as a power factor, there is need of a proper party machine. Something must come from the party for the parliamentary groups. Therefore Joschka has good intentions for the Green party committees. They should professionalize themselves so that they can compete with the parliamentary groups' assistants, for knowledge is power; the executive committees must be geared up to attract the alternative experts, to develop a Green "think tank" so that the parliamentarians can be supplied with material relating to programme and problems. Otherwise the parliamentary group will dry up and with it the whole tulip field of the Green party, and of course even the tulips won't survive that. That all sounds well and good, but if at the end it boils down to helping industrial society into its next orbit (and that's precisely how Joschka seems to see the task of the Greens: we are to be innovative newcomers!) then I would advise the experts – stay away, it's best if you don't make any more expert reports, forget the science which feeds this dragon and enables it to add the next layer to its coat of armour.

Fischer and Huber – that's a Servan-Schreiber type alternative.[6] It suits the great Huber, who is just demanding almost two thousand million marks of investments in the European microelectronic industry, so that in future we can keep up with the Japanese.

Can the Green Party Still Be Saved? A Challenge to the Eco-socialists!

The challenges which the *Eco-Peace movement* is reacting to are one and the same. The suicidal character of our civilization which amounts to the mass extermination of humans, animals, plants and life itself, *will* find a political answer, provided the sword of Damocles does not fall.

The capacity of the Greens, i.e. the ability of the forces which are joined together in our *party*, to fill the big empty gap which is opening up there, is another matter. It is true that we have from the start had universal and fundamental social interests in mind, but each of us in their own particular way, a way also limited by traditions. In the image that we offer, not only externally but also internally, we have so far not reached seriously out beyond our particular origins, beyond the limitations of our respective milieus.

Even so, we were able straight away to occupy the vacant space, at least symbolically, more thanks to our happy choice of name than to our actual vocation of providing society with the necessary organ. There was nothing better than the Greens available, and so the population, with whatever mixed feelings, at least permitted us the claim to be the alternative to the whole traditional party spectrum, perhaps even in embroyo to the entire old institutional system. Now, all too swiftly, we have come to the point where the *subjective substance* that we brought with us, that which we were able to contribute as a direct impulse, is exhausted, quite independent of how good or how bad are our discussion papers. It is dawning on us that we are internally only a particularly exalted microcosm of bourgeois society, a pandemonium of Thomas Mann's "lost citizens" in search of more sense of community than a political party will ever offer. So now we have begun to feel cold in the big forest.

Moreover, in order to reach some kind of agreement – and we needed this, otherwise the various old dogmas wouldn't have let go of us at all – we didn't even dare attempt to achieve an intellectual integration along objectively necessary lines.

Compromises over the programme were always governed by the requirements of demarcation. So far no *unity* in diversity has come into being. Even identical statements and attitudes often conceal not only differing but even conflicting motives. The few who brought with them an identity with roots beyond the old dogmas have only shaped the party image externally, not internally.

There are no guilty parties, scarcely a single one of the participants could have acted in a significantly different manner. It is senseless to tear each other apart over the outcome so far and over the distribution of power in the party, senseless to start a new struggle against the "Z" (who are not even there any more)[7] or anyone else. The expansion of the Greens at Duisburg to include the Berlin Alternative List, and the postponement of the election to the national executive, only reflect the fact that the Greens (and this is something which I, too, among others, had wanted from the socialist conferences at the time) – have become a conglomeration of scattered socialists, even if they have now for the most part become eco-socialists, at least as they see themselves.

Certainly the people who join together in a political party are primarily those who have already lived in a party-political – i.e. power-oriented – way. If now those elements in the party who originally made the ecological start have been forced aside, if people from the former socialist forces are now putting their own previous positions back on the agenda, that is on the whole a development which has come about spontaneously. The process hasn't been ideal. But now the result has to be accepted if something productive is to come from the crisis of the Greens, which has much more to do with psychology than with a particular ideology.

Therapeutic advice is only of limited help. The real issue is the question *from where we can mobilize new substance, a new impulse*. In my opinion we can do this from two quarters, in both cases involving originally "unpolitical" resources, I mean forces which are not set in the old battle orders.

The first are the unconscious, uncommitted inner reserves of those who created the party. Now that it is no longer a case of whether the socialists from the former splinter groups and any other leftists from the 1968 tradition get a foot in the Green door or not, now that – if we still want to use the old categories – we actually are a left party with far too little "right" and "centre", the socialists must finally make up their minds not to persist in a half-baked eco-socialism with the appropriate trade-union insignia, but to "perish" into a true ecologism. I have set myself this task, as you know. If we don't all achieve this in the near future, the whole operation will prove to be a Pyrrhic victory. The Greens will die of a "socialist political initiative" which takes this name seriously, in fact of conceptual sterility. If however on the basis of a socialist "self-sacrifice" – which in essence is a new identification – we do genuinely become an "Eco-Peace party", then we shall win a new "unpolitical" influx from outside too, from the whole of society. It is another theme, to which I will return, that this does indeed presuppose a – properly understood – fundamentalist attitude. Anyhow, at the moment the eco-socialists have in their hand the key to the destiny of the Greens – and also to their own destiny. It would be a notable step forward if they could start by accepting the "non-union" understanding which Gustav Landauer expressed in 1903 in his *Call to Socialism!* (Jochen Sonn of the Daimler-Benz alternative union group reminded me of it):

"The capitalist production process is only in a negative respect a key issue in the emancipation of labour. It does not lead to socialism through its own development and its own inherent laws, nor can it be decisively transformed in favour of labour through the struggle of the workers in their role as producers – but only when the workers cease to play their role as capitalist producers . . . in this role the workers are partners in capitalism, even if their dividend is received not by them but by the capitalists, even if on all significant points they do not reap the benefits but the disadvantages of the unjust system in which they have been placed . . . *There is liberation only for those who put themselves both internally and externally in* a position to withdraw from capitalism, who cease to play *a role and begin to be human beings . . ."*

At Last a Real Debate on Strategy, and an Organ For It!

Going beyond the struggles for self-assertion between 1980 and 1983, we now need a comprehensive discussion on the character of the epoch and its challenges, on the basic line and main direction of our intervention as necessitated by it, and on the particular role of a political and parliamentary party for the Eco-Peace movement. This will result in a realistic strategy in the institutions. Since we are talking about a discussion on perspective and programme, we must create an appropriate council, commission, or whatever the child's name is to be. It is time for an ecological manifesto, and it is clear that such organs as the national executive and the national committee, which were created to carry out ongoing work, and not equipped with programme-making authority, are not able to do this themselves. It is equally obvious that the sum of programme-linked activity allocated to the national work groups cannot yet add up to a whole.

Above all: as yet the inner, social-psychological structure of the work groups still reflects the period of struggles over line which led to the compromise formulae from Saarbrücken to Sindelfingen, and these are no longer sufficiently loadbearing. What we need now is not a settlement on paper which will also do for the future; but to set up a framework for discussion beyond the old trench warfare, where we don't rush once more into action – that is, into adopting compromise papers – but where light is first shed quietly on the whole circle of problems. Such a commission would not simply duplicate the work group themes, nor would it be a place of proportional representation for the various lines – because it would be senseless to work by votes rather than on the consensus principle. It would just be a case of having all lines and their significant nuances represented. Then the first act would be for the participants to offer mutual insights into the motives behind their positions and their intellectual approaches. If for some of us *bürgerlich* is a term of abuse, while others define ourselves positively as *Bürger*, then it is not absolutely certain what is meant in each case.[8] Even then you won't be able to get the definition clarified to the minutest degree, but in a group which is not too large you can recognize what each individual means by the words they select. The commission would also have to organize guest speakers to expound "neutrally" upon a particular topic, from which one could peg out markers. The question is whether in the meantime and in view of the inner-party crisis we think ourselves capable of creating such an organ and of linking its activity continually through well-organized processes of communication with the grassroots, with all levels of the party structure and also with the representatives in parliament.

A true Eco-Peace party will then arise regardless of any structural trouble resulting from ego weaknesses of the participants, and the wrangling will lose its importance. The party will be driven forward by the polarity between its parliamentary representatives and a base which is chiefly movement-oriented but intervenes by means of ballots. Then the executive bodies which lie between the two can happily continue with their debates on structure and ballots for position; it will be of no particular interest to anybody which sentence is accepted and which other one rejected.†

Unless we develop as an intellectually fully independent Eco-Peace party we shall in a very short time have exhausted our symbolic bonus. Our practitioners of realpolitik hardly realize that they would never have got even the minimal chance they have at present without the "transcendental" image of the Greens. Conditioned by our own indecisiveness, the voters want us to square the circle, to horsetrade with the SPD *and* to maintain our credibility. Let us suppose that we had had the will

---

†I don't know whether all delegates have seen the proposal from the Günzberg district association that in future no decisions on line should be taken at the *Länder* or national level, and that even at the national delegate conference there should only be preliminary discussions on the conceivable alternatives at any given time. All the reasons the Günzberg people put forward are sound. Ballots, because they favour both the responsibility of members and their skill, are the nucleus of the proposals. A party which supports the popular ballot in the framework of society as a whole cannot practise anything other than the same principle in its own ranks.

and the strength to insist upon our alternative demand. According to my understanding sufficient people, particularly women, would have accepted that political ability in our case doesn't mean we must be capable of an alliance and ready to compromise with a party pursuing an objective diametrically opposed to ours.

Neither would these people have reproached us for refusing to take joint responsibility for the overall course which we have entered the arena to oppose. If you refuse to contemplate participating in government – and you contemplate it as soon as you start to *negotiate* about toleration or such like – you will once again be as clearly recognizable as the Greens generally were in the beginning. At that time we simply addressed a different wavelength in our supporters' spectrum of expectations. It is not our voters but we ourselves who want the small quick successes. We don't teach our voters about the SPD but allow *ourselves* to be taught that this cat is in the process of becoming vegetarian.

The "shared responsibility" line takes it for granted that we and the others share the same basic consensus. We start from the opposite assumption, namely that the institutions function irresponsibly and can certainly not be corrected in the short term. We do not maintain that this is because someone like Lothar Späth is not a human being.[9] We're not even doing the human being Lothar Späth a favour if we become predictable. Even for his tactical calculations in the CDU/CSU he can make much better use of us as a potential threat. If we get mixed up with the chief minister of Baden-Württemberg, or of Hesse, nothing at all can come of it other than a Green contribution to the business of leading the people as peacefully as possible into catastrophe. Without a break in institutional continuity or a thrust of movement consciousness into the institutional territory, the apparatus *can't* function any differently. Instead of making people ever more deeply conscious of this, we cooperate in nurturing the illusion that the institutions as they are can pursue rescue policies – the citizens can let things be for the Greens are there. During this collaboration many things may "rub off" – if I guide a stream towards the wrong mill, some water still runs wide of the mark and the grass can grow. But in this way we are pursuing our case only by grinding other people's corn, 5 per cent for us, 95 per cent for them. Even the Württemberg and still more so the Baden bourgeoisie were more demanding in the last century.

Within the framework of the material constraints which they have set and which at the same time govern them, the other parties can pursue no other goal than to stabilize our society on its course to catastrophe. To do this they must try to bring the symptoms of the crisis of civilization under control. Our assistance in doing this will always be welcome. If we subordinate ourselves to their perspectives, which with "power sharing" at 5 per cent is inevitable – then we shall not only fail to generate correct awareness, but will help in the generation of false awareness. Whatever we can achieve with our 5 per cent will inevitably benefit the overall course of the other parties, who must produce little consolations to comfort society. Does Winfried Kretschmann[10] believe that he and his friends would in the past four years – if they had had the opportunity to collaborate in government – have been able to remove anything of the fundamental burden of the ecological crisis? Will the state of Hesse in 1987 be closer to or further from ecological collapse? What are we really doing for the general consciousness if by our assistance in patching up we help to conceal that the decisive radical treatment is not being carried out? *That* proof, that measures are being taken to "prevent the worst", is needed by the power structure itself.

Let the SPD Stew Instead of Putting It Back On Its Feet and Helping It Govern

At present we are doing whatever we can to help the SPD stabilize itself around the union type Holger Börner.[11] The SPD for its part sees the object of its *de facto* coalition with us as to tie us up in such a way that we "can do no harm". It is no coincidence that it was Walter Scheel, the ex-President and specialist in state consensus, who even before the change in Bonn insisted that the SPD must go into opposition in order to recapture the Eco-Peace movement and not permit the Greens to consolidate a truly independent alternative to the whole of the existing party system. Meantime the magazine *Kapital* preaches to the stupid people in the CDU/CSU that they should understand that the Social-Democrats must veer even further to the left – of course for the general good!

When after the 1982 Hesse election Willy Brandt expressed an interest in a "majority this side of the CDU" he saw that the SPD only retains a chance of continuing to govern the Federal Republic if it can politically subordinate the Eco-Peace forces. In the long term the Social-Democrats are dependent on us for their ministerial seats in the Federal parliament and the *Länder*. If now we and not the Social-Democrats are suddenly in a tight spot, the sole cause of that is the sycophantic SPD connection in our own ranks, which in the meantime has been openly displayed. From a mistaken reading of the history of the Federal Republic, many of us know no greater spectre than a Grand Coalition. We are trapped by the question of whether we want to permit the right to govern the country when the SPD could also do it with our help, and we don't even take proper account that the movements can always press more strongly upon the establishment with the SPD in opposition than with the SPD in power. The whole right-left question has not the slightest to do with the ecological crisis because the SPD, with the unions behind it, is at least the equal of the CDU as a party of expansion. All those who give priority to the right-left scheme of things subject themselves from the start to the SPD criterion and can only construct a dependent position for the Greens, even if they might have had completely different intentions. That is the case with the Hamburg people and the real reason for their not wanting to relinquish the "toleration" formula.

Because we fear a Grand Coalition, and because we lack a minimum of historical awareness about the old SPD, which has survived from the defunct workers' movement of the nineteenth century, we have not appreciated the trump card we hold in our hand as a result of the dependence – which is more than just numerical – of the SPD upon us. Even if we sometimes somewhere fall below the 5 per cent level, the Social-Democrats will still miss our votes. But we would have lost in any case if in 1987 we seriously have to worry about 5 per cent. For that would mean that we are only of use to the voters as an alibi: *dixi et salvavi animam meam* – I have voted and saved my soul. That can only happen to us if we allow our own image (in case we still have one) to stagnate into the left Social-Democratic/Green blend with which we went into the 1983 election.

Even if we take the point of view that it is a question of changing the SPD, we would – and in this I agree with Hamburg – have to practise the exact opposite of what we showed in Hesse. The idea of a "thorn in the flesh of the SPD" is limited enough, but for Borner we were not even that, but rather a currycomb which made his tangled mane shine again. The fact that the SPD has so far not treated us with the full disdain we deserve can only be explained by its own predicament. Brandt recently hinted at it tactically when he expressed the wish to bring together a majority against the right within his own party alone.

Naturally, after all our wobbling about, a Grand Coalition in Hesse would *now* have injured us more than the SPD (although even that is not absolutely certain). Things would look quite different if we had gone into both Hesse elections with a clear course of unavailability, and had therefore from the start declared to the public: "You know our indispensable demands, they should also be yours. It is not a catalogue of items to choose from.

We want a different overall course, and that should become visible through a change of direction that we cannot realistically expect from the SPD, at least not now – for we have not yet even come close to softening them up, and are far too weak to do so. 'We don't want to act as if a 'red-green coalition'[6] was on the horizon." With this position we would most probably have got a few less first-ballot votes and a few more second-ballot ones than we in fact got. The lack of a clear image which was our striking feature in Hesse and which is attributable to the mediocrity of our self-expectations is a much greater handicap than the same lack of clear image amongst our voters. In their heads it would have said something in our favour that we want to be a party which can wait – if we had only been forthright about it. Anyone who is afraid about whether we get in or not, or who believes we won't come back if we get thrown out somewhere again – even in Baden-Württemberg – simply underestimates us. Or, to put the opposite case: such an easy end to the Greens would merely prove that it wasn't the last word in wisdom to want to confront this unique challenge by means of a parliamentary party.

In Hesse in any case we wouldn't have been thrown out. In that case Börner would have immediately been faced with the dilemma of either continuing to muddle along or of entering into a Grand Coalition. First we would have been blamed for the "ungovernability" of Hesse and threatened with a third ballot. Then we would have had to calmly go through with it. A Grand Coalition is just what he wouldn't have wanted, having regard to Bonn in 1987. I remember the Frankfurt discussion with Peter Glotz[12] in 1982 when the gist of what he said was: "We won't do you the favour of a Grand Coalition, because we don't want you to reach 15 per cent in the process".

Really, our virtue should be the patience to wait. Let us leave the SPD to stew in its dilemma until we can guarantee the necessary change of direction, still from a minority position but one which is historically stronger than theirs. And in the meantime let us make sure that the CDU falls into an analogous dilemma. (The whole of the present discussion bars any broader access to it for us, because even without Otto Schily's generous words we are in the position of junior partners of the SPD; the toleration idea alone is sufficient to hold us fast in a position where we can only tug backwards and forwards between our own and the SPD's voters.)

Anyone who says we can't afford this patience because a) it is "five minutes to midnight" and b) we would lose the contest, is above all mistaken in one assumption, i.e. that the Greens would really be important if these two objections were correct. If we see ourselves as weak people in a hurry and then consider the real dimension of the ecological crisis, it would be best for us to go straight home, for we won't stop anything and won't change any other party. Given the present mentality of the Greens, and if an eco-libertarian toleration concept[13] next comes to join the eco-socialist one, I predict that with the worsening of the whole situation and if we survive our indecisiveness, in the foreseeable future there will be a "responsible" Very Grand Coalition, *with* the Greens, a triumvirate à la Börner/Schily/Späth. There may be other names. It will be an unspoken colonialist plot, of course with a nice development aid policy.

It is Not Toleration but Fundamental Opposition that Will Preserve the Green Project

What is fundamentalism? Externally it puts ecology before economics, and fundamental, long-term interests before immediate short-term ones. (Priority does not mean exclusivity, but keeping to a rank order.) Simply in order to survive it has to be a policy with spiritual impetus and moral standard. A policy of conversion in the metropolises begins with the readiness to change oneself, and in a certain sense with the self-sacrifice of the bourgeois individual, at least in his characteristic of "Roman citizen" who enjoys the advantages of belonging to the exploitative centre of the world. Huber's eco-reformism has for us precisely the function of temptation: to show us once more "the kingdoms of the Earth and their glory". Despite all we know we would still like to continue our tourism around the world and not forfeit any luxury, even if we can't have it all without getting the Bomb into the bargain.

Those who stand for the transition from Having to Being must make it clear that this means a change in values such as can only succeed through what up till now has been described as a religious experience. "Transformations can only come from the transformed." Changes in the material foundation of civilization, a farewell to the Big Machine, the industrial disarmament of the rich countries, presuppose the breakup of the spiritual cement. But that requires a social context which emboldens people to expose their character armour even though (and because) the danger is growing! What is coming goes deeper than all the political and social revolutions Europe has seen since the transition from Antiquity to the Middle Ages. Radical ecologism is only the external side of preparedness for this radical change.

Obviously fundamentalism is made comparatively harmless if you reduce your conflict with realpolitik to the inconsiderable difference between going along with cosmetic measures against the ecological crisis and a merely rhetorical "No". Fundamentalism can never prove itself to be constructive or destructive by the *objects* that are dealt with in parliament because it is aimed at the *attitudes*. The dynamic of the industrial system can only be stopped in external reality after it has disintegrated in its motivation.

Insofar as we have a role to play on the official stage – what is that role? A parable play by Friedrich Dürrenmatt shows the last Roman emperor, Romulus Augustus (looking old: in fact he died very young) in the middle of his flock of chickens. His sycophants are besieging him, begging him to dedicate himself to the affairs of government, above all to military matters. For the leader of the Germanii, Odoacre, is before the gates. Meanwhile the emperor remains stupidly inactive. In the end it turns out that he only took on the office in the beginning so that nobody else could cause any harm by *doing* something. For he came to power with the understanding that Rome was not worth defending.

We are told that we should change the SPD and improve the government. Our actual fundamentalist duty is to nurture in every person we meet in the institutions the mentality of the stage emperor Romulus Augustus. Anyone among us who wants to carve out an up-to-date plan for overall repair, which means quite automatically a solution in the grand style from above, presupposing a well-oiled state, has not understood at all that a world is disintegrating, that this disintegration is the best thing about it and that we must say "Yes" to it and assist it as far as possible. Let us distribute as much as we can out of the coffers of military and industrial armaments, rationalization and modernization! Economic policy juggling instead of sour-faced help with the restoration of bankrupt and anachronistic industries. "Only tribes will survive", that is, new communities, to some extent unprecedented, this time consciously chosen by us, in which we first of all must transform ourselves.

I am deliberately speaking casually and lightly about serious economic matters because the fixation with economics is today *the* Marxist original sin. One doesn't need to be against the 35-hour week in order to place far less emphasis on the flop which is what the campaign as a whole must turn out to be. The solution of the crisis of civilization demands a completely different perspective, and in order to get anywhere near this, we must throw off this craving and sickness for legitimization from the material, bureaucratic and psychological structure of this grave that calls itself the national economy.

Where should one look? Arnold Toynbee in his investigation

into world history generalizes (I am referring here to the introduction by Jonas Cohn to the German edition of Toynbee's *A Study of History*) about what happens at the collapse of cultures or civilizations and what mechanisms repeat themselves in their crises. He speaks of decline and disintegration. Decline is a splitting of society and of the soul. (If society and soul are fatally wrongly programmed, it is naturally lifesaving for human beings to permit this splitting instead of treating it, as we do, as a dark plot of reaction and rushing in to push everything back together again.) It is out of the situation of splitting that Toynbee bases his peculiar concept of the proletariat which differs from the usual one: the great majority of a society sense when the *leading* minority ceases to be creative. Only then is this minority seen as a *ruling* one and loses its actual right. Then the whole of the non-ruling majority gradually becomes an "internal proletariat". "The true mark of the proletarian condition is neither poverty nor humble origin, but rather the awareness of being robbed of one's inheritance, one's place in society, and being unwanted in a community in which one has a native right, as well as the resentment that flows from this awareness. This internal proletarian condition is compatible with the possession of material resources."

Thus this is a *very far-reaching concept of marginalization* which in the next moment turns into something positive.

Toynbee shows that if partially creative forces still remain in the ruling minority, they found a philosophy and the officials trained in it build up a universal state. (In our case the whole political and administrative organization of the "Western" metropolis, with the supranational bureaucracies on top.) But the internal proletariat creates a higher religion which often, as in the case of Christianity, stems from another culture and develops into a universal church; and which explores the transition to a new culture.

From the perspective of the Englishman Toynbee, it would not be particularly surprising that so many Indians now render development aid in spirituality to the Europeans and Americans.

It is natural that other traditions, for example the Indian, will flow into the synthesis, as well as sources belonging to the culture itself – Jesus and Christ, liberated from their churches. A particular reason for something quite new to emerge is the decay of patriarchy, so that a new masculine monotheism is impossible.

This religious renaissance which is not an economic thing, and which in the final analysis will turn out to be a process of *rise* in consciousness and not a regression, is the living seed of the next social order, which for want of a better expression I will call the

"Ecopax formation". This renaissance is as yet not a great river but it is already moving in countless brooks and rivulets. The many new sects (what does it matter, the Christians started as a sect too!) are sure signs. Otherwise it would hardly be possible to explain how even a new *political* party like the Greens has from the start – usually shamefacedly denied – a spiritual component, conspicuous enough in a personality like Petra Kelly. The Greens are clearly a grouping beyond the anti-religious Enlightenment, even if this feature, *the most dangerous for the establishment* and the loadbearing base of the fundamentalist tendency, is for the moment being concealed. In the Eco-Peace movement it cannot be concealed at all, it is its essence!

The Dove On the Roof

If Ecotopia is merely Utopia in the sense of a cheap castle in the air, then we have no future at all. The Eco-Peace movement exists only insofar as there are areas of hope in the psychological energy budget of very many people which push out beyond the whole existing civilization. It is not a case – and Joschka Fischer is right in recognizing this as impossible – of presenting a new state-fixated "total solution". All projects for rebuilding the Big Machine are wrong from the very start. We must let them decay and draw the life blood out of them. We must make a much more comprehensive reality than Karl Liebknecht[14] imagined out of his formula "Not a man (and of course not a woman either) and not a penny for this system!" What we are talking about are "places" located outside the system where we can withdraw from it, in such an attractive concentration of human energy that the Big Machine is abandoned as once were the pyramids of Teotihuacan. External, geographical space is not a problem, for that is there. On a fifth of the arable land in the Federal Republic production is currently being prevented or destroyed. The appropriation and the acquisition of land for it begins *internally*, with the development of psychological preparedness for the departure into new contexts of life and the spiritual joining together of many who give each other the confidence of being able to do without the safety net of the old society.

If there is a social task, and dependent upon it also a political task, it is the task of organizing this departure and of giving it a community character and a political protection. The first is the meaning of the alternative movement in the broadest sense, and at the same time I believe that a special initiatory role will fall to a spiritual community movement. The second is the meaning of the Green party. Anyone who comes to the defence of realpolitik with the argument about the will of the voters is completely bypassing the historical situation and laying down the yardstick of conformism in the alternative camp as an advance guard of the old powers. Even the Green voters only stand outside the old consensus with one part of their energies, and even among them it is completely normal for this share to be *quantitatively* less than 50 per cent. For the Eco-Peace movement is not a crowd of demonstrators that can be counted, but rather the non-integrated sum of emancipatory, system-transcending consciousness, at first usually still atomized, of desires to drop out or change one's path, of preparedness and will for change.

Is there really then no possibility of basically using the parliamentary position only for this function of encouragement of and protection for an exodus from the suicidal system? That does not exclude anything that is currently being done in a merely reformist sense. What is aimed at often doesn't rest in the measures themselves but in the way they are ordered and related. It is not true that there are no proposals for this. I refer you to my contributions of the past two years. I don't maintain these are any more than outlines, but they would have long since been implemented, and not chiefly by me, if the Greens had ever really tackled the basic position from which I am starting. Even in the Frankfurt town hall there have so far been only a few signs of fundamentalist politics. Embedded in the total development of our party, they couldn't avoid allowing themselves to be completely preoccupied with the substance and the feasibility, the handicaps and alternatives of the system. If we want to arrive at Ecotopia we must not work towards renovating Frankfurt but rather towards clearing and dismantling it. Above all our conduct must display this *ideological* orientation. We must leave completely behind us the politics of a "bird in the hand", because this time no bird will be of any use to us if we don't capture the dove on the roof. And by catching sparrows we won't learn how to trap doves – one needs completely different skills for that.

Perhaps one can summarize the problem with a quote from Gregory Bateson of the Esalen Institute in California. In 1970 he wrote: "In medicine, symptoms are treated without an attempt to cure the sickness itself if and only if the sickness either signals a definite demise or else will heal of itself."

Since we are agreed that the disease – and Bateson was referring to the ecological crisis – will not disappear of its own accord, the whole strategy of wanting to "prevent the worst" means that we have accepted death. "Let us alleviate the pain of the patient who is in any case bound to die." Or as the proverb has it: "Eat, drink and be merry, for tomorrow we die." Euthanasia as Green politics. Bateson had ascertained that: "All ad hoc measures leave the deeper causes of the problem undisturbed, and, what is still worse, actually tend to reinforce and concentrate it."[15]

This precisely is the accusation we must raise against the whole line of realpolitik.

In the face of the total catastrophe which is emerging from the womb of Western civilization to fall upon the whole of humanity, and which is inevitable if we don't get at its roots, we cannot afford any more reformist half-measures. Small obstructions and small gains serve no purpose, they rather act as diversions, quite apart from the fact that we can force the others to deliver more of them if we build up a real pressure for transformation. (The comparisons with the KPD/SPD relationship in the Weimar republic, I can't go into more detail here, are wrong both in substance and as regards the structure of the problems.)

The Austrian feminist Judith Jannberg, who came via a completely different path from Bateson to more or less the same conclusion, advises: "Take ourselves and our progress as living beings most seriously and refuse to cooperate in the patriarchal final solution. Thus withdrawal, exit, evading the justice and the tendency to dominate of the man/men. Drain the institutions of the internal and external forces of occupation. Don't squander any forces on reform. Save our strengths and dedicate them to psychological-spiritual growth." That message is valid not only for women. Where and how shall we position our forces? If we impale ourselves on the dead structures, we won't bring about any new culture. Green assemblies and discussions for the most part fit completely into the whole of the rest of the dying culture. We are wasting a lot of energy and time by investing it in postponing rather than exposing the final solution. The only work which will stop the apocalypse is to cleanse and assemble the psychological forces for an Ecopax formation of biophile culture.

Are We Heading In or Out?

Dear Greens,

It would take a good two hours to deliver the whole of the political blueprint which I have brought to this conference. So I must give you a shorter text which concentrates more on the political level – even though our problems can't be solved at this level in the long run. Afterwards my more detailed efforts, of which only a small part could be put directly into my speech, will also be available. But it all belongs together.

At this conference we shall still not be conducting any new debate on our programme, but I hope that we shall trigger one off. My intervention will certainly not be conclusively dealt with here. You will take the paper with you to read and examine at leisure, distribute it and discuss it in your local associations. We urgently need the concept of "think global" to be more systematically associated again with "act local" among our grassroots. Right at the end of their democracy paper, the eco-libertarians quote an old resolution of the Günzberg district association,[1] which I also continued to recommend in our central committee straight after the parliamentary election. It concerns postal ballots on alternative political courses. If indeed every member is to have a say in our political line and if we can concentrate more on actions again and not just on parliamentary work, our party can perhaps still be saved from slipping away.

I have been here five years now. But I feel the same as I did seven years ago – in a position of extreme resistance. I will be as clear now as I was then. I will distinguish between friend and foe in our own ranks as clearly as I did then. Only it is even more important *now and here*, for the headquarters of the destruction of humanity is here, not there.

What I am saying here is not intended as a testament but should point to a beginning. The fundamentalists will either give the whole party a new basic direction – out of and not into the system, and that will be decided in the foreseeable future – or they will go off in their own basic direction. That will be above all a new unification with the movement. Is it dead, as some say? There are flies which only live for a few seconds, but they might have the bad luck to see only the trough of a wave.

If I am not very much mistaken, my present political blueprint, the genesis of which anyone who wants to can understand by reading my writings of the last two years, is in substance getting back to my book *The Alternative*. That also has to do with an alliance, a personal alliance, which I entered into, and which for me is linked with having one's roots in the people. You see, Christine Schröter, since we have become ever closer in the past year and a half, has had a great influence on the spirit and decisiveness of my position.[2]

And now I am not going to talk out of the window but only relentlessly inwards. Those people outside who are open to the message will be able to find out the truth. If some of it should have the effect of putting a bit of a stop to our meteoric climb into electoral favour – so be it, or perhaps even, so much the better. Do we at least all share a strange feeling about it? Plants which grow too fast bend over particularly easily.

The Greens have come into existence at the edge, on the border of this society. They have something to do both with its mechanisms of exclusion and with its decline, which leads to a situation where even without the direct intention of those in power, people fall out of the system or – in the most significant cases – tend to drop out of their own accord, in order to start up something new outside the gates.

One cannot settle permanently on the border. Naturally there are in the field just described people who were mainly unhappy at not being allowed to be in on things, at not being admitted. Now that the movements have forced the system to open a chink in the door, they want to go in. And to some extent the system says: "Hurry, hurry up, and please close the door behind you". Obviously they would like to have a clear separation again: here the fresh green solidarity of all democrats, there the usual small radical minority who want not to repair the environment but to change the system. If at this congress I put my money on a polarization in our party, it is precisely so as not to permit this social polarization again.

The border now for our party is a frontier station. The trains are already standing at various platforms pointing in opposite directions. Or rather, one train, that is our train, is still standing. We linger, resisting. We still haven't got the engine under steam for departure. It is also through our failure that many people who don't quite know exactly where they want to go even though they do want to move, get into the other train, jumping into it as it slowly starts to move, back to the metropolis and up into the power centre of the old world. Should we fundamentalists then perhaps travel along with them as partisans, in order to preserve the unity of the party and to stop the door being closed completely to them? All in all that will mean an even greater flow of power back into the system. What is the point if we devote all our strength to building a bit of a blockade on the line and then settle ourselves in the driving cabin? It must be our goal to get back out of the other train everyone who has seen the faintest glimmer of light that something different should actually be happening. And as for the stokers and drivers of this train, we should without regret let them disappear where they belong. Only they should not be allowed to take the party, these still ever-hopeful Greens, with them. Therefore for the present – and in my opinion until we have got rid of the worst – we need polarization. It should be absolutely clear what is at stake and what decisions each of us is taking. That interests me also in respect of the new elections to the national executive. If you want to elect a committed representative of participation in government like Norbert Kostede from Bielefeld, then please don't do it on the basis of the principle of balance, or because you want to see this position represented, but because you want *him*, because you are in favour of his line. I would be grateful for every bit of truth I discover in this way. It worries me that even Lukas Beckmann seems to be thinking in a state and SPD-oriented way. What I would like from you tomorrow is absolute clarity. You say – at least this is the sort of perspective one picks up from you – that the question of an alliance will be decided by the peace question. Are you going to ask the SPD whether they want to go along with us in "living without arms" – or rather how much cheaper they are going to make the army for us? If the latter, you are helping to divert us from our task of revealing the secret suppressed in the consciousness of the population – that low-flying fighters don't in the first instance signify noise pollution, but above all preparation for war. We can't go on any longer now without this absolute clarity.

Spiritually, the people of our country are still moving – too slowly, but nonetheless quite surely – towards the exit. That is why it is so important for those in power to gather quickly to themselves in the opposite train those Greens who hitherto were ambivalent, as an "anti-party party" (as a party concerned with parliament and the state we are halfway there already, the rest depends on the gradient), so that the population travels politically into a void. As a precaution it is to be robbed and dispossessed of the embryonic political structure which it had in us. That is happening now *inside* the Green party, it is being dispossessed of its original base. Gruhl and Springmann would not have tried to do what Schily, Fischer and Waltraud Schoppe want to do with us.[3]

The ruling bloc from Geissler to Glotz has clearly recognized the problem. Therefore they are trying to browbeat us into sharing responsibility for the death spiral they are fuelling with big money and big industry. In the face of the overwhelming pressure and suction, the previous executive committee has perceived it to be in the interest of the whole movement to resist the trend towards selling out cheaply – however skilfully or unskilfully it did so, there was nothing else it could do. Whether it is emphasized or not, you should not allow to disappear behind this admittedly important question the even more important one, indeed the decisive one, of where the train should be heading – in or out?

Even if most "Realos" [advocates of realpolitik], apart from certain cynics who want nothing but a share in power, somewhere in their hearts want fundamental change – and I still believe that even of someone like Karl Kerschgens[4] – then we must for once clarify right down to foundations what it means for the counter-power – still in a minority, insecure, and unclear in its objectives as it is – to ally itself with one of the oldest main forces of the status quo, a force which has long become totally and with full consciousness a serviceable sub-function of an incomparably more powerful whole. The SPD doesn't weigh even 100 grammes per kilogramme of the system. And even Herr Zimmermann[5] and his policies weigh a maximum of 150 grammes. What a project, instead of setting one's sights on the opponent's bulk, to want to keep on bolstering up this SPD which is dependent upon it. You want to lead it back to unity of word and deed, and then together with you it will fundamentally change the total structure from within, this structure which is thundering towards the valley like an avalanche that has been amassing for 400 years.

For us it is a totally different function of the SPD – and the unions – which is really interesting, namely their function as an institutional prison for people who have entrusted themselves to the protection which the power of organization offers or appears to offer. Prison walls must fall down, rather than being newly cemented by us. That means that we should welcome, encourage, permit this inner decay of these old, state-bearing organizations, which presupposes putting our confidence into something completely different from a junior partnership. Many Greens know already – and even at right angles to the sides in our dispute – that in the final analysis the issue will be fought out between green and black [i.e. Christian-Democrat], and green will be victorious, in whatever manifestation.

But now comes the snag, and I am telling you that we shall

come to a split over it if you carry on as you have been doing – I can't do anything about it, it is inherent in the thing itself. Already now, in the carry-on over an alliance with the SPD – and regardless of what you as individuals write in your papers, for the moment I am not interested in the outcome of negotiations, in the SPD itself it had been decided since 1900 as a result of the general climate what they would do in 1914 – already now you are deciding that we shall afterwards have a similar relationship *with the CDU*, as Joschka Fischer said to Heiner Geissler in his revealing *Spiegel* interview. For the two parties are in complete agreement in their basic decisions on foreign policy, as befits accomplices in the world metropolis which wants to keep at bay the other centre to the East and keep in with the periphery on the South for purposes of exploitation – if only Eastern "totalitarianism" doesn't get in the way. One can then argue about methods, Brandt doesn't want war against Nicaragua either. Fischer – with a catch in his throat, because we have here this ridiculous pacifism – represents the same position as Mitterrand.

"Switching around" – this solution which Klingelschmitt of the Hesse alliance propounds so incessantly in the *Tageszeitung*, will lead to something else which we can't possibly have intended; the Greens will help bring about the final imperial restoration in this country. I firmly believe, no, I know, that most "Realos" go along with this without coming close to realizing it. Yet it is so simple, one can read it in the person of Otto Schily, who at least is no parvenu if Philipp Rosenthal[6] can acclaim him as a future vice-chancellor; this system here has survived "red reformism" fundamentally unaltered, the "red" chancellor Brandt. It will also not only survive, but turn to its advantage, green reformism and a green chancellor.

Jürgen Maier, formally you are right in your criticism of our proposal in the *Tageszeitung*.[7] But this is what Rainer and I want primarily to stop – admittedly in a defensive way, so that in the rush for the state coach they don't carry along from the outset the fundamental basis we once had: of being the alternative to all the old parties, and hence to the whole system whose expression and organ they are. For me this text is only a minimum position. The party should assert that it does *not* want this Green restoration with which we are to rush to the aid of the old power structure at the precise moment when at least its legitimation is melting away like snow in the spring sunshine.

I presume that Rainer Trampert also knows that we can't hold things in check like that indefinitely. What we have to present in response to the "Realos" is not primarily more papers, but a movement in the opposite direction. Exit! Out! Even talk about the contents we are supposed to tie the alliance to is deceptive. *What* are we supposed to tie to the contents? The alliance after all! Our proposal, Rainer, has been publicly interpreted as if we were simply raising the price for the SPD. And others will rightly hold it against us – it contradicts the clarity which I demanded earlier on – if we speak of toleration, but set the price and the pain barrier (even the words indicate the lousy politics) so high that no cooperation – what a pity! – can come about.

We won't win anything in this way, least of all people. And we are obscuring the very break that I want to illuminate. After all toleration is at present the magic hat of those who are *for* and not against going in. The difference between coalition and toleration is the difference between open and bashful collaboration with power. Toleration as a tactic leads to an own goal, as in Hamburg. This kind of tactic is a rudiment of our earlier skateboarding. You will lose everything you have gained or think you have gained by it, if you don't discard it. If all you want is to retain your position, you will soon be collaborating in realpolitik, for want of an alternative.

The question is whether we tackle the central core of the avalanche, its material mass, the industrial hardware and software, so to speak – i.e. whether we want to regard it simply as bankrupt. As in combatting the military system, here too only a basic position of "living without arms" will help. I want to use a real-political proposal, which as far as commitment goes seems genuinely to have been made with fundamentalist intent, in order to demonstrate what it is all about. You dear Lauenburg people, with your proposal about the dying forests, should definitely recognize yourselves in the role I have just attributed to the "Realos". That is why I am hopeful, because it will be the same with the majority of the "Realos": they know not what they do, or what is the actual consequence of their approach.

What is it that the Lauenburg people, fundamentally disturbed by the death of the forests, are proposing? At the symbolic level something radical, which helps to create consciousness! That the foresters should plant no more trees because there's no longer any point in it. Greens against tree-planting! Awake! awake! they say. And how, by expressing yourselves in that way, do you intend to renovate the environment? Not by putting an end to the sources of harmful substances, but by reducing these substances. Faster towards the catalytic converters for the next boom in the car industry? As realpolitikers you compare hopelessly badly with the radical ecologist Joschka Fischer, this windbag in economics, this lover of the money economy which ensures the freedom of the alternative individual! How many *millions* are there then in the forestation budget with which you want first to renovate earth, water, air, so that the forests grow again? I don't know either, but in any case it can only be *millions*. But Joschka is demanding from Geissler 50 to 100 *thousand millions* for the purpose. On top of that, these don't necessarily have to be worked for, they must be got primarily through careful management, from nature, from the world market, or rather the Third World, from women, from the general human resources here – *through industry.*

In the conservative *Wormser Zeitung* there was a series of articles, not just about dioxin and similar super-products which, like the nuclear bomb, sometimes divert attention from the fundamental burden of our whole military and industrial armament, but actually about this fundamental burden itself. The industrial waste that emanates from the Rhine-Main area is causing the water table to stagnate to a depth of 200 metres, and the effect can no longer be controlled. The recorded level of halogenous hydrocarbons – approximately half of large-scale chemical production – is rising, also of course over those who use them. And in agriculture BASF and the Common Market (don't let's withdraw, but get in there too, improve Strasbourg!) ensure that the nitrate content in the water has multiplied tenfold in the past 100 years. The *Wormser Zeitung* basically suggests that there should be more inspectors; and locally we should always have very exact measurement, in order to prove what is evident: that industry will put an end to us if we just wait a little while. Green helplessness is deep-rooted.

A certain Wilhelm Knabe,[8] scarcely to be believed, is of the opinion that we shouldn't try to close down the lignite mines in North-Rhine Westphalia, because that can't be negotiated. Wilhelm *wants* to save the forests. So because he doesn't dare to be shameless, out of the bashful fundamentalist there develops a practitioner of realpolitik. And you *really* don't want to be, Wilhelm, I know that.

You people from Lauenburg, the forestation budget only has any sense at all if lignite is no longer mined and if BASF ceases operation. In any case large-scale chemical industry must not continue production in *this* way. All agreed? Yes. But one can't shut them down from one day to the next – think of the jobs! And after all they need time to switch production. The latter is closer to the real reason why we won't get them shut down overnight. For they must first of all recoup their murderous investments, and that will take a few years. They will play cat and mouse with us until kingdom come if we don't stop worrying our heads over their production-switching problems and the competitiveness of the German economy.

In any case, what is needed first is to force a general halt to research, development and production. That can be achieved by a sort of general *strike*, the possibility of which we must first introduce to the public: General strike against carrying on as before, general strike for life. And we will achieve that more quickly if for example we stuff their waste back where it came from instead of helping to get rid of it "safely".

At this level realpolitik – and our groups concern themselves with very little else – means that we try to make the dragon's armour-plating a little lighter, to clean his teeth and deodorize his bad breath and sort his excrement. If he is still not purring like a cat that's only because of our still somewhat unaccustomed ways. In Leverkusen, where the dragon has the Bayer cross on his coat of arms, he will contemplate his new – Green – deputy mayor for a while and then he will feel at ease and get to appreciate the service. For a while the fools among the parliamentarians he keeps will get worked up over how we want to change the system, whilst we meantime proffer our services as teeth-cleaners. The dragon as a whole is not so foolish, he has for example this somewhat more intelligent deputy mayor, the SPD.

No, we won't let you continue like that without a struggle. The fundamentalists or whatever they want to call themselves will get together, clarify amongst themselves how far they can unite on the position indicated in my speech and my accompanying text and then, with various emphases, turn it into a theme for debate at the grassroots. Anyway, I hope that's what will happen. Then we shall see how it progresses. We won't just loyally tolerate your march off into the institutions. You will have an insecure, if not a hostile, hinterland, and we shall try to make contact again with the autonomous forces and with those who have already left the Greens in disappointment. We shall behave like this so that at least we cannot be confused with you. If this is what we want we shouldn't bother ourselves now with places on lists. One can put a brake on the various groups better from outside than from within. We shall also be concerned with making the departure in the opposite direction into a practical proposition.

The contrast is deep. Bonn is not Hesse, where we got no further than words. *You* want participation in government and joint responsibility for this richest, most powerful European province of the empire with which the white man, irresistible through his capitalist system, has overrun the whole of humanity and driven it towards the end of history. *We* on the contrary would like to dissolve this empire, to liquidate it in the same way that one liquidates a bankrupt business, in order to save something for a new start. *We* want to keep the party in working order until the next wave of the movement. *You* would like to make it into a dependable partner for the SPD. With all your talk about authority not being won in two years and the party not putting it at risk you are hiding the real issue. The parliamentary group's report shows that in contrast to the movements you have already reached the point, collectively, where it has become a *principle* to want to "limit" everything – from armaments to experiments on animals – instead of doing away with them. So you are becoming a greater evil than the SPD, because one wouldn't think it possible that you would do the same as them in green guise.

On the question of rotation, our motives should be absolutely clear. Even two years in that spaceship are too many, or at least enough to transform half of you. We must stick resolutely to the biennial rotation, and indeed as a permanent measure.[9] But the office community of successors must be dropped, because with that it becomes exactly four years. And no colleague should stay there longer than two years. If you decide differently, it won't even come close to being a group of *our* representatives.

Even the Hesse alliance not only expressed the demobilization of the movements, but actively advanced it. What on earth will happen in the case of Bonn! In the case of an obvious change to the side of power! When even the present group treats the movements, whose representatives are not even allowed to go there any more, as troublesome beggars! Exceptions prove the rule. But hatred is welling up against us, and is only too justified.

What have we done if the typical grassroots activists are now supposed to be those shown with obvious relish in the *Tageszeitung* lobbying our glorious Wiesbaden parliamentary group and asking: "How can we realize our objectives now?" You little darlings, inside and outside the regional parliament! But there is a method to what the *Tageszeitung* is doing. The newspaper is to a great extent part of the business. I am saying that because in their position one is not a mirror but an amplifier.

In the paper Heinz Suhr, press spokesman of our parliamentary group and therefore responsible for imparting any news it has, quotes from our proposal – Rainer's and mine – the point about the link with the extra-parliamentary forces, and then goes on: "Fine – where are they, these wonderful forces? Where is the 'urgent pressure from the social movements of resistance'? If anyone has seen it anywhere, please let me know". There in classic fashion speaks the counter-attack from within one's own team. There speaks a positive interest in the death of the movement. Cynical triumph of the legacy-hunter over the very thing which has put him in that position.

At the same time how mistaken are all our people who have with such relief taken off their blockade overcoats. Previously there were movements, now there is the trough of a wave – the movement is just coming! Let us hope that we then have a Green chancellor in the next parliamentary group in Bonn, who can provide police protection for you. Many seem to have no idea of what is already happening and what is still to come.

We are no longer needed as we were in the beginning, based on the individual campaigns, to identify the individual heads which the hydra stretches out towards us. Well and good, treat them as topics for discussion in competition with the experts of the others. I fear that what Waltraud Schoppe can learn from her very esteemed SPD colleagues will help her in future to admonish the dragon even better: "Please don't spit out your fumes so unrestrainedly into the atmosphere". Our whole parliamentary group is learning well and Waltraud is one of the best.

You reformists, even you can't seriously believe that the Big Machine which is pressing us ever harder against the wall can be stopped by anything else than a popular uprising, for which our Brokdorf and Frankfurt runway demos can only have been a prologue. It is the time not of reformists, but of a reformation, which has now commenced. There is a small difference, namely that the original Reformation included something which Engels once called the most radical fact in German history, the great Peasant War. It is not only Luther who can be emulated. There was also Thomas Münzer. He led the peasants into battle under a rainbow banner, with an invisible peasant Christ at the head, after their masters had left them with no other choice but rebellion. The peasants were defeated. It is written that he who lives by the sword shall die by the sword. So next time it's better to do it differently. But we must be more like Münzer, not like the soft-living flesh at Wittenberg as he called the later Luther, not an eco-liberal party which starts by dancing attendance on the ideal type of representative democracy as the future Bismarck liberals did on constitutional monarchy in 1848–49. For them the most important thing was that the people, the wild mob, should be able to speak only in measured doses. Now the so-called moderates have a much neater hammer. To talk of "the people" – and wanting to treat them as an autonomous force – is "totalitarian". They need to make sure Hitler has this final victory, that now in Germany one may never again refer to "the people".

But we had only peasant conspiracies in recent years, encounters like the crowds around Hans Behaim in Niklashasen,[10] though these had at least one thing more than we do, namely their naive vision of the kingdom of God. As I said, they were only puffs of wind, the storm is yet to come!

At present a "data processing" is being carried out of a kind which the masters had never thought of. The people – and *that* in the end expresses itself in the votes for us – see: forests dying, dioxin, low-flying fighters, ground water pollution, pseudo-croup,[11] experiments on animals – in each case it concerns the totality and everything belongs together. The population – and the peasants although there are not so many of them any more are still the best indicator for this – are beginning to add it all up, are beginning to understand what they have already suspected for a few years: that the daily horror stories in reality announce a *single* total catastrophe and that this also has *one* underlying cause, even if it is not a completely simple one. It is precisely the peasants who know how actively they are involved with this sort of cattle torture and soil poisoning – *and why*. The common agricultural policy is a hard teacher. Anyone who understood the various levels of the logic of self-annihilation would also know about the character of the *one* movement for salvation which is coming.

Now I am almost at the end, exactly at the point where Jürgen Maier, previously referred to, will ask: "So what now?" I have a lot to say on that but for now I will just mention the problems.

First I would like to speak for another half hour about the relationship between the Eco-peace movement and fascism, but differently from the way you would venture to do so. *Formally*, structurally seen, movement, state and society stand in relation to each other quite similarly to the time of the Weimar republic, and *formally* the Greens are rising according to a quite similar pattern to the Nazi party. In order for there to be a good outcome this time, i.e. for the popular uprising to be non-violent, the Greens must not be lost. If they allow themselves to be coopted, and if then afterwards, when the storm has reached its greatest strength and the wave its full height, they remain coopted and are just one more party of the system – there couldn't be a better preparation for civil war and the ensuing dictatorship. But there would be much more to say on that, above all on the fact that the movement for a peaceful transition needs a different structure working from within than a political party: certainly not the party as vanguard, that would be asking for trouble for a new culture; the party may only be the political arm which at the decisive moment engages the political arm of the opposing side, let's say the CDU/CSU, in shadow-boxing, so that the state machine is paralysed, naturally through the movement which divides the army right up to the officer corps and then lets nothing out of the barracks. I recall how in late 1967 Novotny called upon the army and the security forces – they didn't come because they were divided.

Then and only then would I have something to say about the most important positive thing, the social alternative, or at least a sketch of it. For the monstrous thing is that a policy which does away with large chemical industries, etc. also does away with jobs as a means to support life. That's where they got stuck in Hamburg, and that is why they will sooner or later also march off into realpolitik – or chase their own shadow. Here is the bottleneck of fundamentalism. Do we want to begin to build up a self-sufficient society beyond jobs with BASF and the common agricultural policy – and indeed as our main objective, *this* our positive project! – or not? That is the crunch question *to you.*

Or perhaps your mental block lies one level deeper? Human beings don't live in order to produce. Or rather, the fact that they do so is precisely the reason for their destruction. I would like to talk for a last half hour about the fact that the alternative republic will be above all an association of communities, that is of living communities with God or Goddess in the middle, and why. And to add a few words about the fundamentalist network which we should still build up throughout the whole country behind all structures of the party and movement, conceived as reaching far beyond their present area to all sensitive nonconformists in all social and political camps. The fundamentalists – even those who deny this prove it by resisting or even by leaping forward – are still rooted in another reality which we all have in us, but which is daily covered up by our own involvement. The contest with the apocalypse can only be won if this becomes a great era of belief, a Pentecost with the living spirit poured out as equally as possible over all.

Only from there, in the last analysis, can politics be founded anew, so that it does not lead back into the old vicious circle – the politics of salvation can only come from there. A friend quoted me from the prophet Hosea the central message which must emanate from us: "Assyria shall not save us, nor will we seek horses to ride; what we have made with our own hands we will never again call gods: for in thee the fatherless find a father's love." Contrary to all appearances what ecological politics means is precisely: Away with the safety belt, away with all the arms we bear. Then we shall live. Then too everything is possible politically. The idol is already tottering, it will also fall.

Speech at the Hamburg congress, December 1984
Kommune, *January 1985*

Some Ideas for a Green Campaign in the Rhineland

BEWARE POISON!
(Skull and Crossbones Symbol)
EVERYWHERE IN EARTH, WATER, AIR AND FIRE!

Chemicals are killing us!

A question to everyone: Can you think of a better solution than to get out of the chemical industry?

I. The Objective

This is to expose and make people conscious of the enormity and complexity of the danger which emanates from the chemical industry. We want to move people to protest and action and also to seek alternatives, in fact to seek a *fundamental alternative*.

The Seveso poison which led to the closing down of Boehringer in Hamburg is just the tip of a whole range of icebergs: of large-scale chemical production itself. Like the Bomb it is a symbol for the death sentence our civilization has passed upon itself. Evils like pseudo-croup, cancer, contaminated breast milk, deformed babies, male infertility and dying forests cannot be traced back to specific instances; even where this may seem possible it is only too easy to overlook the structural context in which the cause is embedded. All these effects can only be understood against the background of a *general poisoning* of water, air and earth. We won't be able to overcome them by putting restrictions on effluents. It is futile to imagine the possibility of a different industrial system. The current industrial system will kill us sooner rather than later unless we are prepared to reduce it to a completely different scale.

This suicidal logic has penetrated the regular industrial, scientific and state institutions of our society. In the case in question we are dealing with a German industry second in size only to the car industry, an industry which is not only in the lead in poisoning the world but also in making profit. It is the most expansive of the "old" industries. It is grouped round the three great sharks – Bayer, BASF and Hoechst. Each of the three has surpassed in terms of power and influence the war criminal concern of IG Farben in which they have their origin: they at least emerged victorious from the Second World War.

Nothing significant has changed in the structures which enabled them to play their ominous role at that time. Their output alone shows that. If BASF produced Zyklon B for gassing the Jews during the Hitler period, then after the war they contributed to the development of the Agent Orange poison which was used for defoliation during the Vietnam war and has been responsible for the birth of countless deformed children.

The empire of the German chemical and pharmaceutical industry has at its disposal not only gigantic material resources but also extensive psychological resources and will be prepared to use any means at its disposal to continue and keep expanding its work of devastation. As a result of its high profit levels it possesses the power to tie its workforce socially. Whole towns are but appendages to it. When problems arise, not only the state – as in the formaldehyde case – but also the whole trade-union bureaucracy will spring to its assistance. The president of the chemical industry trade union behaves in such a way that at least it is not doing *him* any injustice to talk of the "poison union".

To challenge this industry means in effect to begin drilling through the plank at its thickest point. But if this can't be stopped, then nothing can be stopped. Without changing the system by overcoming the superior strength of the chemical giants, the environment and indeed life itself cannot be saved. We must in addition remember that in other parts of the world they operate much more shamelessly and cause much greater damage to people and the environment than they do here at home. We share the responsibility for that; and anyone who does not take an interest in the situation will tomorrow find out that we are hit by the rebound of biological destruction all round the world so much the harder for its being a little bit later.

Our opponents are not the people in the chemical industry, but the logic of development which they serve. Our opponents are the representatives of this development logic in their role as functionaries of the Big Machine. We must try to make the split in consciousness which is now taking hold of the population as a whole spread through the factories too: the people who work for the catastrophe and are at the same time horrified by its consequences (how much longer will they express this only in private?) are one and the same. Let us ask the people in the managerial offices, in the finance and marketing divisions, above all in research and technology, whether they feel no responsibility for collaborating daily in ruining the elements of earth, water, air and fire. Mothers in the Mainz area now have to be advised not to use the mains water supply for small children – where are the origins of the poisoned water sources to be found? And let us punish with outrage and scorn those people who still hypocritically demand proof that the "firm" can do something about it! We can always reckon it up for them.

Nevertheless it wouldn't be enough merely to restrict ourselves to blaming all the evil onto the industry, because we ourselves, as a result of our work and interests, our habits and comforts, our dependencies and willingness to compromise, are at the least co-conspirators. Even in many Greens acceptance of the industry outweighs the opposite motive. We still permit more or less anything because we have not taken the decision to risk a true alternative to the suicidal system of big industry.

Whether or not there is any salvation depends upon whether and how quickly a consensus is achieved within the population and not least in the factories of the chemical industry itself. In the final analysis what has to be decided is whether we are prepared to risk the abolition of the chemical industry and to seek a different basis for life other than the wage-earning job. At first the pressure to close down many production lines will give rise to diverse search operations to find out what practical steps might be possible to lead us out of the vicious circle. In order to put forward an *attractive* alternative we must guide people away from material standards: human progress must no longer be measured by whether we travel quickly by aeroplane or slowly by bicycle. Then the many people who form the minority among whom these ideas first catch on can experience the end of their jobs as liberation from dependency on the "benevolent" dragon and an escape from its poisonous circle of fumes. We must no longer accept that we have to destroy the world in order to live.

And yet this will continue to be the case as long as we have to look to the state for support; after all, where is it supposed to come from? It will also continue if we keep on dreaming of creating different types of jobs by "alternative investments in the future" which the state and the large corporations are supposed to come up with. All that will lead to is an "ecological modernization" of the whole industrial nonsense and a continuation of our journey towards the abyss.

What we must demand is start-up assistance for building a new way of life – that is, a grand redistribution of means and resources out of the system. Would we not need land to be able to begin producing food for ourselves? And wouldn't we therefore need the means to buy it out of the absurd European Common Agricultural Market?

But stop, first we must contemplate this comprehensive change of perspective: away from "super-free" wage labour and towards the reunification of human beings with the land and with their basic conditions of reproduction in general: land and tools to those who have to use them to feed themselves. How real this change in the direction of development is will depend entirely on how many people want it and actively push for it.

In truth abolition begins with spiritual release from the traditional system of values in our own being. So long as we still care about playing some recognized role in the current system our energies will stay committed to it and all that will come about is a cosmetic change. We must get together to fill the vacuum left behind in us by Coca-Cola culture. Those who desire a quality of life in which there is room for something that uplifts the spirit and the heart will take the lead and carry others with them. In this way people will come together who fit in well with each other, and together they will create examples of a different culture, worthy of existing and capable of surviving. At least, they will try to do so.

Abolition of the industrial system will be a complicated process. But only if there is this alternative polarity between traditional jobs on the one hand and the type of examples mentioned above on the other will it be possible for a new direction to emerge quickly enough out of the variety of makeshift measures and attempts to break out.

It all depends much more on intellectual decisions than on material resources, which are after all available – securing them is primarily a question of intellectual and cultural power.

The struggle against the chemical industry is important. But we only have a realistic chance of winning it if at the same time we set about building up an alternative way, not only of earning one's living but actually of life itself. Otherwise any gains which the people affected do manage to wrest from it will only lead back into the universal supermarket.

Maybe not the initial impetus, but certainly the full extent of a campaign against poisoning the world will depend on whether we can give credibility to a total alternative instead of just to adjustments within the system.

Without vision we shall come to a standstill. What the Greens need is on the one hand an extra-parliamentary practice of resistance and on the other the building of a new culture – not least for themselves – unless they want completely to lose their function as a political arm of the movement.

The campaign against poisoning may be supported by the Green structures but should not remain a Green party issue: and we should not be taking over any initiatives. On this issue we must regard ourselves not as a party but as a component part of the whole movement. We should set up a co-ordinating group linking all the participants, insofar as they are interested in joining it.

II. Framework, Steps and Measures

We ought to concentrate on the chemical industry in the Rhineland, above all on BASF, but could also include neighbouring areas of Hesse (Darmstadt, Grossgerau, the whole area as far as Frankfurt) and Baden-Württemberg (Manneim, Heidelberg). For purposes of exchange of information and cooperation, it is important to have contacts with Hamburg, Leverkusen, Hoechst, etc.; we shall also involve individuals from supra-regional contexts. But for the organization of the whole campaign and for actions we must rely entirely on our local and regional forces.

The PR machine is already fully committed to defending the industry against "attitudes hostile to progress" (see for example the BASF film about their "achievements", advertizements for animal experiments, associations along the lines of the pro-nuclear power initiatives, etc.). To oppose this we have to strengthen our attack on the foundations of this destructive industrialism. Our motto should be to show the other side of the coin, the coin which more and more frequently turns up harm rather than good, pain rather than well-being.

In order to do this we must first gather together all relevant facts about the pollution of the region and of the individual districts and localities.

Secondly we must demonstrate that the production and research establishments of the large-scale chemical industry are the places from which this pressure on human beings and nature primarily emanates. We must achieve a state of affairs in which the sight at night of the chimneys and flames above them is perceived as being ominous. This will be connected to particularly blatant examples of products, by-products and waste products which damage and threaten our health and the environment, and traced back to the expansionist policies of the chemical firms in research, marketing, profits, etc.

This debate must be conducted concretely and in a way which is strongly symbolic. We need posters and leaflets bearing such phrases as "Poisoned wells" – with a kitchen tap over which there is a notice saying "Water not suitable for drinking"; or the old picture entitled "The Poison Mixer" with a chemical distillery in the background and the words "What is poison mixing in the witch's kitchen when measured against the workings of a chemical plant?"; or the Wicked Queen offering Snow White a poisoned apple; a factory chimney which is simultaneously a dragon belching fire; or the Earl King's veil of mist related to pseudo-croup, etc.

In particular we should prepare a leaflet which has printed on the reverse the reply which Willi Tatge got from the corporation (which says that they will not give us any more information) and on the front an invitation to people to reveal to us, anonymously or otherwise, in writing or by telephone (we should make our address and telephone number widely known) any information they have from the belly of the monster.

For the time being, the campaign itself will have three phases:

a)   Functions organized by district associations at which there is discussion on the local chemical industry; and in connection with these, local actions at particular places we wish to highlight (as for example the Gerolsheim waste dump in Worms).

These local activities will serve principally to train and mobilize our own forces. They should be addressed to all activists and groups connected with the ecology and peace movement and should involve them. If need be the district associations can invite speakers from other parts of the country (for example national executive members such as Willi Tatge, Erika Hickel, Willi Hoss; Thea Bock from Hamburg, Bettina Krems-Hemesath of the pseudo-croup campaign, etc).

Against this background, chemical poisoning will be a focal point for the next provincial delegate conference at the beginning of 1985 and we can then orientate ourselves for the next phase:

b)   An Anti-Chemicals Conference in Ludwigshafen,* to run as follows:

—starting with a hearing in which the extent of the complexity of poisoning is put forward, BASF is characterized from the ecological standpoint and clarification is given on how an alternative start could be made: how do we intend to work and live if we abandon the kind of jobs which Moloch has to offer us?

—continuing with discussions on a strategy for action and education: what kind of approach will bring success in averting harm and forcing the chemical industry to retreat?

---

*This is already in preparation as a dioxin conference, with a somewhat more limited objective that outlined here.

–leading to a resolution to organize a mass rally in Ludwigshafen in order to confront the population, including those employed by BASF, with the consequences of their daily acceptance of the practice of industrial suicide;
–flanked by a symbolic siege of the BASF research establishment, whereby access to the buildings is hindered but not prevented, and the main purpose is to remind the people in the laboratories that they are culprits and responsible for incalculable consequences. "Do you still believe you can control what happens as a result of your discoveries? And is not your experimental science, in the form in which it functions at present, a work of the devil?"

c) The mass rally itself, which on the day it takes place will define the image of the whole town and should have a similarly catalytic effect to that which the hindering of NATO manoeuvres had on the majority of people in Fulda who were still trapped in the old way of thinking. It should lead to a re-evaluation of BASF in the town and by so doing radiate throughout the whole region.

A Lesson in Compromise

A Green Animal Protection Law Based on Alternative Concentration Camp Logic?

The animal protection law is about to be amended in parliament, and our concern is with two key points which expose the nerve of our scientific-industrial barbarism: factory farming and animal experiments. The Greens will of course say an unqualified "no" to the current practice of systematic and large-scale animal torture and use the opportunity to put forward their plan for a fundamentally different policy on health, research, agriculture and industry.

In fact the opposite seems to be the case. Up till now both in the parliamentary group and in the working party on this question the people who have dominated are those with the same attitude towards the use of concentration camp methods and torture upon animals as the Social-Democrats have towards nuclear power: they would like to "restrict" and "start doing without", but at the same time assume responsibility for the rest of the evil which they represent as being unavoidable. And they check critics in their own ranks in just the same power-oriented way as we are accustomed to expect from other parties (after all nobody who supports a Green parliamentary initiative can get past them). Up till now they have not been persuaded by arguments, but only by extra-parliamentary pressure and by the very same "lack of objectivity" and "emotionalizing" which all the other established parties always complain about.

I only want to deal here with one of the two key points, that is, animal experiments, and in doing so I have to thank Christine Schröter for important stimuli bearing on the spirit and content of this contribution.

Resistance in the parliamentary group to a straightforward ban on animal experiments is so strong that the Greens' national working party on Human Beings and Animals almost allowed itself to be pushed into a "compromise" advocating *the regulation of animal experiments instead of banning them*. The draft paper they put forward is a really brilliant example of the Green "political feasibility" which has been springing up all over the place recently. There is a lesson for us here about the nature of the compromise culture which a few influential people in the parliamentary group are advocating so strongly. We have reached the point where we can even tolerate plutonium as long as it enjoys impeccable legal sanction and the official who happens currently to be responsible promises that it will be used "for peaceful purposes". No wonder the more radical campaigns against animal experiments and the nuclear state are beginning to say that the Greens don't *make* mistakes, they *are* the mistake.

"Restrict to Abolish"

The very first paragraph of the Green draft paper proves that we can already lie at least as well as any established party. Right at the beginning of a law which even in its proposed new form permits animal experiments so long as it is proved that they serve "a scientific and/or medical purpose of outstanding general significance" they want to insert the pious phrase "by radical restriction and the promotion of alternative approaches to completely abolish experiments on animals".

Yes, there you have cunning politicians at work, and you have a Green version of the language of the disarmament diplomats and arms controllers, of those cobblers who try to convince us that they want to do away with shoes. And of course this particular variant meets with the approval of the Social-Democrat Ilja Weiss who assumes the same role for the opponents of animal experiments as does Jo Leinen for the citizens' initiatives in general: that of facilitating their efforts through SPD policies.[1] This is the same Ilja Weiss of whom the pharmaceutical industry can say that "even he" is not opposed to all animal experiments. So the nature of Green intervention against animal experiments had been settled with him in advance and he is annoyed now that his partners in our parliamentary group have been blocked.

All the same, the experiments are to be "radically" restricted, even Ilja Weiss is in favour of that. And so the seven pages of text about animal experiments include fifteen lines which could be understood by the uninitiated who don't read on to mean that in future it would be impossible to carry out a single experiment without breaking the law. April Fool! For those lines are followed by a full six pages on "individual justified exceptions" which very invitingly open a back door for each and every "reasonable", "responsible" and "humanistically justifiable" animal experiment.

These "exceptions" are to be permitted when the applicant can prove that there are as yet no methods or processes which could replace the experiment. Thus so long as no competing scientist has invented anything better, human beings retain the right to use animals as guinea pigs, and there will continue to be at least debatable instances of this kind until kingdom come. But it's all to be perfectly rational. As our dear Chancellor recently stated, very appropriately, it must be clear that the results have not already been obtained or approved elsewhere. Finally, the results are also to be of genuine service to humankind, that is, they are to be transferable to human beings, though it is known that there are deep differences of opinion on this between the supporters and opponents of animal experiments. From the outset the text puts the supporters in the right by making transferability a basic condition whilst only periodically wanting the argument to be heard as to whether this is relevant to a particular case or not.

By means of these "exception" regulations we are creating jobs; jobs for a very busy and well-fed licensing bureaucracy which provides the opportunity for organized opponents of animal experiments – who must from the start have accepted that exceptions are inevitable – to be drawn into accepting a share of the responsibility. These commissions will have an exciting long-term job opposing the politics of secrecy and suppressing the facts as practised by the interested parties.

One particularly nice sub-section requires that "all operations which may involve pain, suffering, damage or fear may only be carried out by people who have completed university level education in medicine or veterinary medicine, or by graduates in biology with a specialization in zoology who have the necessary expertise". Thus if the exponents of torture have a degree everything will be alright. And actually that is correct – only physicists should be allowed to tinker with nuclear bombs.

According to another passage, animal experiments are to be selectively banned for cosmetics, tobacco, alcohol or drugs, in the field of military technology and military medicine, and for purposes of teaching and instruction in schools and colleges. Let's suppose that as a result of this passage the cosmetics, tobacco and alcohol companies really did have to search round for cover addresses and deceptive wording; and in the field of education the mood may change as a result of the sensitization of the younger generation. But one thing is certain; the "responsible peace-lovers" in the CDU/CSU and the SPD will hardly accept that the "safeguarding of peace" through military deterrence is *not* of "outstanding significance for humanity in general" and therefore needs reinforcing by animal experiments.

Inevitably, this draft reaffirms the ideology by which the place of a living being on the evolutionary ladder determines which is selected first for torture: "experiments on vertebrates which are zoologically classified as higher animals are only permitted if it can be proved that experiments on lower vertebrates do not suffice for the objective being pursued. Warm-blooded animals may only be used if experiments on cold-blooded animals will not serve the objective. Experiments on non-human primates are forbidden." Here you have the logic of the West: "There are many violent things in existence, but nothing is more violent than human beings!" (Sophocles).

One thing is quite obvious: influential people in the Green parliamentary group don't want to ban animal experiments – at least they want to make sure that *not all* animal experiments are banned. Many of them even expressly state that in this case they wouldn't want to see anything banned. As a representative of the people one is after all an advocate for the people affected, who will sometime or other find themselves without the next life-saving drug if the pharmaceutical industry is not allowed to continue dissecting and injecting.

So the very people who are already hopelessly dependent on the big medicine machine must be used as the excuse for the monster to be properly reproduced! Our parliamentary representative Sabine Bard, who is clearly a veterinary surgeon first and a Green afterwards, injects a note of panic into the discussion with the argument that we would soon have to be operated on without anaesthetics. A representative of the pharmaceutical industry couldn't have put it better. In any case the "justified" experiments must continue until "alternative approaches" (in the promotion of which the research ministry is to play godfather) have produced a substitute for every "necessary" animal experiment – so that the proud edifice of science does not reveal any cracks.

I think I have proved one thing: the general tenor of the Green draft law is indirectly to legitimize animal experiments and to safeguard them by introducing a few measures to prevent the worst *excesses* and *superfluous* cruelty. According to the book, then, everyone should be satisfied, because everything will be ok if we make sure the law is obeyed. It is well known that there were concentration-camp doctors and other collaborators with the annihilation machine who "sincerely" convinced themselves they should stay in their posts in order to exert a mitigating influence and prevent somebody worse from taking their place. After all what more could they do? The contribution of the people responsible in the parliamentary group on the question of animal experiments is along the same lines as this alternative concentration camp logic.

How Has This Come About?

How is it possible for this "compromise" draft still not to have been got out of the way? How – in this case – has the Green parliamentary group functioned as the last cog in the government machine, to reduce the necessary major change to such a minimum that the system can digest it without ruining its stomach? First, the history. The story began when the above-mentioned Sabine Bard, who considered animal experiments to be indispensable in certain cases and clearly doesn't want to violate her professional code of conduct either, threw a few personal suggestions for modest changes to the parliamentary group without even consulting the national working party on Human Beings and Animals. The incompetent and fanatical people there would only have upset our lady specialist. However, a discussion was forced retrospectively on the Bard proposals (which according to the working party would reduce animal experiments by 1.5 per cent) and on 11 September [1984] a rump group, under pressure from the activists present, decided – on the second vote – to withdraw this contribution to the continuation of ecological catastrophe. Up till then Sabine Bard, supported by Armin von Gleich, had steadfastly withstood massive criticism from the grassroots both inside and outside the Greens. In doing so she had at least formal protection from the parliamentary group leadership. The debate had obviously not the slightest influence on her way of thinking. The fact that the draft described above, which in the meantime one section of the working party also wanted to help push through for "realpolitical" reasons, could appear at all as a "compromise" is attributable to her unchanged position of veto: maybe it will reduce animal experiments by a few more percentage points.

Horrified by the outcome which they had almost let themselves in for as a result of the pressure of the situation within the parliamentary group and of "feasibility" within the Greens, Dieter Plagemann and some other members of the national working party at the last minute quite erratically inserted right at the beginning of all the "exception" regulations – which were actually intended to provide for an indeterminate "long-term abolition" – the sentence that they should only apply for four years, after which there should be a complete stop to animal experiments. So everyone who looks at this draft now ought to know that this sentence, inserted as an emergency brake, stands in opposition to the spirit (or rather the evil spirit) of the whole text and certainly does not correspond to the intentions of those who consider the licensing arrangements necessary. My advice to

Dieter and the others is: "Go for broke, friends, don't try to cover the breach, withdraw that sentence. If necessary let the parliamentary group keep to Sabine Bard's original proposals: as things are undisguised farce is preferable to the veiled kind."

The present stand is indeed typical for the constant *danger* that our parliamentary group will give in to the pressure of prevailing circumstances and ideologies from which we ourselves are often necessarily emancipated. Yet the story wouldn't have been like this if only our parliamentary group as a whole had concentrated just for a moment on the real substance of the conflict between the working party and some of their members. That didn't happen because most Greens – not only the parliamentary group – preoccupied with other aspects of the approaching total catastrophe, have too little intuition as to the importance of the animal experiments issue in relation to our political programme as a whole. I fear that our MP Erika Hickel, who inclines towards an unconditional ban on the experiments, assesses her colleagues quite correctly when she requests them to pay heed to the animal protectionists so that they are certain to vote for us. What that actually means is "At least be clever enough to take care of the clientele; don't get excited about the real issue."

Last time the issue was debated in parliament (on 11 September) the chamber coincidentally emptied just before this item came up. Apparently the only people who stayed were the declared supporters and opponents of the ban. One can see that other important office-holders of the Greens also laugh disparagingly or feel embarrassed as soon as the Human Beings and Animals working party is mentioned.

Many of us have simply missed the point that what we are faced with here is something basically different from "Grannies Against Animal Experiments" (though they should certainly keep their right to be included in our efforts). The problem of whether the miller may beat his mule or not will be adequately dealt with even by the CDU – after all no type of "progress" is dependent on mules nowadays. But how blind and defensive are those Greens who deflect – in the way Jo Müller, about to become one of our MPs, has done[2] – the efforts of the militant opponents of animal experiments with the accusation that they are based on a children's story mentality. That may play a role in one or other individual case, but it is of little overall significance.

The same blindness – but if anything even more disastrous in its effect – is shown by the people who bring in the misery of the Third World in order to tell the animal rights activists that their energy should be spent on a more worthwhile cause, whereas in fact this has even more to do with us and our responsibility than does "Food for the World". Animal experiments have an extremely important role in underpinning, facilitating and justifying the machinery of progress with which we are working on our own annihilation.

Ever since the explanations put forward by Alfred Sohn-Rethel[3] it has been evident how science and capital, the spirit of research and money, are analogous and related from the very foundation of our civilization. When will we Greens at least say loud and clear that our science – reduced to its professed intention of "relieving the toil of human existence" – is in both structure and function just as fundamentally a work of the devil as is our financial system. Scientists and entrepreneurs are twin brothers and right from the beginning their common work as war-horses of capital accumulation has been carried out all round the world. Quite contrary to the current assumption and despite many individual examples to the contrary, the fact remains that every pause in the laboratories will ultimately *save* a large number of lives, including above all human lives all over the world.

A Fringe Area of Green Politics?

As far as I can see, animal experiments are one of the most political questions we have ever had to deal with. To become a radical in this area means to slaughter one of the holiest cows in modern Western idolatry, the "freedom of science". Science, which along with money was originally one of the main means for our escape from impotence, disease and death, has now joined capital as the chief agent of these very factors in human existence and has allowed them to become all-powerful. Thus do our "God complex" (see the book by Horst Eberhard Richter)[4] and our compensatory desire for omnipotence avenge themselves.

Animal experiments occupy a central place in the material and spiritual edifice of our whole civilization. We are speaking here of one of those foundation stones whose removal could cause the whole house to collapse. Or should I say rather that they play more or less the role of the infant's blood which in olden times was mixed with the mortar for the foundations and ramparts. The discontinuation of this practice and the imposition of a complete taboo on it had more of a moral and intellectual significance than a material one. If we really wish to foster the split in consciousness in our society and particularly in its scientific and managerial "elites", I know no more sensitive way in. It is not accidental that we are dealing here with an issue which will cause us to come into conflict with the various bodies responsible for protecting the constitution, because the social control of science is just as firmly anchored in the constitution as is enormous wealth with its supposed social responsibility.

Of course the Bomb, nuclear power stations, dioxin, world hunger and police terror are more directly dangerous than animal experiments. Defence against such dangers means a *postponement* of the death sentence which humanity has passed upon itself. But if we are talking of *repealing* this death sentence then my effort in writing this article, which at the present time entails no risk, is more important than the moderately risky act of opposing torture by the despots in Ankara. All the swords of Damocles which we have hung over ourselves are merely *products*, materializations of a total structure which is inimical to life. Animal experiments – ostensibly intended to relieve human pain and suffering and to protect human life – belong in essence and at a further remove to the *production process* of evil itself.

If we want to understand their significance we should not ask any specialist – at least as a specialist or expert – not even an "alternative" specialist, even one who is an adviser to the Green parliamentary group. Even many opponents of animal experiments are too involved in the spirit of our present conditions to follow the thing through to its conclusion. We may very nicely, and for the most part very correctly, prove that contrary to their stated objective they are *not* useful to human beings. The offical experts will still manage to dispute that, simply because they rest their arguments on the old, basic values of Judeo-Christian cosmology rooted in popular prejudices.

And so what if certain experiments *are* useful, at least indirectly? After all, both knowledge and the reality reflected in it are part of a continuum. Do we then wish to maintain that the whole development of Western science, of which animal experiments have always been a part, would have brought us no tangible advantage nor led in the same time to the same results without these laboratory practices? It is a fact that in countries like ours, life expectancy was rising until a short time ago. Perhaps we just want to say that enough knowledge has *now* been accumulated through animal experiments and that they are therefore *no longer* necessary? We can say that as a sort of preliminary emergency brake.

In my opinion a critique on a purely scientific level can only ever lead to restrictions, to a "reasonable" reduction in animal experiments. It won't do simply to remove this unhappy torture practice from the system of science as if it were a chance foreign body which needn't have been there in the first place. Anyone who relies solely or mainly on proof – which can anyway always be disputed by the parties interested in particular cases – that the results of animal experiments are not transferable to human beings, silently acknowledges the validity of one decisive precondition: that if they were transferable or if it could be shown that they were otherwise useful to human beings, they would then be justifiable. Our specifically European humanistic utilitarianism, the basis of which is that human beings are the measure of all things and the lords of all creatures, is not cast into doubt by this line of argument.

We shall scarcely be able to defeat the type of science we are familiar with on its own territory. Moreover, there will always be sufficient people who for the time being prefer an inconsistent critique of the status quo. So let *us* only point to non-transferability in the really relevant cases and in doing so emphasize that in these cases the experiments are, even according to their own canon, nonsensical. We shall then just need to unmask and identify the direct interests which lie behind these crimes against the animal world. But in order to achieve our aim we must *always* go further, even if by doing so we are making excessive demands on half-hearted animal-lovers: for it is these very people who need this kind of impetus to drive them forward. As in all other sensitive areas of radical cultural change, minimal consensus tactics are in this case counter-productive.

Chief Seattle's Reply

If we want to get to the bottom of animal experiments and our generally destructive science (destructive even at the experimental stage), we come up against two quite elementary facts of human existence: on the one hand our inadequacy as natural beings in comparison with other better protected species; though we have in our brains the instrument to compensate for our "inadequate" equipment. On the other hand, nobody except human beings *can* find out how to blow up a frog's stomach through a straw. Probably these two elementary factors have more to do with the results than we generally think – that is with the fundamental *possibility* of the ecological catastrophe.

In any case we are a species so far excluded from communion with itself or with the forms of life closest to us that almost any one of us can be trained to carry out torture without feeling anything. The bridge between our rationality (of which Goethe says: "He calls it reason and uses it to be more bestial than any beast") and the bosom from which it springs is so broken that we hardly hear the warning voice of our own unconscious as representative of nature any more. Science toughens its priests and servants, as well as its clients, even more reliably than the dragon's blood toughened Siegfried in the *Nibelungenlied*. In my opinion animal experiments, quite regardless of whether or not their results can be transferred to humans and whether or not they help us in some direct or indirect way, are in principle part of the logic of self-destruction. It is the same as with the army. The principle of "security first" which underlies these dealings with disease and death, as indeed almost all their practices to date, will only lead to destruction.

And we have not sufficiently understood the issue if we deal with the problems of animal experiments primarily in terms of sympathy or respect for life, much as these sentiments point in the right direction. We shall harm ourselves not only spiritually and morally, but physically as well, if we maltreat the animal and plant kingdom simply because we are afraid of disease and greedy for life.

As early as 1979, Hans Jonas published his *Principle of Responsibility: towards an ethic for technological civilization*. Whereas our parliamentary representative Sabine Bard considers the crucial question to be "May we allow animals to suffer *because it is useful for us humans?*" (my italics): Hans Jonas started his book with the sentence (again my italics): "Prometheus, definitively unbound, to whom science has given untold power and the economy a tireless impetus, calls for an ethic which by means of voluntary curbs prevents his power from *becoming an evil for humankind.*" It is a long book and important for us particularly in respect of its critique of the Marxian utopianism of Ernst Bloch. But perhaps the following few sentences from the completely untheoretical speech of Chief Seattle in 1855 before the American President will suffice to substantiate the only correct decision:

"We are part of the Earth and it is part of us. The fragrant flowers are our sisters, the deer, the horse, and the eagle are our brothers. The rocky heights, the luxuriant meadows, the body heat of the pony – and of human beings – all belong to the same family.

"Whatever befalls the Earth befalls also the sons of the Earth. Mankind did not create the fabric of life, it is only a thread within it. Whatever you do to the fabric you do also to yourselves.

"Whatever happens to the animals will happen soon also to human beings. All things are bound up with one another. Even the white man will pass away, maybe before all other tribes. Continue to soil your bed and one night you will suffocate in your own waste. But in your downfall you will shine brightly.

"I have seen a thousand rotting buffalo left behind by the white man – shot from a passing train. I am a savage and cannot understand why the puffing iron horse should be more important than the buffalo, which we kill only in order to stay alive. What are human beings without animals? If all animals ceased to exist, human beings would die of a great loneliness of the soul."

I consider the first and the last sentence here to be the most important indications of the other culture which we must develop. We shall only save ourselves if we adopt this attitude ourselves and anchor it in our everyday lives; if we do so it will not be only animal experiments which become constitutionally impossible. "One does not exploit a nature with which one identifies" (Hans Peter Duerr).

Chief Seattle's attitude has nothing to do with a special love of animals or with condescending sympathy. It has to do with a cultural state of mind wich has no need for animal protection as a special arrangement. Laws always come into being only after order has been fundamentally disturbed. As Lao Tzu says in *Tao Te Ching*: "Favour and disfavour both instil fear . . . favour is bestowed upon the subordinate, who accepts it fearfully and loses it again equally fearfully."[5] Animal protection and favour are both indicators of something wrong in our culture which we must no longer be satisfied with if we are to live. There is a yawning abyss between Christian-Western humanism on the one hand (which has about as much to do with Christ as Christ did with the Pharisees in his own lifetime) and the attitude of Lao Tzu and the North American Indian on the other.

There is a film titled *Treblinka Each Day for the Animals*. When measured against the Western image of a world where human beings as God's emissaries are in principle set above nature and all other living beings, the title along is provocative: "How can one place the annihilation of animals and humans on the same level?" But anyone really seeking information should see this film, and anyone in danger of deciding to support the "responsible" Green position which is in favour of continuing with animal experiments, *must* do so.

Is It Right for Us to Ban Something?

When pressed, our friends of science and practitioners of realpolitik turn libertarian. They say we must not support the banning of something in which many people have a vital interest (however manipulated this may be!). From this point of view one can also imagine a nice Green military policy: "Living without arms" is at the present time an unreasonable demand on most people, so let us spare them the trouble of hindering manoeuvres, unilateral disarmament, and doing away with the army. After all the need for military security is also a vital one. Our medicine and our military are in any case comparable with one another, for they are both allies of death, both necrophiliac.

An unconditional ban on animal experiments would in any case be for the time being no more than a freeze in a specific sector of the death machine. The propaganda that the Greens shouldn't ban anything is pure demagogy all down the line. Presumably any party which is in a minority will at first only have a minority of the population behind it when it puts forward a bill. Does the parliamentary mechanism, which after all we accept through cooperating with it, give rise to the danger that we shall break through too quickly or too slowly? Why do we participate at all in the legislature? In such a situation our main function is to bring its suppressed facts and open secrets to the surface in the long term interest of society as we see and represent it. Only a position of complete abolition (similar to unilateral disarmament and a rejection of the army in the case of military matters) will permit us to draw attention to the essence of the issue because then and only then will the opposing side duly start to howl. Only thus shall we achieve the necessary swift breakthrough in public opinion.

What makes the pseudo-libertarian argument all the more absurd is that the majority in parliament won't even pass the proposed "compromise" bill. But on this occasion the argument will only be about the scale of restrictions, not about the principle. It is not the necessity of conversion or of a break with the imperial world view of the white man which will be brought to the fore, but the idea of allowing a bit more reason to prevail on the basis of scientific achievements. Is that to be *our* role in the change of epoch which has already begun and which will lead either to the apocalypse or to the transition to a new civilization? How much time have we actually got to lose? And are we really so stupid – I can't call it anything else – when, as they say, it is already five minutes to midnight, that is, five minutes before the patient's demise, as to try to gain time by treating the patient's scratches? Everything which diverts us from our task of building up consciousness towards a reversal of consensus, towards turning it against this whole pattern of behaviour, contributes to our downfall.

Quite honestly, Green defenders of even a single animal experiment shouldn't be talking their way out of it by referring to the "justified needs" of *other* people (who for the most part did not vote for us), but should say that they consider them necessary in order for *themselves* (whether for direct medical reasons or because of their general world view) to be buffered against disease and death. The means already discovered as a result of research – insofar as they have not retrospectively been found to be harmful to human beings – are after all still available; the knowledge invested in them isn't lost the moment we distance ourselves from the way in which it was gained. But the opposition we are coming up against in our parliamentary group doesn't seem to me to be concerned with arguments. They simply support the old culture against the new. And in my opinion anyone who doesn't think we should manage without animal experiments as a means of acquiring knowledge should be confronted with the proposal that they offer themselves as guinea pigs. We must stop allowing "lower" substitutes to suffer in our place. Maybe the experts will think of something to confine the damage within more narrow boundaries than "lower forms of life". And the development of substitute methods would be very much expedited.

I know this is a "vicious" attack. But it is not at all philanthropic to be nice to people who have concerned themselves fairly closely with the problems of animal experiments and still argue for their continuation, however "restricted" this might be. If we – because we were not firm enough at the right time – are unsuccessful in forestalling an ecological civil war, this would be one of its more important fronts. It would in any case be intellectually sounder to blow up laboratories than lamp-posts, or even munitions transports. For this kind of science, which in any case functions in such a way that it is pretty meaningless to distinguish between military medicine and civilian medicine, lies so much nearer to the source of evil that do the murderous end products.

In reality what we need to blow up in good time is not the laboratories but the consensus for this murderous "freedom of science": we need to bring about a state of affairs where the general public, right down to the narrow circle of the perpetrators themselves, consider it immoral to have anything to do with this scientific barbarism, even at a distance. In it the development of human consciousness is so satanically deformed that the representatives of this alienated rationality urgently need a general halt in order to rethink. In this respect dawn is already beginning to break, but now the Greens have turned up just in time to defend enlightened reason – as if it was attacking reason and promoting some kind of obscurantism to want to restrain the scientists who are messing about as the paid agents of Moloch.

In any case the question of animal experiments is so central to testing whether we are really ready for conversion that there is no better litmus paper by which we can find out what we really want and what we no longer want. Up till now the supporters of the status quo have had reason to come to the soothing conclusion that the Greens are turning out to be a party with a broader appeal, useful for repairs to the facade of the political and social system.

Obviously in this way they will save neither animals nor humans – which in fact they would like to play a part in doing. The ecological crisis will simply provide them with a sinecure for their own political advancement. Anyone who wants things to be different will have to live in a constant state of rebellion inside their own party. That would not be futile, because the population is becoming increasingly radicalized in the face of the looming catastrophe, and if necessary will surpass the Greens in radicalism. I see increasing opportunites for preventing the party from being devoured by the system.

Statement on My Resignation From The Greens

What people are trying to do here[1] is to save a party – no matter what kind of party, and no matter for what purpose. The main thing is for it to get re-elected to parliament in 1987. It has no basic ecological position; it is not a party for the protection of life and I know now that it never will be, for it is rapidly distancing itself from that position. Yesterday, on the question of animal experiments, it clearly came down in favour of the position taken by the speaker who said, more or less: "If even one human life can be saved, the torture of animals is permissible". This sentence expresses the basic principle by which human beings are exterminating plants, animals and finally themselves.

Gerda Degen spelled it out yesterday – in the words of Jürgen Dahl.[2] You listened, you applauded, you know it – "really". There is not a single issue where the Greens are taking seriously the purpose for which they ostensibly entered the political scene. You can blame it if you like on "Realos" or "fundamentalists", or – more narrowly – on the paedophile issue.[3] We are in decline because the people who had placed their hopes in us realized, at least when they saw the behaviour of the North-Rhine-Westphalian Greens after the Saarland elections, that their course is not a sincere one; they are like everybody else, only they are trying to kid both others and themselves that they are different.

The Greens have identified themselves – critically – with the industrial system and its political administration. Nowhere do they want to get out. Instead of spreading consciousness they are obscuring it all along the line. They are helping to patch up the cracks in the general consensus. The theorists of realpolitik state directly that nothing else will do but to "rule out" extremes. Lafontaine is better at Green ministerial politics.[4]

It once looked as if some kind of salvation would come from us – but the applause for Petra's speech, which reminded us of this, won't bring it back. All that will be left is a normal party along with all the others. I can't carry on in it in that situation. After what happened yesterday am I still supposed to try to win serious animal protectionists onto our side? With us they will just waste both time and energy. Or cleaning up pollution. The proposal accepts that alternatives must be "competitive" in the market. "Mission to nowhere" *with* the chemical industry. I feel all the more sad in that some of the people involved would "really" like things to be different.

I want above all to ask those people who genuinely regret my departure and have pleaded with me not to go, to be clear as to their motive. Do you need me so that despite your doubts you have something to hold on to? That can't depend on me. Everyone has to reach their own decision. I can't carry on as if nothing had happened, as if nothing were happening, as if the exit were still open. Michael Stamm is telling the truth.[5] His solution is the only one left if we admit to ourselves what we really are as a party. Bankrupt.

This experience is the end of traditional political existence for me altogether. At last I have understood that a party is a counterproductive tool, that the given political space is a trap into which life energy disappears, indeed, where it is rededicated to the spiral of death. This is not a general but a quite concrete type of despair. It is directed not at the original project which is today called "fundamental", but at the party. I've finished with it now. I wouldn't consider it right just to withdraw silently. I am not becoming unpolitical. I am not saying goodbye to the intellectual process. I want to contribute to creating a new place and a new practice. Clearly we have to take a longer run-up. We must risk some cold water if we want to assemble the necessary substance for our withdrawal from the industrial system, first of all within ourselves.

Tageszeitung, *19 June 1985*

Notes

Basic Positions of The Greens

1. See note 5 to "We Need a Lot More Empty Space . . ."
2. The national congress of the Greens met in Hagen in November 1982, and placed eight conditions for the "toleration" of an SPD government in the event of that party's victory in the Federal elections to be held in March 1983. The prime condition was the rejection of the Euromissiles.

Human Beings are Not Ants

1. Erhard Eppler belongs to the left wing of the SPD, with pronounced leanings towards the ecology and peace movements. He is the author of *Wege aus der Gefahr (Ways out of Danger)*, Rowohlt, 1981.

This Time The Greens – Why?

1. Gustav Heinemann was the first President of the German Federal Republic on its foundation in 1949, later joining the SPD.
2. The *Berufsverbot* is the ban on radicals holding government employment, introduced in the early 1970s and still a major issue in West Germany, though its enforcement varies widely between the different *Länder*.
3. The national congress held in Sindelfingen adopted an economic programme which gave priority to creating new jobs, at the expense – in Bahro's view – of radical ecological measures.

Overcoming the Gravitational Pull of the Industrial System

1. Rainer Trampert, an eco-socialist from Hamburg, is a member of the Greens' parliamentary group and national executive committee, and one of their three Federal spokespeople. He was formerly aligned with the "Zentrum" group (see note 5 to "Fundamental Thoughts on the Crisis of the Greens"), and is the co-author (with Thomas Ebermann) of *The Future of the Greens* (1985), which gives clear priority to the ecological issue.

No Stand-In for Eppler

1. i.e. the decision on the Euromissiles.

To What End Are We Consolidating Our Forces?

1. Otto von Lamsdorff was the leader of the liberal Frei-Demokratische Partei (FDP), which sank below the 5 per cent barrier in the March 1983 election.
2. The Saarbrücken congress of the Greens in November 1980 adopted the party's first programme, since extended but still in force. In Bahro's (subsequent) view it was an inadequate compromise between ecological and left-socialist positions.

If Only the Thing Was More Stable!

1. Like Rainer Trampert, Thomas Ebermann hails from Hamburg and the "Zentrum" group, and is co-author of *The Future of the Greens*. See note 1 to "Overcoming the Gravitational Pull . . ." and note 7 to "Fundamental Thoughts on the Crisis of the Greens".
2. Johannes Rau is the SPD leader of the *Land* government of North-Rhine-Westphalia, and likely candidate for Chancellor in 1987.
3. Ignaz Kiehle is the CDU's agriculture minister.
4. Joschka Fischer symbolizes for Bahro the "Realos" within the Green party, and their haste to seek an accommodation with the established parties (in particular the SPD) that will give them a share of political office.
5. Williamsburg – the NATO dual-track decision on the Euromissiles in November 1979.
6. Lothar Späth is the CDU leader of the *Land* government of Baden-Württemberg and champion in his party of "ecological modernization".
7. Friedrich Ebert, a leading member of the SPD, became the first Chancellor of the German republic in 1918, and notoriously proceeded to the brutal repression of the revolutionary movement.
8. Dany Cohn-Bendit, a leading personality in the Paris *évènements* of 1968, has for many years been settled in Frankfurt and is active in the Green party there.
9. The Sozialistisches Büro is a grouping of left intellectuals formed in the late 1960s but no longer significant.
10. Norbert Blüm is minister of labour in Helmuth Kohl's conservative government.
11. Richard von Weiszäcker is the current President of West Germany.
12. Krefeld was the scene of a demonstration against the US vice-president George Bush in June 1983, marked by some violent clashes with the police. Similar confrontations took place on several occasions during the campaign agianst building a second runway at Frankfurt

airport. At Krefeld, it was later proved that a Federal intelligence agent had helped initiate the violence.

13. August Haussleiter, a co-founder of the Greens, and publisher of the Munich paper *Die Grünen*, was instrumental in establishing the compromise between different political tendencies that brought the Green party into being at Karlsruhe in January 1980.

14. Franz Alt, *Frieden ist Möglich; die Politik der Bergpredikt* (*Peace is Possible: the Politics of the Sermon on the Mount*), Piper, 1983.

15. Werner Raith, *Das verlassene Imperium* (*The Abandoned Empire*), Wagenbach, 1982.

16. Volker Fröbel is an economist concerned with North-South issues.

Dare to Form Communes

1. The "long march through the institutions" was the slogan of the non-violent wing of the German new left after the defeat of the student movement in 1969, particularly associated with Rudi Dutschke.

Why Communes?

1. Luise Rinser is a well-known German writer, who campaigned on the Green slate for Federal president in opposition to Richard von Weiszäcker.

2. Dorothea Mezger is a Third World economist from Munich.

Withdrawal From the World is No Solution

1. Luise Rinser, *Mirjam*, Fischer, 1983, a book about Mary Magdalene.

We Need a Lot More Empty Space in Our Minds and in Our Feelings

1. See "Three Questions on Peace from the West German Radio", *Socialism and Survival* (Heretic, 1982), p. 140.

2. Lewis Mumford, *The Myth of the Machine* (Secker & Warburg, 1967).

3. Bahro cites Thoreau, but not this particular sentence, in *The Alternative in Eastern Europe* (NLB, 1978) p. 281. He does however quote it in his talk "Ecology Crisis and Socialist Idea", *Socialism and Survival*, p. 42.

4. This building in Berlin was described to us by Bahro as "a horrendous battleship-like palace of congresses".

5. Mike Cooley, director of technology at the Greater London Enterprise Board under the Labour GLC, was the leading figure in the Lucas Aerospace workers' campaign for an alternative (i.e. non-military) corporate plan, and author of *Architect or Bee* (Langley Technical Services, 1980).

The Third World and Us

1. Johan Galtung, the Norwegian economist and specialist in problems of development, is the author of many books and evidently a thinker whom Bahro takes very seriously. He is as yet little known in the English-speaking world.
2. Josef Huber is a social-democratic writer and champion of an "ecological modernization" to be led forward by industry and science. His books include *Die verlorene Unschuld der Ökologie (The Lost Innocence of Ecology)*, Fischer, 1982.

We Are Defeated. That Is Not Exactly Unimportant

1. Cf. J. Servan-Schreiber, *The World Challenge* (Collins, 1981).

Notes for a Lecture on "Dimensions of Exterminism and the Idea of General Emancipation"

1. Bahro's first book, *Die Alternative*, was significantly mistitled in its English translation, *The Alternative in Eastern Europe*. As Bahro makes clear in *Socialism and Survival*, p. 18, his book bears equally on the situation in the West. The chapter referred to here is chapter 10.
2. Carl Amery, author of *Natur als Politik*, was a leading figure in the Green movement in its early years.
3. Bahro quotes here from Jonas Cohn's introduction to the German edition of Toynbee, *Der gang der Weltgeschichte*, Deutscher Taschenbuchverlag, 1979 (p. 25).
4. Horst Eberhard Richter, *Der Gottescomplex*, Rowohlt, 1979.
5. *The Alternative in Eastern Europe*, p. 253. Marx and Engels wrote in *The German Ideology* that the communist movement "for the first time treats all naturally evolved premises as the creations of hitherto existing men, strips them of their natural character and subjugates them to the power of the united individuals". It must make it "impossible that anything should exist independently of individuals, insofar as reality is nevertheless only a product of the preceding intercourse of individuals" (*Collected Works* vol. 5, Lawrence & Wishart, 1976, p. 81).
6. Erhard Eppler, *Wege aus der Gefahr*, pp. 119 ff.
7. Herman Daly, *Steady-State Economics* (Freeman, 1977).
8. Agnes Heller, *The Theory of Need in Marx* (Allison & Busby, 1976).
9. Karl Marx, *Theories of Surplus-Value*, Part One, chapter 4, section 16 'Nassau Senior'. Our translation.
10. *Collected Works*, vol. 5, p. 31.

Fundamental Thoughts on the Crisis of The Greens

1. This is *Pfeiler am anderen Ufer (Bridgehead on the Other Bank)*,

Befreiung, 1984, from which several texts in the present volume are translated. "Fundamental Thoughts . . ." was addressed to the national congress of the Greens at Karlsruhe in March 1984 (not to be confused with the founding conference there in January 1980). The Duisburg conference in November 1983 had no major significance.

2. Marie-Luise Beck-Oberdorf, a Green member of parliament.

3. See E. P. Thompson et al, *Exterminism and Cold War* (NLB, 1982).

4. Otto Schily, a lawyer and Green parliamentarian, has taken a position still more firmly for collaboration with the SPD than that of Joschka Fischer. See note 4 to "If Only the Thing Was More Stable".

5. See note 2 to "The Third World and Us".

6. See note 1 to "We Are Defeated . . ."

7. The "Zentrum" group split away from the Hamburg Communist League to join the Greens, originally with a somewhat manipulative perspective, though this later faded and the group disbanded. Rainer Trampert and Thomas Ebermann are its two most significant former members.

8. In German *"Bürger"* means both "citizen" and "bourgeois", and *"bürgerlich"* is the corresponding adjective.

9. Lother Späth. See note 6 to "If Only the Thing Was More Stable".

10. Winfried Kretschmann, a former Green deputy in the Baden-Württemberg *Landtag*, is a leading "eco-libertarian", essentially an eco-liberal.

11. Holger Börner is the SPD leader of the *Land* government of Hesse.

12. Peter Glotz is a leading national official of the SPD.

13. Eco-libertarian, i.e. a similar "toleration" practised towards the FDP.

14. Karl Liebknecht, prominent socialist, anti-militarist, and subsequent co-founder of the German Communist Party, took a solo stand in the German Reichstag on the outbreak of the First World War by refusing any kind of support for the imperial government.

15. Bahro quotes from a German edition of Bateson's collected essays, and this passage is retranslated.

Are We Heading In or Out?

1. See footnote on p. 166.

2. Christine Schröter, a member of the Greens' steering committee. In late 1984 Bahro moved from Bremen, where he had lived since his arrival in West Germany in 1979, to live with her in Worms.

3. Waltraud Schoppe, like Otto Schily and Joschka Fischer, is a leading "Realo" and advocate of collaboration with the SPD. Until the 1985 rotation she was a member of the Greens' parliamentary group. Herbert Gruhl and Baldur Springmann were co-founders of the Green party from a Christian-Democrat background, but soon left because the party was too left-wing and insufficiently ecological.

4. Karl Kerschgens is the leading "Realo" in Hesse, where he was a deputy.

5. The CDU minister of home affairs; see p. 49.

6. Philipp Rosenthal, an industrialist and political host linked to the SPD.

7. Rainer Trampert and Bahro had proposed a resolution designed to block the drift towards collaboration with the SPD.

8. Bahro is being ironic. Wilhelm Knabe is a member of the national executive committee.

9. The biennial change-over, i.e. the replacement of the Green members of parliament by a second line of "successors" midway through the parliamentary term.

10. Hans Behaim, a charismatic peasant leader of the early 16th century, a generation before the Reformation erupted.

11. Pseudo-croup, an infant disease spread through air pollution which has recently claimed several fatalities.

A Lesson in Compromise

1. Ilja Weiss is chair of the League Against Animal Experiments, with a "moderate" position of step-by-step abolition. Jo Leinen has long been chair of the Association of Citizens' Initiatives, and is now minister for the environment in the SPD government of Saarland under Oskar Lafontaine.

2. Joachim Müller, who became a Green member of parliament at the 1985 rotation, is described by Fritjof Capra and Charlene Spretniak in *Green Politics* (Dutton, 1984) as "a manager type, concentrated and efficient" (p. 88).

3. Alfred Sohn-Rethel, *Intellectual and Manual Labour* (Macmillan, 1978).

4. Horst Eberhard Richter. See note 4 to "Notes for a Lecture on 'Dimensions of Exterminism' . . ."

5. As at several other points in this book, Bahro refers to the Chinese classic *Tao Te Ching*. Since English editions vary considerably, we have translated from Bahro's German.

Statement on My Resignation from The Greens

1. Bahro resigned from the Green party at its Hagen congress in June 1985, abandoning his attempt – along with other "fundamentalists" – to bring the party back to its mission of total opposition to the industrial system. The issue of animal experiments, treated above in "A Lesson in Compromise", was for him the litmus test of the Greens having become "a party like all the others".

2. Bahro describes Jürgen Dahl as "a brilliant ecological thinker".

3. A contingent feature that allegedly contributed to the defeat of the Greens in the North-Rhine-Westphalia elections in spring 1985 was a debate in the party on paedophilia.

4. In the Saarland, the SPD under Oskar Lafontaine stole some of the Greens' clothes and drove their vote down to 2.5 per cent.

5. Michael Stamm is a Hamburg eco-socialist, who has called for unconditional support for an SPD government in the 1987 general election.